Y0-CRS-052

Out of Touch

Out of Touch

The Presidency and Public Opinion

Michael J. Towle

Texas A&M University Press
College Station

Library of Congress Cataloging-in-Publication Data

Towle, Michael J., 1962–
  Out of touch : the presidency and public opinion / Michael J. Towle.—1st ed.
     p. cm. — (The presidency and leadership ; no. 16)
Includes bibliographical references and index.
  ISBN 1-58544-273-9 (cloth : alk. paper)
  1. Presidents—United States—History—20th century. 2. Presidents—United
States—Public opinion—History—20th century. 3. Public opinion—United States—
History—20th century. 4. Truman, Harry S., 1884–1972—Public opinion.
5. Johnson, Lyndon B. (Lyndon Baines), 1908–1973—Public opinion. 6. Carter,
Jimmy, 1924—Public opinion. 7.
Presidents—United States—Biography. 8. United States—Politics and government—
1945–1989. I. Title. II. Series.
E176.1 .T69 2003
973.91'092'2—dc21
                        2003010954

To Liz
who walks life's paths with me

Contents

Figures

Acknowledgments

This book was written, on and off, over a period of many years. Needless to say, I am in debt to several people for their counsel, advice, and encouragement over the years.

This project grew out of observations in my doctoral dissertation. I would like to thank the members of that committee for helping to start me on the line of inquiry reflected here. I would especially like to thank my dissertation chair, Bruce Buchanan, for his assistance and support, and Terry Sullivan for introducing me to archival research. Walter Dean Burnham, Ben Page, and Jeffrey Tulis provided lots of feedback and good suggestions when this project began.

Over the years, Ken Collier and James Endersby have been very helpful as sounding boards and in encouraging me to piece together and complete this project. Ken has also been great company when we have set out together to rummage through presidential archives.

Two institutions of higher learning have helped cover the research costs involved in visiting presidential libraries. Mount Saint Mary's College has been very generous in supporting my travel and visits to the Carter and Truman Libraries, and providing me with a sabbatical to put all of my thoughts together. The University of Texas at Austin provided funding for research in the Johnson Library.

The archivists at the Truman, Johnson, and Carter Libraries have always been extremely helpful in locating documents and dispelling confusion. I appreciate their eagerness to help and their professional demeanor.

Two anonymous reviewers offered insightful analyses of the first draft of this book. Their suggestions significantly improved the project.

The friends I have made at Mount Saint Mary's College and the University of Texas at Austin are too numerous to mention here. But I appreciate them all not only for supporting me in this project, but also for being good company and great friends.

I have been blessed with the loving support of a large, supportive, high-spirited family. I am especially indebted to my mother and father, Kate and Ed Towle, who provided for my formal education and have served as role models for me over the years.

While working on this project I met and married Elizabeth Skeffington. Her loving companionship, her sense of fun, and her ability to put everything into perspective have been blessings to me.

Out of Touch

Introduction

Much has been written about the relationship between the American president and the American people. This is not surprising. American presidents are under constant scrutiny from their constituencies, and the modern ability to gather and process information has allowed for the continuous reading of the citizenry's attitudes about incumbent presidents and their policies.

Indeed, the opportunity for discussing the relationship between the American people and their chief executive has not been lost. Commentators on Sunday morning talk shows speculate on how well the president relates to the public. Scholars examine such things as how public attitudes about the president affect presidential success in dealings with other political actors. And politicians score points by either showing how the president is or is not "one of the people."

But most of this analysis is one-sided. While we know a considerable amount about the public's attitude about the president, we remain woefully uninformed about the president's attitude about the public. As Doris Graber notes: "What do . . . presidents know about their publics? We know their sources of information about their constituents but little else . . . . Presidents listen to the many voices that claim to speak for the public: pressure groups, the media, and scholars. They watch public opinion polls and commission studies to analyze the nature of their support and opposition, particularly at election time. They count the yeas and nays in their mail. But what they reject and what they accept from these sources and how they use it remains largely unknown."[1] Yet this is an important question in a democracy. For a president to act according to the public's will, to be constrained by public pressure, or even to manipulate the public's passions, he or she must operate according to an understanding of the public. In short, the relevance of our abundant knowledge of public opinion remains unclear without knowing how it is viewed by the occupant of the Oval Office.

This book aims to examine this topic. Through the use of materials from three presidential archives, the following chapters will address two questions. First, what motivates a presidential administration's interest in public opinion? Second, how is information about the public interpreted? Answers to these questions will shed light on the responsiveness of the modern presidency to public opinion.

Ultimately, this work explores a great irony. Despite the fact that modern technology and polling techniques allow presidents to monitor public opinion continually, many of the post–World War II era presidents have left the White House unpopular and seemingly disconnected from public opinion. Lawrence Jacobs and Robert Shapiro observe the "apparent paradox" of politicians' becoming more devoted to "tracking public opinion" while "ordinary Americans have increasingly perceived policymakers as unresponsive and out of touch with them."[2]

Many presidents have been accused of being out of touch. What explains this disconnection between the people and their president? No doubt there are many causes, including the fickle nature of public opinion. Perhaps politicians themselves can be blamed for leading the public to expectations that cannot be fulfilled.[3] Also, some presidents have plausibly lost public support because they chose to do the right things over the popular things.[4]

Richard Waterman, Robert Wright, and Gilbert St. Clair observe the image problems that can lead presidents to being labeled "out of touch." They argue that the careful creation of image has become central to what they call the "image-is-everything-presidency." George H. W. Bush, for example, suffered from the "out of touch" public image in 1992 while running against the "in touch" Bill Clinton.[5] While a president's administration attempts to create a positive image of the chief executive, the partisan opposition attempts to create an unflattering image. "Thus Ronald Reagan successfully presented an image of toughness, while the Democrats largely failed (at least prior to the Iran-Contra affair) in their attempts to portray the president as a man who was seriously out of touch with the nation's problems. On the other hand, unsuccessful politicians, such as Carter or Bush, have ultimately been defined by their political opposition: Carter as vacillating and ineffective and Bush as out of touch with the needs of ordinary Americans. Somewhere along the way, both men lost control over their own public images."[6] Clearly, an administration's opposition is motivated to portray the president in an unflattering light.

Image problems no doubt lead to an accusation that some presidents are out of touch with the public. And the public's perception that the government is unresponsive to them can not be taken lightly. Jacobs and Shapiro observe that politicians since 1980 are in fact less inclined to seek the public's guidance when making policy.[7]

This volume will argue that presidential administrations have a difficult time being responsive to public opinion even if they want to, and this is not simply because public opinion is fickle and hard to understand. The conditions under which the contemporary presidency operates contribute to the strained relationship between the president and the people. While public opinion has become such a key factor that presidents must be constantly mindful of it, the way that administrations look at public opinion slowly alienates them from the public they seek to know. In fact, the importance of public approval for a president's success in dealing with other political actors may force more attention to superficial issues of popularity and less attention to a richer analysis of the underlying public opinion.

The central role that public support plays in the modern presidency is widely acknowledged among presidency scholars. Richard Neustadt's classic work *Presidential Power* deals at length with the importance of the president's prestige in the public at large. According to Neustadt, presidents must protect their public standing because it is a critical persuasive tool to be used against those who would otherwise oppose them. Neustadt's discussion of how presidents relate to the public primarily focuses on how they should project their image, not on how to read the public. Although Neustadt emphasizes the role of the president as a "teacher" to "students . . . who are habitually inattentive," his theory clearly explains why presidents believe it is wise to be attentive to the public.[8]

And attentive they are. For proof, one need only look to the size of the White House public relations apparatus. By 1977, according to the leading scholars of this topic, between 60 and 85 percent of the 500–600 persons employed as White House staff were used to publicize the president. Of the forty-nine presidential aides with the highest annual salaries, slightly over 30 percent had positions directly involving media relations.[9] Although the names and structures of personnel offices in the White House change from administration to administration and even from year to year, in the first year of the George W. Bush administration, the White House Office included the Office of the Press Secretary, with a subdivision dedicated to media affairs; the Office of Communications, with a subdivision dedicated to speechwriting; the Office of the Public Liaison; the Office of the First Lady, including her communications office; and the Office of the Vice President, including his communications office.[10]

With the exception of the Office of Public Liaison, such White House communication offices are primarily charged with aiding presidents in their role as the *leaders* of public opinion, not *readers* of it. Leadership is the aspect of the presidential relationship with the American people that gets the most attention. But leadership of public opinion—or even manipulation of public opinion—first requires an *understanding* of public opinion. To lead the public successfully, a president must read the public correctly.

Public opinion, it should be noted, has no readily agreed upon definition. Susan Herbst states that "a multiplicity of distinct conceptualizations can be found in the social science literature" for public opinion. Herbst, citing a 1965 work that "discovered scores of different definitions" of public opinion, observes that the term had been used differently depending on which aspect of the "opinion communication process" was being examined. "Some studied the way opinions are formed, or how our attitudes are influenced by those around us. Others were concerned with the relationship between public opinion and public policy—how and whether mass opinion is reflected in legislative action or the nature of political systems. Finally, many of the researchers were interested in the ways in which opinions toward particular issues changed over time. Each of these projects demanded a unique definition of public opinion." Herbst argues that the term has come to have a narrower meaning in the era of public opinion polls. Today, due to the pervasiveness of public opinion surveys, public opinion is commonly thought of as "the aggregation of anonymously expressed opinions."[11]

Although the term "public opinion" seems to have emerged in the late eighteenth century, an understanding of the importance of this complex concept extends to ancient times.[12] As noted, the development of survey research has caused many scholars to narrowly use the term "public opinion" to denote the proportions of people on competing sides of contemporary issues. Public opinion can be conceived of in more abstract terms as well. In 1934, for example, one scholar defined public opinion as "a deeply pervasive organic force . . . . It articulates and formulates not only the deliberate judgment of the rational elements within the collectivity but the evanescent common will, which somehow integrates and momentarily crystallizes the sporadic sentiments and loyalties of masses of the population."[13] Such an abstract definition is of little practical help to a government official. However, the definition does serve as a reminder of something that modern survey techniques have allowed us to forget: there are many manifestations of public opinion that may affect a government official other than polls—including popular culture, fashion, political writings, protests, riots, and election outcomes. To understand public opinion, therefore, one may need a sense of the abstract "evanescent common will," including such things as public attitudes about the role of government, the legitimacy of the current government, beliefs about the role of the citizen in the political order, and attitudes about policies and governance. For politicians, this understanding can be quite important, because political fortunes can depend on their notion of public opinion.

Presidents and Public Opinion

Public opinion has long played an important role in the American political system, including the presidency. In James Bryce's classic work, *The American Commonwealth*, first published in 1888 and subsequently updated several times through 1914, 13 of the 123 chapters discuss the role of public opinion in the United States. Bryce includes the executive branch in his observations. For example, in chapter 78, titled "How Public Opinion Rules in America," he writes, "Towering over presidents and state governors, over Congress and state legislatures, over conventions and the vast machinery of party, public opinion stands out, in the United States, as the great source of power, the master of servants who tremble before it."[14]

Significantly, for his time period, Bryce contends that public opinion even plays a role in the United States *between elections*. For example, when the branches of government encounter "stoppages" over an issue, and "the mind of the country [is] clear upon" the issue, "the master . . . is at hand to settle the quarrels of his servants." Bryce asserts that "government by checks and balances" demands the "arbiter" of public opinion, which must be "frequently invoked." In chapter 79, Bryce is even more explicit about the role of public opinion: "in America public opinion is a power not satisfied with choosing executive and legislative agents at certain intervals, but continuously watching and guiding those agents, who look to it, not merely for a vote of approval when the next election arrives, but also for directions which they are eager to obey, so soon as they have learnt their meaning."[15] Bryce says that public opinion guides not only the legislature but also the executive. Presidents, it seems, were look-ing to public opinion in the late 1800s when Bryce was formulating his obser-vations about the American system.

Even in his time, Bryce was aware of the problem of losing touch with public opinion. "Anyone who has made it his business to feel the pulse [of pub-lic opinion] of his own must be sensible that when he has been travelling abroad for a few weeks, he is sure, no matter how diligently he peruses the leading home papers of all shades, to 'lose touch' of the current sentiment of the coun-try in its actuality." Bryce—writing before the emergence of scientific surveys—identifies newspapers as one of the primary "organs" by which public opinion is expressed. Interestingly, Bryce's text errs in its expectation about the possi-bility of polling but is prescient in regard to the role that public opinion would play in the era of polls: "even where the machinery for weighing or measuring the popular will from week to week or month to month has not been, and is not likely to be, invented, there may nevertheless be a disposition on the part of the rulers, whether ministers or legislators, to act as if it existed; that is to say, to look incessantly for manifestations of current popular opinion, and to shape their course in accordance with their reading of those manifestations."[16] Bryce, it seems, saw a republic in which politicians were constantly mindful of public opinion.

Bryce comments on the role of public opinion in guiding American polit-ical actors, but other writers focus on the role of these politicians as leaders of public opinion. Jeffrey Tulis suggests that many of the problems observed with the modern presidency stem from an incompatibility between current expecta-tions of popular leadership and the office's original design. According to Tulis, the presidency went through a fundamental transition in the twentieth century, especially since the presidency of Woodrow Wilson. Tulis argues that at the time of the founding there was an expectation that the president would be "rep-resentative of the people, but not merely responsive to popular will." Further, presidents were expected under normal circumstances to avoid speaking di-rectly to the people about policy matters that were currently under consid-eration, thus reserving the deliberative process to Congress and the interplay between Congress and the executive. But Woodrow Wilson's dislike of the sep-aration of powers in the American system resulted in his conscious effort to change the expected role of the president. According to Tulis, Wilson believed that the president should act as the leader of the public and should "sift through the multifarious currents of opinion to find a core of issues that he believed re-flected majority will even if the majority was not fully aware of it. The leader's rhetoric could translate the people's felt desires into public policy." Tulis asserts that Wilson acted on his beliefs as president and created the modern expecta-tion that presidents would speak directly to the people about public policy and attempt to use the people as a political force for policy change. But, according to Tulis, the new expectation of presidential leadership does not fit well with the original design of the Constitution: "Instead, elements of the old and new ways frustrate or subvert each other." Tulis believes that the new tendency to measure presidents according to their skill at leading the people for public policy purposes has led to problems: "One never examines the hypothesis that there are limits to popular leadership as an institutional practice or to the system's ability to function well under the auspices of popular leadership."[17] Thus, the underlying tension between modern expectations of popular leadership and the original design of the constitutional order have been fundamentally problematic for the presidency and the polity as a whole.

Tulis's assertions have their detractors. David Nichols, for example, examines arguments made at the constitutional convention and concludes that the presidency *was* designed to be an office of popular leadership. Terri Bimes and Stephen Skowronek disagree with Tulis's claim about the role of Woodrow Wilson in American political development. By examining Wilson's writings, they deny that Wilson sought to end the framers' proscription against popular leadership. Instead, they suggest that Wilson himself was critical of those who used rhetoric to fuel popular passions and believed that good leaders should "discern the present conditions of the nation and take it no farther than it was already prepared to go."[18]

The debate over the development of the rhetorical role of the president underscores the importance of the history of the relationship between the president and the people. Whatever the case, the presidency today operates in an environment in which public opinion has become a critical factor in the operations of the office.

In addition to their general attention to public opinion, presidential administrations are also concerned with maintaining the president's "public approval rating," the pollster's device for ascertaining the percentage of people supportive of the president's overall performance. This concern is more than just vanity; it is also perceived as strategically necessary. Several scholars have measured what presidents seem to know intuitively: they are much more productive in their dealings with other political actors when they have the backing of the public. Bruce Buchanan calls public support "the core resource" and asserts that support "empowers the contemporary presidency and is extraordinarily important to its vitality." Buchanan observes the role of public support in dealing with Congress, conducting foreign policy, receiving favorable media coverage, assisting presidents in their work within the executive branch, and enabling presidents to have "faith in themselves and their works." Dennis Simon and Charles Ostrom have observed the numerous studies that have examined the role of public support and have concluded that the "politics of prestige" is a "major feature of the modern presidency." According to Simon and Ostrom, scholars who have studied public opinion and the modern presidency have clearly demonstrated that presidential effectiveness rests upon high levels of public support. Thus, the public approval level has been shown to correlate with such things as the probability of successfully preventing veto overrides, minimizing losses during midterm elections, maintaining a high "box-score" (the percentage of time that Congress passes legislation supported by the president), and winning a bid for reelection.[19]

Many decry the obsession with public opinion and public approval that characterizes the modern presidency. Twenty years ago, for example, Sydney

Blumenthal dubbed the phenomenon "the permanent campaign." Theodore Lowi too has observed that the modern presidency operates under conditions analogous to a perpetual campaign. Lowi scornfully notes the growth of what he calls the "plebiscitary" or "personal" presidency—"an office of tremendous personal power drawn from the people." The subject has also been studied by Paul Brace and Barbara Hinckley, who examine the impact of public approval ratings on the presidency. They observe the many ways that popularity affects presidential activity, illustrate the consequences, and call for a "new realism" in the expectations placed on presidents. In this same line of thought, Richard Waterman and Hank Jenkins-Smith observe the oft-cited "expectations gap" between what the public expects from presidents and what it actually perceives in its presidents. They note the negative impact of this on incumbent presidents.[20]

The preeminent role of public opinion in the presidency presents several interesting questions. One important question is whether modern technology and survey techniques have made the presidency more responsive to public opinion. Scholars have been divided on the issue. John Geer argues that the advent of public opinion polling has allowed modern politicians to operate with more complete information. Rational actors, therefore, will be able to adapt their views toward the public's median position. Furthermore, according to Geer, modern survey techniques have made it harder for presidents and all politicians to allow their own biases to impede their understanding of the public's desires. Geer asserts that modern politicians follow the public's lead on salient issues and reserve their own leadership to non-salient issues that will allow them to claim credit and attract voters. The result is that politicians in the era of the scientific survey are more responsive to the public than their information-poor predecessors. Jacobs and Shapiro, on the other hand, dismiss the popular notions that modern political leaders "slavishly follow public opinion" when making policy and engage in "pandering" to the public to attract support and votes. They argue that a confluence of political events since the 1970s has resulted in a system wherein politicians place the policy goals of their partisan supporters over the policy preferences of the general public, and they explain political attention to public opinion as a method whereby politicians determine the best strategies for presenting their predetermined policy objectives. They label the result of politicians' attention to public opinion as "crafted talk," designed "as a strategy to win the support of centrist opinion for their desired policy positions." The consequence is that politicians "simulate responsiveness" by acquiring support for their positions and by moving the public to positions they would not hold if they had fuller knowledge. In contrast to Geer, Jacobs and Shapiro hold that "the influence of public opinion on government policy is *less* than it has been in the past." The main exception to this is during the presidential campaign season. Jeffrey Cohen, like Jacobs and Shapiro, denies that the prominence of public approval polls has made the presidency more responsive to the public. Cohen seeks to explain how presidents use public opinion when making public policy and argues that presidents are responsive mainly in symbolic and non-substantive ways.[21]

Whether one accepts arguments like Geer's, that presidents do follow public opinion when making policy, or arguments like Jacobs and Shapiro's, that politicians follow public opinion in order to alter public perceptions and "simulate responsiveness," one is left with another question: how do presidents and their staffs settle on an interpretation of public opinion? For presidential administrations to act according to the public's will, or to be constrained by public pressure, or even to manipulate the public's passions, they must operate according to an understanding of the public. But how do they come to an understanding? The answer is elusive.

The president's sources of information about the public are often unreliable as indicators of mass opinion. Citizens' opinions are often poorly articulated, and even when they are expressed they may not be instructive for the policymaker. For example, if campus protesters really wanted Lyndon Johnson to stop all American involvement in Vietnam immediately, how useful was that opinion given the complexities of the situation? Clearly, protestors expressed dissatisfaction, but they provided few positive indications for policy direction. Because the protesters' views were not the same as the American majority's, Johnson was left in the unenviable position of attempting to choose between a vocal issue-articulating minority and other less vocal but (perhaps) more supportive elements of society. For Johnson, the Vietnam situation may not have had any potential path that would have decisively satisfied the public. In the words of V. O. Key, "The voice of the people may be loud, but the enunciation is indistinct."[22]

Some claim that public opinion polls have come to the rescue of bewildered politicians. For example, George Gallup once wrote, "Polls can report what all the people think about an issue—not just those who take the trouble to vote. And polls can identify the groups who favor and those who oppose a given issue with far greater accuracy than is possible by examining election returns. In addition, polls can report the reasons why voters hold the views they do."[23] According to Gallup, elections are not adequate gauges of public opinion, because the citizenry often does not stand for all the issues expounded by the winning candidates, who will interpret their elections as mandates. John Geer also sees polls as helpful to politicians, arguing that "with the development of the sample survey, politicians began to have access to much more precise and accurate estimates of what average citizens were thinking on a wide variety of political issues."[24]

White House attention to polls has grown steadily during the modern presidency to the point where presidents now have an official pollster who measures public opinion.[25] But despite Gallup's optimism, opinion polls have shortcomings for a president attempting to use them. First, while polls do provide a measure of existing opinion, there is no reason to believe that the respondents' opinions are carefully considered. In fact, poll results themselves call into question the depth of public attention to affairs of state. Some foreign policy examples are instructive. In 1994, as the future of democratic governance in Russia was a major concern of American foreign policy, only 47 percent of the country could identify the president of Russia.[26] Despite being a major controversy of the Reagan presidency, for example, a 1986 *New York Times*/CBS News poll revealed that only 38 percent of the American people knew which side the U.S. government supported in the war in Nicaragua.[27] In 1979, only 23 percent of the public knew that the Soviet Union and the United States were the two countries negotiating SALT II.[28] In 1964, 62 percent of the American people were unaware that the Soviet Union was not a member of NATO.[29] In 1945, as the United States was in the final months of its war with Japan, one poll indicated that only half of the American public could identify Emperor Hirohito.[30] An administration attempting to use polls to ascertain public opinion will be forced to speculate on the quality of both the survey technique and the responses.

Another shortcoming of public opinion polls is their inconclusive meaning. In 1988, when asked, "Are we spending too much, too little or about the right amount on welfare?" only 22 percent said "too little." But when the same organization substituted the words "assistance to the poor" for "welfare," 61 percent also responded "too little." One 1981 poll found that while 95 percent of the respondents believed that the Clean Air Act may need amending, 70 percent of the same respondents confessed knowing little or nothing at all about the act.[31]

Presidential administrations are at a particular disadvantage in interpreting the meaning of the president's public approval rating. Despite its apparent importance to the modern presidency, the poll numbers themselves offer no guidance. Why is a president popular or unpopular? For example, Bill Clinton's Gallup approval rating during his impeachment trial was, by historical comparison, in a rather high range, between 65 percent and 69 percent.[32] Was this because the economy was good? Was it because the public sympathized with the president? Perhaps the public was reacting to a sense that the House Republicans had overstepped their bounds? Was his popularity attributable to something entirely unrelated to these things? The public approval rating itself offers no guidance to questions like these.

Presidents and their advisors cannot escape the task of interpreting public opinion. Any attempts to understand public opinion, even with the help of sophisticated polling techniques, will necessarily involve their own views and biases. They must weigh their own understanding of public opinion against various measures that support or repudiate their views. They may have to decide what a fully informed public would want or attempt to separate opinions according to the intensity with which groups hold them or articulate them. They may even need to determine which group of the population has the "best" opinions. Even the most attentive public officials will feel uncertainty about their understanding of public opinion.

The Foundations of This Study

In order to ascertain why presidential administrations look to public opinion and to understand how they settle on an interpretation of public opinion, this book will rely on a comparative case study of the Truman, Johnson, and Carter administrations. Through the use of archival sources, the institutional dynamic of these presidencies can be compared as they looked to public opinion. This study seeks to provide an explanation of the process by which presidential administrations grow "out of touch."

Several scholars have used case studies to analyze the implications of presidential attitudes about the public and public opinion. Doris Graber examined how early presidents' beliefs about public opinion affected their foreign policy decisionmaking. Melvin Small has observed the ways that the Johnson and Nixon administrations reacted to the antiwar movement during the Vietnam conflict. Kathleen Turner has made extensive use of the Johnson archives to analyze how Johnson's efforts to communicate to the public about Vietnam were affected by (and sometimes confounded by) his relationship with the press. Bruce Altschuler has examined President Lyndon Johnson's use of polls and his relationship with pollsters. And Jacobs and Shapiro have examined the role that public opinion played in the Clinton White House's efforts to create health care reform.[33] The research presented in this book attempts to add to this body of scholarship by comparing several administrations' reaction to public opinion.

Most scholars who have studied the connection between the public and individual political officials have focused on legislators, and some of their observations may be applicable to executives as well. In the late 1950s, for example, Lewis Anthony Dexter conducted more than a hundred interviews with members of Congress to ascertain how representatives acquire beliefs about their constituents. Two of Dexter's observations are equally plausible for White House officials: "some men automatically interpret what they hear to support their own viewpoints," and "what congressmen hear and how they interpret what they hear depends on who they are."[34] Like the adage "where you stand depends upon where you sit," the individual interpretation presented to a president (or other officials) may be tainted—consciously or unconsciously—with self-interested or otherwise prejudiced analysis.

One prominent scholar of the Congress has made observations similar to those made about presidential scholarship at the beginning of this introduction. Richard Fenno, in the introduction to his *Home Style: House Members in Their Districts,* observes, "One question central to the representative-constituency relationship remains underdeveloped. It is: *What does an elected representative see when he or she sees a constituency?* And, as a natural follow-up, *What consequences do these perceptions have for his or her behavior?* The key problem is perception. And the key assumption is that the constituency a representative reacts to is the constituency he or she sees." In an attempt to close this gap in knowledge, Fenno traveled extensively with eighteen members of Congress and congressional candidates. By a research method he called "soaking and poking," Fenno developed a typology of self-presentation of members of Congress based on their perceptions of their constituents' attitudes.[35]

Fenno's research should be inspirational to scholars interested in the linkage between the president and the public. Analyses like Fenno's need to be conducted on the presidential level in an effort to understand contemporary American politics. The plebiscitary nature of the contemporary presidency, the crucial role of the presidential-public relationship in the formation of the national agenda, and the twentieth century's growth in the policymaking responsibilities of the president make such research essential.[36]

Most people cannot act as a participant-observer to a presidential administration. Fortunately, presidential archives allow us to review the discussions that have taken place in the White House. Although archival materials are not generally available until many years after an administration has ended, presidential archives are still a treasure trove for those seeking to understand the discussions within a presidential administration. While scholars cannot follow presidents the way that Fenno followed members of Congress, they do have the option of "soaking and poking" in extensive archives in order to ascertain modern presidents' perceptions of the American people.

Basing a study on individual administrations—as will be the case here—has shortcomings. There are two fundamental difficulties that plague an examination of this kind. The first difficulty stems from the uncertainty involved in reconstructing the perceptions of other individuals. The availability of archival sources makes this task simpler when studying the presidency. Indeed, archival research can be a superior method to interviewing or using memoirs, because it allows an analysis not only of day-to-day operations but also of the development of attitudes, ideas, and concerns over the course of an administration. Furthermore, presidents and their advisors are seldom accessible for scholarly discussion while they are in the White House. As Bruce Altschuler observes, "Access can best be gained by studying a presidency whose internal memoranda have been opened to the public." Similarly, Jacobs and Shapiro note, "Focusing on archival evidence concerning the behavior of authoritative government officials like U.S. presidents offers a promising approach to explaining changes in political behavior and strategy."[37] In fact, archival sources may be less likely than other sources, such as memoirs and interviews completed after a finished term, to be tainted with selective memory or an attempt to sway the judgment of history. Research on this topic, therefore, *requires* a basis of archival sources from which to reconstruct an administration's thoughts.

A second major difficulty stems from the fact that the presidency is an idiosyncratic office. Peculiarities of the individuals observed make generalizations more problematic. Ideology, personality, and intelligence will affect the beliefs and perceptions of any administration, and the researcher might have difficulty separating quirks within an individual administration from other more significant discoveries.

Despite the second difficulty, is it possible that there are features of the modern presidency as an institution that may tend to bias the beliefs and perceptions of any presidency similarly situated? If so, then generalizable statements can be made that would partially compensate for the undeniably individualistic nature of the office. This book contends that the condition under which the modern presidency functions forces presidential administrations to ask certain questions about the public and biases them toward particular interpretations of public opinion. These institutional features of the modern presidency could be responsible for the many presidents in the post–World War II period who have been accused of growing "out of touch" over the course of their terms.

This study examines the *administrations* of three presidents rather than three *individual* presidents. Presidents and their top aides are in constant communication with one another. By exploring the dynamic of these discussions within the White House, the following chapters will illustrate how the institution of the modern presidency led to the "out of touch" phenomenon and limited the possibility of presidential responsiveness to public opinion.

The Truman, Johnson, and Carter administrations were selected for comparison, in part, because they were all Democratic administrations whose public support steadily declined over the course of their terms.[38] Because they each suffered the same fate with the public, they can be compared during the times that their public support was high, moderate, and low.

The primary method of measuring public support is the public approval rating, a technique begun in 1939 by the Gallup Poll. Consistently since then, the Gallup Poll has been asking, "Do you approve or disapprove of the way _____ is handling his job as president?" The question is followed up by "Is that approve/disapprove strongly, or approve/disapprove somewhat?" Other pollsters have since adopted similar measures of public approval, though often with different wording.[39]

The three presidents studied here faced similar patterns of public approval. Of the three, Truman was the only one whose decline was interrupted by a more than brief recovery in public approval, but he too eventually faced a serious decline. Truman's first Gallup approval rating was 87 percent, in June, 1945, as the war in Europe was ending and Truman was starting out in office after Franklin Roosevelt's death. His approval stayed above 75 percent in 1945 but then slowly sank as low as 33 percent in September, 1946. By March, 1947, it had recovered to 60 percent, but it dropped again to 36 percent in April, 1948. After his surprise reelection, his approval rating shot up to 69 percent in January, 1949, and continued on a slow, steady decline, achieving a record low of 22 percent in February, 1952. His approval rating never got above 33 percent after that. Lyndon Johnson had a longer period of high approval, but it steadily declined over his five and a half years in office. Johnson's first Gallup approval ratings were very high, ranging between 74 percent and 80 percent for his first seven months in office. They averaged 70 percent over his first two years in office, a time that included his election with over 61 percent of the popular vote. But Johnson's popularity dropped after 1966. During the final seventeen months of his administration, Johnson's average approval rating was a fairly low 42 percent. Jimmy Carter faced a similar pattern. His approval ratings were above 60 percent from his inauguration through August, 1977, but then began a precipitous drop. They fluctuated between 37 percent and 52 percent between February, 1978, and April, 1979, and then varied between 28 percent and 38 percent until November, 1979. In November, American embassy personnel in Teheran were taken hostage, and in December the Soviet army invaded Afghanistan. At first, the public rallied to the president's side, with his approval rating climbing to 58 percent in January, 1980. Unlike Truman's popularity rise, however, Carter's was short-lived. It never got above 43 percent between April, 1980, and the end of his term; it had fallen as low as 31 percent.[40]

Because these three administrations faced similar patterns of declining public support, comparisons of their administrations could help develop not only an understanding of how presidents interpret public opinion but also of what motivates their attention to it. Shapiro and Jacobs specifically call for such a comparative approach. Suggesting that scholars move beyond single case studies, they advocate studies that attempt to "synthesize in-depth research in order to unravel *historical trends* in the causal relationship between public opinion and policy. The strategy requires finding trends over time in the extent to which policymakers seek out or otherwise get information on public opinion, and respond to, or are otherwise affected by this information."[41] The study here will compare patterns seen within three different administrations over a thirty-six-year span of time.

Public Approval and the Reaction to Public Opinion

By using archival sources, one can observe a striking change in the ways that administrations interpret public opinion over time. Chapters 2, 3, and 4, will focus on how these administrations interpreted public opinion when their popularity was high, moderate, and low for their presidents.[42] To explain these patterns of interpreting public opinion, these chapters will rely, in part, on explanations based in cognitive psychology.

The Congratulation-Rationalization Effect

One observation stands out above all others for these administrations: their attitude about the American people seemed to depend upon what the American people thought about them. It should not be surprising that clear and distinct patterns of thought occurred depending on their level of public approval. When the level of public approval drops, for example, a president might be expected to be frustrated and sense that negative external forces are increasingly beyond control.

Such an observation is not without precedent. John Kingdon, in his classic article "Politicians' Beliefs About Voters," observed patterns in candidates' beliefs about voters that depended upon the success or failure of the individual candidate's bid. Kingdon interviewed winning and losing politicians of various state and federal offices in Wisconsin after the 1964 election. According to Kingdon, "Winners tend to believe more than the losers that the voters in their district decided how to cast their ballots not by blind party voting, but according to the issues of the election and the man who was seeking the office." Furthermore, "losers are inclined very strongly to believe that voters are not informed about the issues of the election, while winners tend to believe that voters are much better informed. A full quarter of winners even think that voters are very well informed about the issues, most of these being safe winners." Kingdon calls his observation the "congratulation-rationalization effect."[43]

Interestingly, Kingdon observes both the congratulation and the rationalization effect within the same individuals. When seasoned politicians were asked to name the factors that led to their previous victories and defeats, 91 percent contributed their defeats to such uncontrollable things as party makeup of their district, lack of money, family name of their opponent, etc. On the other hand, 75 percent of their victories were credited with such controllable factors as hard work, reputation, constituency service, and campaign strategy.[44]

Modern presidents may face two elections, and it is plausible that the congratulation-rationalization effect would apply equally to presidential administrations as to lower offices. Furthermore, the nature of the modern presidency could exacerbate the influence of this effect. As many observers have maintained, the modern presidency operates under conditions analogous to a perpetual reelection campaign. Theodore Lowi, for example, describes how the American citizenry has formed a personal relationship with the occupant of the Oval Office, and how that relationship is based on a continuous judgment of the ability of the president to fulfill political expectations. As discussed earlier, one continuous measure of the public's satisfaction with its personal president is the public approval rating, which has been demonstrated to have an influence on presidential success or failure in dealings with other political actors. Cohen observes the effect: "Small movements in popularity are tracked [in the White House], even though they may . . . not represent true change. In a sense, the polls have become a running barometer of the presidency, almost a running referendum or interelection 'election.'" Cohen notes that this "heightens presidential sensitivity to poll results."[45]

Does Kingdon's congratulation-rationalization effect apply to the continuous state of reelection of the modern presidency? The following chapters will argue that it does. The popular times for these administrations were clearly marked by self-congratulatory tendencies in the White House. When they were unpopular, on the other hand, these administrations were clearly rationalizing; low approval and public discontent were seen to have several causes outside of the White House's control. As chapters 1, 2, and 3 will contend, these attitudes about the public affected the interpretation of and the judgment about the value of public opinion.

Cognitive Psychological Variables

Some early works in the field of cognitive psychology also offer some explanation for the observed changes in these administrations' patterns of interpreting public opinion. Indeed, a simple analysis using Leon Festinger's theory of cognitive dissonance will prove powerful.[46]

Festinger's theory is quite straightforward. When individuals have two or more belief sets in conflict, they experience a psychological discomfort in their thought processes that Festinger labels as "dissonance" or "cognitive dissonance." The existence of dissonance, according to Festinger, if sufficiently uncomfortable, will motivate the individual to resolve the inconsistencies. These attempts at resolution can take numerous forms, including "behavior changes,

changes in cognition, and circumspect exposure to new information and new opinions."[47]

Festinger has also observed the phenomenon of post-decision dissonance. Doubts about the wisdom of a decision will result in dissonance and attempts to reduce it. Festinger postulates that dissonance reduction can result from "attempts to increase the relative attractiveness of the chosen alternative, to establish cognitive overlap, or possibly to revoke the decision psychologically."[48]

The administrations studied here fell victim to some of the classic symptoms of cognitive dissonance as public approval dropped. As a result, they had difficulty accepting the various indications that their actions were not in accord with public opinion, especially after the early years of strong public approbation. The declining approval rating resulted in dissonance about their domestic and foreign policy decisions. The Truman, Johnson, and Carter administrations dealt with this, in part, by creating the belief that the public still supported their actions. As the support declined, the pressures to reduce the dissonance increased, manifesting themselves in the selective perception of information about public opinion. Selective perception, in fact, is an essential concept of cognitive dissonance theory. According to S. T. Fiske and S. E. Taylor, psychological research into selective perception has focused on three areas: "*Selective exposure* (seeking consistent information not already present), *selective attention* (looking at consistent information once it is present), and *selective interpretation* (translating ambiguous information to be consistent)."[49] These phenomena will be clearly observable in the administrations studied here.

Public Opinion and Strategic Concerns

It is not just the interpretation of public opinion that results in administrations' growing out of touch. The very factors that cause them to look to public opinion change over their terms. As we shall see, the changed nature of what they want to know about the public also leads to their alienation from it.

Presidential attention to public opinion is motivated, in part, by strategic necessity. Scholars and presidents alike have observed the hazards that can befall an administration that fails to interpret public opinion correctly or that loses public support. The public approval rating, for example, has become a conspicuous constraint on the modern plebiscitary presidency. Strategic considerations demand presidential attention to public opinion.

Yet there are tremendous variations in the strategic concerns that animate an administration's attention to the American public. For example, presidential administrations may attempt to ascertain the public's opinion on a policy for majoritarian reasons; that is, policies may be pursued to satisfy the majority will. An administration's concern with public opinion may also stem from the desire to determine whether there exists sufficient public support to allow for an unpopular action without unacceptable levels of political damage. Further, an administration may wish to use public opinion as a political club to beat potential opponents in Congress; this is generally noticeable in the early stages of an administration when a president declares that he or she has a mandate to pursue particular policies. In short, the strategic concern that forces attention to public opinion may vary according to the strategic uses meant for the information obtained.[50]

Chapter 4 will examine the strategic motivations behind these administrations' attention to public opinion. The chapter will suggest that these administrations concerned themselves not only with the public's *issue agenda* when support was high but also with *maintaining and expanding* their public support base. As public support declined, the primacy of the goal of ascertaining the issue agenda of the public was set aside as the administrations sought to *define and stabilize* their support base. Finally, when public approval was low, they sought to *consolidate and protect* what remained of their support bases and completely dismissed (sometimes contemptuously) the public's preference on policy issues. This pattern narrowed the scope of public opinion deemed sufficiently serious for analysis in the White House.

Chapter 1

Interpretation in Popular Times
Self-Congratulatory and Cautious

The circumstances under which Truman, Johnson, and Carter entered the presidency were quite different. While Truman and Johnson ascended to the presidency on the death of their predecessors, their times were dissimilar; Truman began his term as the United States was about to emerge triumphant from the rubble of World War II, and Johnson began after the murder of his predecessor. Of the three, only Carter entered the White House as a direct consequence of an election.

Yet one thing is similar about the beginnings of these presidencies. As with most presidents, each was popular early in his term. Truman and Johnson were especially popular, perhaps because of the difficult circumstances under which they began their terms. Gallup published three approval ratings for Truman in 1945, and all were 75 percent or higher. Similarly, Johnson's popularity averaged over 75 percent during his first six months in office. While Carter was never as popular as the other two, all of Gallup's approval ratings for Carter during his first seven months were over 60 percent.[1] Each administration, therefore, could begin its term with the assurance that the president had a temporary cushion from the wrath of public disapproval.

The Popular Times of the Truman Presidency

It is hard to imagine more difficult circumstances under which to assume the presidency than those faced by Harry Truman. Truman became president during one the most turbulent times in U.S. history; having served only eighty-one days as vice president, he was relatively unknown to America. Furthermore, Truman had only seen the president twice while serving as vice president. It was by no means clear how the public would react to Truman; his folksy style contrasted sharply with the reassuring patrician manner of his twelve-year predecessor, Franklin D. Roosevelt. When Truman became president he was thrust onto the world's center stage as the United States was helping to defeat Nazi Germany; as plans for a United Nations organization were being developed; as the world was on the dawn of a nuclear age that would start with the unconditional surrender of the Japanese Empire; as the future of Europe was in doubt; as twelve million Americans were serving in the armed forces and more than 200,000 American lives had already been lost; and as an embryonic cold war was developing unnoticed.

Figure 1.1
TRUMAN (EARLY — HIGH APPROVAL)
Source: *The Roper Center for Public Opinion Research*

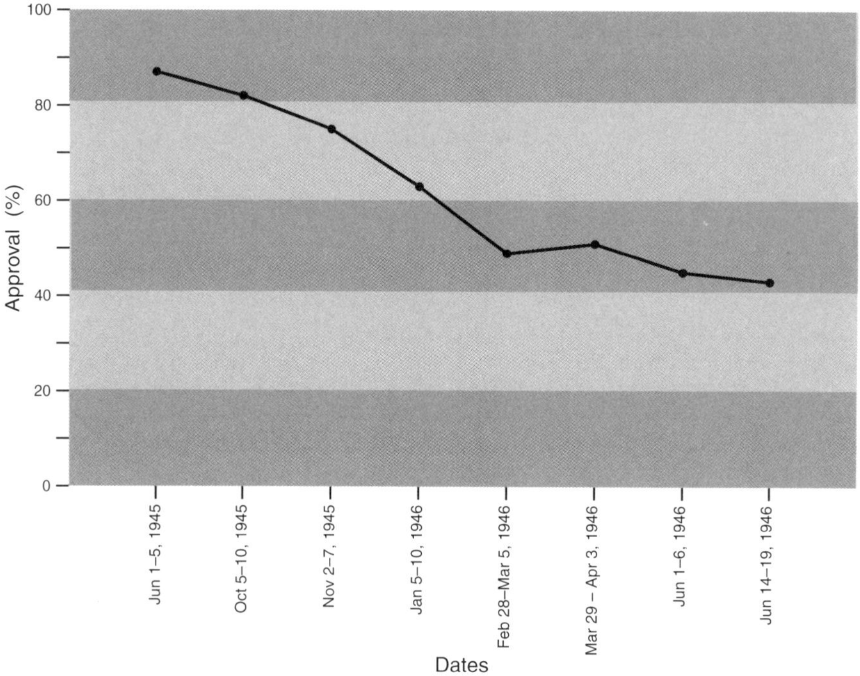

But the euphoria that accompanied the end of four dark years of war certainly worked to Truman's advantage. As figure 1.1 shows, the public's immediate reaction to the new president who oversaw the end of the war was understandably favorable.

The Popular Times of the Johnson Presidency

Johnson's ability to ameliorate the fears of the nation at the time of the Kennedy assassination no doubt contributed to the high levels of support for him during his early years in the presidency. Figure 1.2 shows that Johnson was able to sustain fairly high support ratings, generally well over 60 percent.

A single word to describe these early years of the Johnson administration might be "action." From the start it was obvious that Johnson would be a driven, active president. The activity and urgency of the early years permeates the archival records and published accounts of the administration. One striking example of this is Johnson's handwritten scrawl below a December, 1963, memo to Walter Heller, chairman of the Council of Economics Advisors: "Work, think, work, think, hard on the State of the Union. I depend on you. Hurry your thoughts."[2]

Figure 1.2
JOHNSON (EARLY — HIGH APPROVAL)
Source: *The Roper Center for Public Opinion Research*

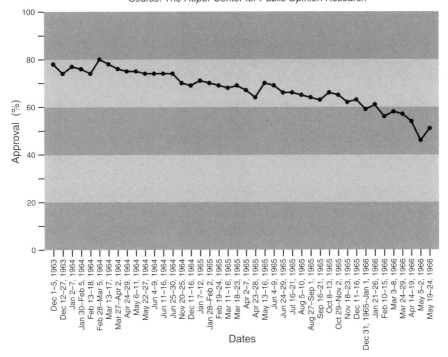

But his early efforts paid off and established his reputation in the public mind as a president who understood power and the workings of Congress. With the dramatic slaying of President John F. Kennedy, Lyndon Johnson inherited a legislative program whose future was in doubt; Johnson's youthful predecessor was becoming increasingly less popular at the time of his death, and his dealings with Congress reflected his position. Approximately three months after Johnson took the oath of office, however, he successfully pushed through Congress the first of Kennedy's remaining major programs, an $11.5 billion tax cut. Within another five months came the historic passage of the 1964 Civil Rights Act.[3] The passage of these two bills firmly established Johnson as a leader to be respected. Within a year, Johnson had launched his Great Society programs, designed to reduce the conditions of poverty.

Johnson's early legislative success is perhaps partially attributable to the outpouring of sympathy and support from the American public after the Kennedy assassination. Indeed, Johnson's handling of the situation was generally highly acclaimed as dignified and able.[4] And Johnson knew that quick actions in the wake of high public support were essential to achieving his goals. Soon after taking office, Lyndon Johnson told Special Counsel to the President Harry McPherson that he was pushing legislation through Congress so hard immediately after taking office rather than waiting until the summer of 1964, "Because they'll [members of Congress] all be thinking about their reelections. I'll have made mistakes, my polls will be down, and they'll be trying to put some distance between themselves and me."[5] Johnson began his presidency with the understanding that public opinion should be used as an important strategic resource. In fact, he considered it important enough to assign aides the responsibility of analyzing polls; originally, this task was given to Hayes Redmon and Richard Nelson, then to Frederick Panzer later in Johnson's term.[6]

The Popular Times of the Carter Presidency

Jimmy Carter's 1976 campaign was considered unique at the time. By taking advantage of the changes in the Democratic Party's nominating rules, Carter, an obscure former governor of Georgia, was able to parlay media attention from his victory in the New Hampshire primary to front-runner status. And the country seemed to like the genteel manner of the born-again Christian peanut farmer.

Carter had a very different style from most of his recent predecessors. He lacked the strident manner of Nixon and the larger-than-life style of Johnson. Coming to office in the aftermath of the Watergate scandal and the Vietnam conflict, Carter set out to make the presidency seem closer to the people. Carter had based his 1976 campaign, in part, on the theme of reestablishing trust in government. From the earliest days of his presidency, Carter wanted to make it clear that his administration would be open to public input. He chose his symbols well. In his inaugural parade, he walked from the Capitol to the White House to reinforce his message that he would be open to the public. To appear more like the common person, he carried his own suitcase aboard Air Force One. He allowed himself to be photographed in blue jeans. In the seventh week of his presidency, Carter even held a call-in radio show so that citizens could talk to the president personally about their concerns.

As figure 1.3 shows, Carter remained relatively popular through his first six months in office. Although he had a short honeymoon with the public, with his Gallup approval rating dipping below 60 percent for the first time in September, 1977, his approval rating would remain around 55 percent for the rest of 1977, with the exception of one reading of 51 percent in late October.

Self-Congratulation and the Fear of Support Loss

These administrations knew they had public support, and they knew the accompanying advantages of it. But to what did they attribute their popularity? And how did they react to public opinion when they were popular?

A look at the archives of these three administrations suggests that they believed that the public closely identified with them, and that this was the root of their popularity. As discussed in the introduction, such a reaction is consistent with Kingdon's "congratulation" effect for winning politicians, who Kingdon suggests will explain their elections in terms of personal actions. Similarly, for

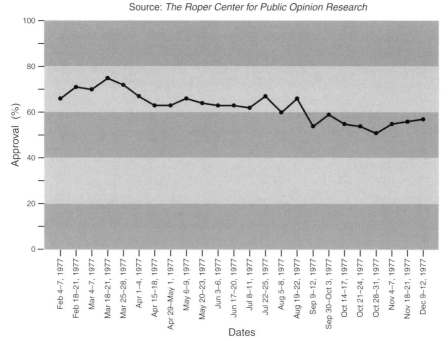

Figure 1.3
CARTER (EARLY — HIGH APPROVAL)
Source: *The Roper Center for Public Opinion Research*

these presidents self-congratulation was evident while they were popular and were continually "winning" the battle for public favor. These administrations' political beliefs and their understanding of public opinion were cognitively consonant. This may have made them more attentive to public opinion. As Kingdon observed, the self-congratulatory tendency of winning politicians and their corresponding belief in a well-informed electorate will make them more responsive to public opinion: "He [the politician] might pay greater attention to his constituency than otherwise, because he believes that his constituents are paying greater attention to him."[7]

The remainder of this chapter will focus on two dominant trends evident in these administrations' reactions to their high public standing. First, they attributed their public support to their ability to align with public opinion and convince the public of the worthiness of their actions. In essence, their assessment of public opinion was self-congratulatory. Second, these administrations tended to fear that their president's support would soon decline.

Truman

The Truman administration began with the confidence that the public closely identified with it. Truman, of course, took over the presidency near the end of one of the United States' most difficult challenges. Within four months, the war was over and Americans saw themselves and their allies as victors in one of the world's greatest struggles. The war-weary public was relieved and joyful—happy to support the occupant of the White House.

Truman could operate with a sense that the public was behind him. Even when economic conditions began to make things rough for the administration, its leaders could congratulate themselves that the public was on their side. On January 3, 1946, for example, Truman's press secretary Charlie Ross forwarded to Truman a "very reassuring" advance copy of an article by George Gallup that was to appear in the next day's paper. The article was to show that "rank and file" labor union members were siding with Truman, not the union leaders, on a proposed labor policy that would call for a thirty-day, cooling-off period before workers could go on strike. Truman knew of his high levels of support. A proposed agenda for the January 11 cabinet meeting, which was covered with Truman's handwriting, was attached to another advance copy of a Gallup report that indicated that the public was supporting Truman on most of the policy positions he espoused.[8]

Those around Truman reinforced the notion that the public was identifying with the president. Minutes of the January 18 cabinet meeting reveal that Secretary of Commerce Henry Wallace told Truman to "continue to carry his fight to the people," because he was "convinced that people are behind the President." Wallace "urged the President to keep on fighting." To this, Secretary of Agriculture Clinton Anderson responded that "people are delighted with [the] fighting leadership displayed by the President."[9]

As would be expected, the theme of self-congratulation also occurred after the stunning surprise victory in the 1948 election. Leon Keyserling, vice chairman of the National Housing Authority and member (later chair) of the Council of Economic Advisors, wrote to Special Counsel to the President Clark Clifford that Truman's 1949 State of the Union draft showed that it might "be the most significant State of the Union Message in many decades." Reinforcing the connection between Truman and the people, Keyserling referred to the president's mandate, indicating that he believed it was a "splendid idea" to begin "the Message with a ringing statement of what the people's mandate has been and of the intent to carry it out."[10]

The self-congratulatory comments sometimes occurred in the same conversations with statements that revealed a fear of support loss. For example, a cabinet meeting on September 7, 1945, focused on the question of whether the United States should continue its policy of conscription for universal military training in the postwar era, a policy that Truman favored. Truman believed that he needed to act fast while he still had public support, because "the longer the matter is delayed the more forceful would become the exponents of passivism and isolationism." But there remained the self-congratulatory sense that Truman's position was the same as the public's: Secretary of War Henry Stimson was "certain that the true attitude of the people of the United States is not what the opponents of universal training say."[11]

Others, besides Truman, feared support loss. At the cabinet meeting on

January 11, 1946, Secretary of Commerce Henry Wallace expressed his concern that the Congress would go Republican if it were not pushed to support the president's program.[12] While Wallace's concern would certainly prove prescient, Truman was still relatively popular at this time. Indeed, Gallup Polls in December, 1945, showed a 75 percent approval rating, followed by a lower but still respectable 63 percent in January. The fear of support loss came at a time when there was little evidence of public abandonment.

Johnson

It would have been impossible for President Johnson and his associates not to realize his tremendous popularity. As noted earlier, published Gallup approval ratings hovered between 60 percent and 80 percent through 1965, and Johnson won his 1964 election with the highest percentage of the popular vote in U.S. presidential election history. LBJ's popularity was evident from the earliest days of his presidency. On January 14, 1964, Special Assistant to the President Horace Busby evaluated the analysis of Johnson in the *Public Opinion Index for Industry,* a publication that "all major U.S. corporations subscribe to—and religiously believe in," and concluded that "the Johnson administration begins with a strong plus in the personal image of the President." Assistant to the President Richard Nelson reported to Johnson a telephone conversation with George Gallup from March 25. Gallup informed Nelson, "The President is doing a fantastic job. We all thought that the honeymoon would last 30–45 days and then the polls would drop off sharply. But this has not been the case. The President still has a fantastically high national rating, and it looks like that rating is going to continue. He is doing a great job, and the people know it and are willing to express it. We just polled Republican county chairmen, and they nearly all secretly feel that the G.O.P. doesn't have much of a chance in November." The good news also came from his life-long constituents. Busby reported on a survey completed in Texas: "The most marked change is the waning—and virtual disappearance—of the highly negative ratings long characteristic of opinion polls in Texas as Senator and Vice President. Only 6 percent give the 'worst possible rating' . . . *Only 13 percent are 'unfavorable' in any degree.*[13]

Of course, Johnson's term began three years after his election with Kennedy into national office. Perhaps for this reason, the administration's self-congratulation became even more prevalent late in the 1964 campaign, when it was increasingly clear that Johnson would be a decisive victor on his own. On October 12, Busby informed Johnson of his popularity with the campaign press corps. "You have not, at any point, enjoyed the respect and admiration of any segment of the press to compare with the sentiment running among this traveling contingent now." Busby explained that Johnson's popularity was the result of various acts of political courage; primary among these was an October 9 New Orleans campaign speech that passionately expressed Johnson's belief in the civil rights movement to a southern audience. Johnson concluded his speech with an ad lib that momentarily shocked, then won over, his audience. It was about an unnamed Democratic U.S. senator who left Mississippi as a young man. When an old man, the senator expressed a deep desire to then Representative Johnson and Speaker of the House Sam Rayburn. "I would like to go back down there and make them one more Democratic speech. I just feel like I've got one in me. Poor old state, they haven't heard a real Democratic speech in thirty years. All they ever hear at election time is nigra, nigra, nigra."[14] Johnson's willingness, as a southerner in an election year, to take on such a politically divisive issue, was seen by many as a sign of Johnson's willingness to stand for his principles. Busby explained the reason for Johnson's support:

> The New Orleans speech was courageous—and, most especially, *courageous politics*. People dislike or distrust politicians as synonymous for non-courageous, devious acts. Thus, overnight, they are speaking of you—as once of FDR—as the "master," "the champ.". . .
>
> Several men discoursed on this theme: "I can see now why they say Johnson is [a] leader—I'd follow him now myself." The press . . . is seeing you through new eyes. Virtually all of it comes from this one factor: a show of deliberate courage.[15]

The administration's self-congratulation remained after the 1964 election, as Johnson's public approval rating was consistently high. Even the Vietnam War was seen as a source of Johnson support; an accurate observation at the time.[16] Another memo from Busby to the president reveals this.

> The temper of the people is difficult to assess from the White House. My premise for this memo may be far wrong. However, my own intuitive conclusions are these:
>
> The indicated high level approval for your handling of Vietnam stems from your willingness to give "prompt, adequate, and fitting reply.". . .
>
> The public confidence in you rests heavily on the man-in-the-street's instinct that while you want peace as he does, you also will not allow the Communists to push the U.S. around, as the man in the street believes he would not.

It is important to note the self-congratulatory nature of the perceived reason for public support: the people and the president are believed to be thinking as one. This memo eventually makes that connection explicit. "The people, as you said so often during the Korean War, are probably ahead of the Congress—and certainly equal in their understanding to the Executive."[17] Two June memos from staff aide Hayes Redmon reinforced the idea that the bold actions in Vietnam were bringing support. Pollster Louis Harris privately informed Redmon that his polls revealed "a clear mandate for the President's course of action." A later memo explains, "[There is] support for air raids and

[a] clear, overwhelming mandate to send as many U.S. troops there as necessary to withstand the Vietcong attacks during monsoon season."[18]

There was also a strong belief that the domestic policies of the Johnson administration were widely hailed by the people. A December, 1965, memo, for example, lists the five most popular issues that elicited public support. Of these five, four are domestic: Medicare, civil rights, anti-poverty, and increased Social Security benefits. The same memo notices the similar thinking of the administration and the people: "A Harris poll showed that people blame crime on social problems rather than a breakdown in law enforcement. Asked to list the causes of crime, people named such things as slum life, restless youth, poverty, racial discrimination. This is a good tie with the Great Society programs in anti-poverty, education, civil rights, etc." Even fifteen months after the election, the administration could continue to gloat. Hayes Redmon reported to Special Assistant Bill Moyers about an "interesting and factual" report of the Republican National Committee. The report noted the severe defeat of 1964 and acknowledged that most traditional Republican groups had voted for Johnson, and non-voters (often said at that time to be a silent source of Republican support) overwhelmingly supported Johnson over his opponent, Barry Goldwater. Similarly, Bill Moyers was informed in late January, 1966, that support for the Eighty-ninth Congress, which passed large segments of the Johnson program, was "widespread and bipartisan," with support for Medicare, education, and the tax cut being most favorable.[19] Johnson was particularly proud of his domestic legislative achievements, and during his early years his administration credited these achievements for his popularity.

According to published Gallup Polls in the early days of the administration, the president had good cause for self-congratulation. In February, 1964, 61 percent approved and only 14 percent disapproved of Johnson's foreign policy record. Although it dropped to 50 percent approval and 28 percent disapproval in February, 1965, it rose to 60 percent approval and 25 percent disapproval by July, 1965. Johnson's forte was certainly domestic policy, and polls showed an impressive standing. In February of 1964, 70 percent approved of Johnson's domestic policy record, with only 12 percent disapproving. One year later, the figures were still impressive: 60 percent approval versus 20 percent disapproval. By July, 1965, 63 percent still acclaimed Johnson for his domestic policy achievements, while only 27 percent disapproved.[20]

Despite these impressive levels of public approval, the administration often showed signs of fear that the support was illusory or transient. Sometimes others would attempt to create fear, in a deliberate effort to change the president's policy objectives. For example, Secretary of Commerce Luther Hodges of North Carolina and Tennessee Governor Buford Ellington warned Johnson of white "backlash," a movement to Goldwater in "distressingly great numbers," because of Johnson's support for civil rights legislation. Johnson ignored them. Other fears were probably typical campaign jitters, as when Horace Busby cautioned Johnson against an "'easy win' theory": "My own feeling is that many within the Democratic Party apparatus have a naive, immature, unreal view of what the Party is up against . . . . Confidence is rested too casually on polls, press, and pros who have already badly misjudged the country's temper in their estimates about Goldwater's delegate bid. If they missed these, their bias—or naivete—is no service to the Democratic cause."[21]

Such campaign jitters would remain when approaching the 1966 elections. An early 1966 memo that discusses the crushing defeat of the Republicans in 1964 cautions against "over-optimism about 1966."[22] They feared that some unknown public opposition might exist.

The topic of Vietnam seemed to instill the most fear of support loss; despite the early approval, the administration anticipated problems that its policy would cause. In February, 1965, for example, Horace Busby informed Johnson that increased controversy over the Vietnam policy made him "genuinely fearful of several possibilities" including "a rising acceptance of the pro-isolationist, pro-negotiation, pro-withdrawal position." In the early years of the Vietnam conflict, Johnson was also apprehensive of hawk sentiment. In a meeting with his Vietnam policy advisors on May 16, 1965, Johnson revealed his nervousness about a recent bombing pause. "My judgment is [that] the public has never wanted us to stop the bombing . . . we don't want to do it too long else we lose our base of support." Similarly, on August 4, 1965, Special Assistant to the President Douglas Cater held a meeting to discuss the "information problem" stemming from press reports of American activities in Vietnam. The notes record Cater's saying at the start of the meeting, "Our public posture is fragile."[23] Johnson noted in a December, 1965, meeting with his Vietnam advisors, "The weakest chink in our armor is public opinion." The following day, Special Assistant to the President Jack Valenti sent Johnson a memo discussing public perceptions of decisions on Vietnam, noting, "You have said yourself that our support is wide but thin."[24] The administration believed that its Vietnam policies could cost the president his public support.[25]

This fear affected policy advice to the president. Notes of a National Security Council meeting in February, 1965, for example, indicate Bill Moyers's support for a retaliatory bombing strike "to meet the demands of domestic opinion requirements."[26] Hayes Redmon, in a memo to Bill Moyers in February, 1966, also discussed his concern about the loss of support from those who wanted to escalate the Vietnam conflict. "In order to bring the moderate hawks back with us, we should, in Louis Harris' phrase, 'bloody it up a little.' We must show the public we are getting somewhere. Recent publication of Vietcong killed and wounded rates was helpful in this regard."[27] The administration's fear of support loss contributed to its decisions about policies and public presentations of information.

Carter

Despite his low margin of victory in the 1976 election, Carter's administration also partook in the notion that it closely identified with the prevailing public mood. Before the inauguration, Patrick Caddell, the president's pollster, told Carter that his staff needed to "be made sensitive to the implicit contract made during the campaign between the Governor and the electorate." As could be expected, the administration was quite sensitive to its good public standing immediately after the inauguration. Special Assistant to the President Barry Jagoda, for example, noted that "we are currently basking in public favor." Gerald Rafshoon positively gushed to the president about the administration's public standing. Referring to several recent events that gained favorable publicity, Rafshoon wrote: "Right now we are basking in the afterglow of wonderful media saturation. The inaugural walk . . . the speech . . . the gala (especially the gala), the pardon, the thermostats, the refreshing open cabinet meeting, Mondale's trip . . . etc. . . . etc. Your ratings could not be any higher than right now."[28] Pat Caddell contributed to the flattery of the president. On February 3, 1977, in response to a nationally televised speech to the nation the previous night, he wrote, "Last night's was a truly first rate performance. We're all really proud of you." The president himself congratulated his administration on February 24 by passing along some poll results to Press Secretary Jody Powell and Assistant to the President Hamilton Jordan that showed the increased public trust in leaders of various segments of society (including companies, religious groups, labor unions, and the government) since a year earlier. Later that year, young people were seen as gravitating to the president. A July 1 memo described young people as "an ally of the Carter administration" on several of the "most critical" issues of the administration's agenda.[29]

But despite its public standing, the Carter administration's enthusiasm about public support during the early days of its administration was tempered by the concern that the public support could easily drop. Prior even to the inauguration, Pat Caddell had warned the incoming president that his popularity could be short-lived. Specifically, Caddell warned Carter that approval from "the non-traditional groups which supported him in 1976" needed to be "compensated for among other groups" to protect his "political future."[30]

The extent to which the administration was concerned about future support loss was surprising. Only two months into the administration, Hamilton Jordan was warning Carter about a possible challenge for the 1980 presidential nomination by California Governor Jerry Brown! Looking ahead to the next presidential election, Jordan cautioned Carter that while a strong economy "will make you unbeatable in 1980," a poor economy "might permanently erode your popular support with the American people."[31]

Carter was amenable to the argument that he could lose public support. This can be seen in the president's favorable reaction to a memo he received June 14, 1977, from Gerald Rafshoon, warning him that "although you are still *personally* popular, your performance is perceived as inconsistent." Rafshoon advised the president that he was becoming overexposed to the public and that he was "running the risk of *boring* the people." He told Carter to use other sources to communicate to the public. Rafshoon's memos states, "The risk [is in creating] a personally popular, populistic Jimmy Carter, thought of as a good guy, but with support that is not deep." The president must have been attentive to the memo, for it was covered with Carter's handwriting, including the notation: "Jody and Ham. Good advice. J."[32]

Others contributed to the ominous warnings. A memo from Ted Van Dyk, of the Agency for International Development, reminds Carter of the popularity slides of Truman, Johnson, Nixon, and Ford, and informs the president that "your standing is high; but . . . it can plunge overnight when the first real setbacks occur (and they will)."[33]

These administrations began with the belief that the public was supportive of them and with the conviction that they could act on their agenda because their opinions were consistent with public opinion. They feared the day that public support would decline.

The reaction of these administrations to their popularity is similar to the reaction of one of Kingdon's winning politicians. All three administrations identified themselves with the public during these times and partook in self-congratulation about their levels of public support. Their policy pursuits were cognitively consonant with their general belief about the wishes of the public.

The belief that their actions resonated with the public kept these administrations attentive to public opinion. Perhaps this is why they were so aware of the potential for support loss. The concern for a potential downturn in public approval was significant, because it created a motivation for continued attention to the attitudes of the people. Because they did not want to lose their cause for self-congratulation, the administrations were open to the possibility of public discontent and nervously watched for the potential erosion of support.

During their popular times, these administrations fulfilled John Geer's expectation that modern politicians would be responsive to public opinion. The administrations were concerned about the public's judgment and thus attentive to public opinion.

The high degree of attention to the opinions of the general public is remarkable for its contrast with the later days of these administrations when they exhibited the signs of having lost touch with the public. As the next two chapters will indicate, these administrations were never as broadly attentive to the public as they were during the peaks of their popularity. As time passed, they subtly dismissed aspects of public opinion.

Chapter 2

Interpretation in Times of Declining Approval
Optimistic and Presumptuous

Invariably, presidential popularity declines after the passing excitement of a new presidency. Presidents know this too, and they try to push policy proposals while they are still popular. The decline in public approval does not negate the importance of the public to the administration. Given the nature of the modern presidency, a presidential administration still must ask about the public, and it still must interpret the meaning of public opinion.

This chapter will examine how the Truman, Johnson, and Carter administrations changed their interpretation of public opinion as public approval declined. An explanation for these changed beliefs can be found in cognitive dissonance theory. The earlier belief that public desires and presidential actions were in accord had become strained.[1] As a result, members of these administrations embarked on dissonance reduction. Two beliefs resulted: (1) the optimistic belief that they would experience an imminent rise in popularity, and (2) the presumptuous belief that their problems stemmed from their image and their poor communication techniques. Both of these beliefs were more palatable than believing that the public support loss represented real disenchantment with the administrations. But at the same time, they led these administrations to an estrangement from the possibility of a richer understanding of the American public.

Harry Truman's Declining Popularity

Truman's times would prove turbulent. While the public supported him in the immediate aftermath of World War II, his popularity was fleeting. Figure 2.1 shows that Truman's Gallup public approval rating dropped sharply after his first year in office, falling to 33 percent in September, 1946. The decline was perhaps partially attributable to the economic troubles that occurred as soldiers returned home to seek employment and as price controls were lifted.

Although the Republicans in 1946 won majorities in both houses of Congress for the first time since 1928, Truman's approval rating would rise in 1947. It reached 63 percent in late March and early April after he gave his Truman Doctrine speech. The speech to Congress was a statement of America's cold war intent, declaring that the United States would support people struggling for freedom. In late May, Truman's public approval peaked at 65 percent. In June, Truman vetoed the Taft-Hartley Act, which placed restrictions on

Figure 2.1
TRUMAN (MIDDLE — MODERATE APPROVAL)
Source: *The Roper Center for Public Opinion Research*

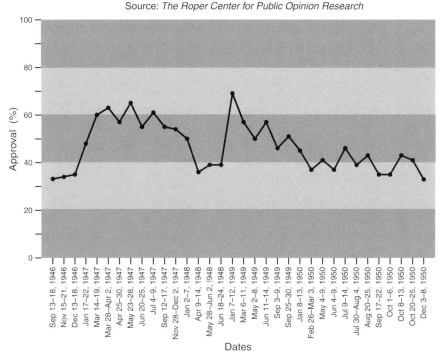

labor unions. Congress overrode the veto. But Truman's defiance of Congress was popular among many Democrats, particularly labor union supporters. Truman's popularity remained above 54 percent through 1947.

Although Truman's approval rating was 50 percent at the beginning of January, 1948, his fortunes would soon decline. Gallup's three public approval measurements that year—one in April, one in May/June, and one in late June—showed that the president's support had slipped to 36 percent, 39 percent, and 39 percent, respectively. A number of things may have dampened public enthusiasm for Truman. In February, he called on Congress to pass civil rights legislation, alienating southern Democrats. That same month, the Soviet army assisted a coup in Czechoslovakia that led to the installation of a pro-Soviet government. In March, Truman reinstated the draft. In June, the Soviets blockaded all traffic in and out of Berlin, and Truman ordered an airlift that would last through September, 1949.

In July, the Democratic convention proved to be an inauspicious beginning to the presidential campaign as southern delegates walked out over the party's civil rights plank. But Truman had an ace up his sleeve. Announcing that he would call a special session of Congress so that the Republicans could pass programs of the type favored by their nominee Thomas Dewey, Truman effectively set a trap that would expose a division within the Republican Party. By

September, the president was able to use the special session as an opportunity to denounce the "do-nothing" Congress.

Truman's historic surprise election in November boosted his public approval. Gallup's published public approval rating for the president was 69 percent in January, 1949, and all but one reading was above 50 percent for the year. By 1950, however, Truman's fortunes began to sag once again. In January, his public approval rating was 45 percent; by early March it had dropped to 37 percent.

North Korea's invasion of South Korea on June 24, 1950, started a new crisis that would remain throughout the president's term. Truman's rapid military response gave him a brief jump to 46 percent public approval. But as the number of troops in Korea increased, the public grew weary. In February, 1951, Truman's approval rating fell below 30 percent for the first time, to 26 percent. (See figure 3.1, in the next chapter.)

Lyndon Johnson's Declining Popularity

In May, 1966, Gallup's public approval rating for Johnson had fallen below 50 percent for the first time, and the White House became concerned about the declining level of support. In early June, Press Secretary Bill Moyers informed the president, "Conversations with Gallup, Harris, and other professionals in the poll business confirm only one thing: that our standing is down and likely to drop further."[2] Moyers was right. The decline was steady and undeniably significant. By October, Gallup's published approval rating for Johnson had fallen to 44 percent, and by September, 1967, it had dropped to 38 percent. Johnson's earlier years of support had become the halcyon days of his presidency, with levels of approval that he would not again equal. Figure 2.2 illustrates Johnson's status during his middle years in office.

The change in Johnson's political climate in late spring of 1966 was subtle at first. The decline in his support could not be clearly attributed to any single factor. There was some growing discontent about U.S. policy in Vietnam from both those who wanted to escalate and de-escalate American involvement in the conflict, although the strongest opposition was still fairly isolated. There was a growth in inflation, from 1.7 percent in 1965 to 2.9 percent in 1966, significant by the standards of 1966. Nonetheless, the economy was still strong for the average American, with an unemployment rate of only 3.8 percent.[3] Johnson's dealings with the press were strained, but he was hardly the first president to suffer that.[4] Perhaps the public was simply becoming disinterested in the colorful Texan with his seemingly endless supply of energy. Although the source of the decline was not obvious, the decline was, and it would definitely have its repercussions.

By the second half of 1967 the mild distrust of early 1966 had grown into a more serious problem for the Johnson administration. Campus groups were protesting the Vietnam War; Republicans were decrying the high inflation rate; and Johnson's policies—which once seemed to sail through Congress—were now caught in quagmires of compromise or a complete lack of support.

Figure 2.2
JOHNSON (MIDDLE — MODERATE APPROVAL)
Source: *The Roper Center for Public Opinion Research*

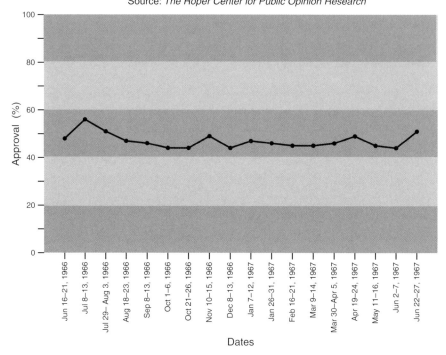

Published Gallup Polls revealed many problems for Johnson's attempts to convince the public of the worthiness of his Vietnam policies: the number of Americans in 1967 that thought American fighting in the war was a mistake grew from 32 percent, in February, to 37 percent, in May, to 41 percent, in July; in June, only 48 percent said they had "a clear idea of what the Vietnam war is all about"; and in July, 52 percent of the public disapproved of Johnson's handling of the Vietnam situation.[5]

The Johnson administration faced significant evidence that it had lost its high levels of public support.

Jimmy Carter's Declining Popularity

Although Carter's support base began eroding in late 1977, he still maintained moderate levels of support through early 1979, according to figure 2.3. Between February, 1978, and April, 1979, the Gallup public approval rating for Carter fluctuated between 37 percent and 52 percent. Several factors may have contributed to Carter's support loss. For one, the country was experiencing economic difficulties, with the inflation rate at 7.7 percent in 1978 and 11.3 percent in 1979. The unemployment rates were 6 percent and 5.8 percent. The country also had an "energy crisis," with gasoline prices rising from an average

Figure 2.3
CARTER (MIDDLE — MODERATE APPROVAL)
Source: *The Roper Center for Public Opinion Research*

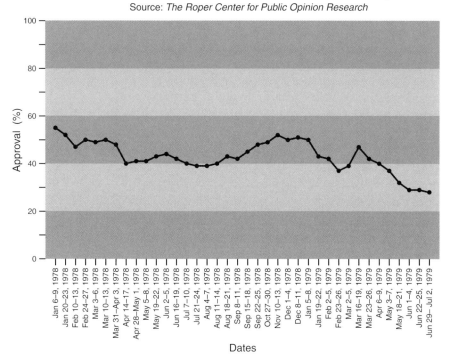

of 67¢ per gallon in 1978 to 90.3¢ in 1979.[6] Carter also took on the divisive is-sue of returning the Panama Canal to Panamanian control, and although the required treaties passed the Senate, the debates in early 1978 were contentious. (Carter's approval rating fell from 50 percent in mid-March to 40 percent in mid-April. The first of the treaties was passed in April.)

Carter's support bounced back modestly after the conclusion of the Camp David Summit in September, 1978. The summit, which brought together the leaders of Egypt and Israel, resulted in an important peace treaty between Israel and its Arab neighbor to the south. Carter kept Israeli Prime Minister Menachem Begin and Egyptian President Anwar Sadat at the negotiating table for thirteen days in the presidential mountain retreat, and he is credited with skillfully negotiating a deal. Perhaps due to the new-found respect for Carter, his approval rating edged to 52 percent by November, 1978. The approval lev-els were not sustained, however. Between January and June, 1979, Carter's ap-proval rating fell from 50 percent to 28 percent.

In early July, 1979, Carter invited several prominent Democrats, who had experience in Washington, to Camp David for an assessment of his administra-tion. This was followed by subsequent discussions with other national leaders.[7] Then, on July 15, Carter spoke to the public in a televised address about the "crisis of confidence" in public institutions and the need for the nation to unite to deal with its problems. The speech was well received in some circles. William Holland writes, "Initial polls revealed a jump in Carter's popularity of approximately eleven percentage points. Telephone calls and mail received at the White House were overwhelmingly favorable. Carter's follow-up speeches on energy in Kansas City and Detroit captured the front pages of the large national newspapers. Pictures of the shirtsleeved President hammering home his points . . . allowed the President to be portrayed in a position of strong leadership."[8] The beneficial effect of the speech would prove to be short-lived. On July 17, Carter asked for the resignations of everyone in his cabinet in an effort to restructure his administration. The unintended consequence was to make it seem as if Carter's presidency was in crisis, and it undermined the gains the president had made.[9] Some began to criticize the speech for suggesting that the country's faults lie with the public's malaise, and the label "the malaise speech" stuck despite the fact that the word did not appear in the speech. The polls showed the reaction; Carter's Gallup public approval rating would remain below 33 percent through early November. (See figure 3.3, in the next chapter.)

Popularity Is Just Around the Corner

As support levels tapered off for these administrations, each believed that the declining support was temporary or not as bad as it seemed. Often this belief manifested itself in statements indicating that opposition was from a vocal minority, and therefore did not constitute a real threat. On other occasions individuals would assert, without substantiation, that although people disagreed with some of the president's policies, they could still be considered supporters. The archives are also riddled with comments suggesting that public support would increase soon, but these predictions were seldom true in the short run and ultimately wrong over the long term. This represents a curious switch from the earlier times, when the fear of support loss motivated the administrations to be more attentive to public opinion. Instead, these administrations subtly closed themselves off to emerging public opinion through their confidence that a return to popularity was imminent.

Truman

When the Truman administration's support levels declined, staff members believed at first that their situation was temporary. By late 1946 it was quite apparent that Truman was no longer popular. Robert Hannegan, Democratic National Committee chairman and postmaster general, nonetheless managed to elevate spirits at an October 11 cabinet meeting. Minutes of the meeting reveal Hannegan's decidedly positive outlook after a public statement made by Truman. "Political situation is improved since President's speech. Rep[ublicans] are still trying to answer speech. There are no glowing reports around the country, but it is not as bad as press reports. We will lose some seats but we will also gain some. Thinks we will retain control of Congress. Cabinet members should follow up our advantage."[10] Note Hannegan's conviction that things were not as bad as they seemed. This view came from other sources as well, even after the loss of the Democratic majority in the 1946 election. Clarence Cannon, in his final days as chair of the House Appropriations Committee before the Republican takeover, managed to give Truman some good news about the Democrats' losses. Cannon had been back in their mutual home state of Missouri and told Truman, "Before I left Missouri I noted unmistakable signs of a change in sentiment—and the mail from the State since I have been in Washington corroborates that view. . . . a lot of farmers are beginning to wonder why they voted the Republican ticket." He added, "As a matter of fact—while the Republicans seem to have won a tremendous victory in Missouri—they carried most of the state by the narrowest margins. . . . If the election was held today we could carry the State. And we can certainly carry it in 1948."[11]

Optimistic statements about Truman's future do not become noticeable again for several years. During this time, he was unexpectedly elected to another term in 1948, resulting in a temporary recovery of his popularity. By 1950, however, the public was again tiring of Truman. Gallup Polls that year showed his approval rating fluctuating between 37 percent and 46 percent; with the repeated slide in approval, the administration's optimism returned.

One optimistic reference by the president occurred at a cabinet meeting on May 19, 1950, which the president began by comparing the Republican Party to the Whigs and the Federalists. The GOP did not go extinct, however, and—as 1950 rolled on—White House officials began to think increasingly about how to deal with the Republicans. As the midterm election approached, they maintained their optimism. In fact, a memo by Special Assistant to the President Ken Hechler in staff aide George Elsey's files indicates a fear of *too much* optimism. Referring to Captain Victor Hunt Harding, the executive secretary of the Democratic Congressional Campaign Committee, Hechler notes, "Captain Harding's office reports that the prospects for November now seem so good that they are frightened by the overconfidence and complacency which seems to have gripped the political leaders in many localities."[12] On November 6, election day, Hechler passed on "Captain Harding's Fearless Forecast," an upbeat set of predictions for the election. The election ultimately resulted in Democratic losses in both houses. Even so, a post-election report by Hechler maintains that the problem was essentially turnout, and that the country would elect a Democratic president if the turnout were higher. Similarly, a memo from Special Assistant to the President Philleo Nash to Ken Hechler in late November reports that despite the Democratic losses in Wisconsin, Democrats were in fact on an "upsurge" in that state! The memo blames low turnout.[13]

Johnson

The tendency to give a rosy view of the political climate after a decline in approval is quite noticeable in the Johnson administration.[14] For example, in May, 1966, after informing Bill Moyers that pollster Oliver Quayle found in North Carolina a 53 percent disapproval of Johnson's handling of the Vietnam War, Hayes Redmon relayed the pollster's view that "the negative rating does not

mean that there is anything approximating public support for the noisy minority voices of [Vietnam policy detractors such as Arkansas Senator J. William]
Fulbright, [Oregon Senator Wayne] Morse, [General James M.] Gavin and the
New York Times."[15] Another example demonstrates how the administration
could optimistically drown out bad news with the good. On July 26, Hayes
Redmon sent Charles Roche a memo listing the "political moods" that congressional candidates would face in the 1966 election:

> 1) A trend of opinion favorable to the President as regards his job
> in general and his handling of Vietnam in particular.
> 2) Public frustration over the duration of an unpopular war in
> Vietnam.[16]

On February 17, 1967, Staff Assistant Fred Panzer, who was responsible for research on public opinion, informed the president of his latest Gallup approval
rating, which was 46 percent. Gallup published the numbers in such a way as
to demonstrate that fewer people "strongly approved" (down to 16 percent
from 23 percent in September, 1966) or "strongly disapproved" (down to 17
percent from 26 percent) of the president. Despite the fact that there was no significant improvement in the rating and there was actually a decrease in strong
supporters, Panzer explained it optimistically:

> What does this mean? Apparently, the public is marking time. Most
> significantly, the violent opposition is beginning to soften, perhaps
> because
> • people have more understanding of the President's problems.
> • people are impressed with your post–State of the Union posture.[17]

(As we will see, this quote also reveals another phenomenon that occurred during the middle levels of popularity for Johnson—the belief that the people need
only "understand" the administration to support it.) The beginning of another
Panzer memo is blatant in its attempt to accentuate the positive: "Here's a better way of interpreting the Gallup release for yesterday, March 12, 1967."[18]

The middle levels of popularity are marked by a faith in an eventual
upsurge in the polls; few of these predictions had even short-term validity. On
May 26, 1966, for example, the White House staff took note of one of Oliver
Quayle's observations in Wyoming. "Olly says he feels confident, despite these
unhappy figures, that the president will 'come back' by September." No comeback occurred. In January, 1967, Assistant to the President Jim Jones informed
Johnson that a negative Gallup Poll, which seemed to repudiate a positive Harris Poll, was inaccurate: the Gallup data were a month old and predated some
significant changes including "the favorable response to your State of the Union
Message." The implication, of course, was that improvement would be evident
in the next poll. It was not. Similarly, Panzer's analysis of a February poll inspired him to write to the president that "a breakthrough on the upward side is

highly likely if things keep on the way they are." There was no breakthrough. On April 5, Robert Kintner informed the president that he was feeling positive about the future. "I sense a greater upsurge over the next few months. I don't know, obviously, the reasons for this, and I think they are probably rather complex factors." Kintner did little more than relay positive "vibes," but the president reacted warmly. "Tell him, 'The President liked that very much,'" Johnson told his secretary. Of course, there was no upsurge. On May 12, 1967, Panzer informed LBJ that some positive Harris Poll results slated for publication the following week might "seriously jolt the hopes of the two G.O.P. front runners" and "take the Vietnam war out of the campaign."[19] Neither occurred. Optimism like this would become more difficult to muster with passing time.

The administration was susceptible to anyone who could play off the desire to return to cognitive consonance about the administration's stance with the public. George Reedy, in *The Twilight of the Presidency,* notes the importance of emphasizing the positive. Reedy, who worked in the Johnson White House at various times, as both press secretary and special assistant to the president, notes that a strong president "has a propensity to create an environment to his liking and to weed out ruthlessly those assistants who might persist in presenting him with irritating thoughts." In comparing the contemporary White House to Versailles, Reedy observes, "The sensitive mind boggles at the revelation that the . . . assistant who shows up at the bed chamber at 7:15 in the morning with a Gallup poll demonstrating a five point rise in popularity is displaying the total sum of the court wisdom of a Richelieu (who, of course, had other forms of wisdom as well)." One wonders if Reedy had Fred Panzer in mind. Panzer was often instrumental in presenting information in a more palatable way. Altschuler notes that Panzer's reports to Johnson were typically "searching out the most optimistic possibilities rather than telling the president just how serious the problem was."[20] This trait, which could soften the blow of bad news, would become even more common and have more serious consequences as the public disapproval levels increased and as Panzer became more central to the integration and interpretation of poll data for the president.

Carter

The Carter administration also appraised its public opinion situation optimistically, though perhaps not as frequently as the Johnson staff.

One early example of optimism occurred in February of 1978, when Assistant to the President Stuart [Stu] Eizenstat advised Carter that if he made regular statements to identify himself with the administration's efforts to make the government more efficient and less regulatory, "that identification should redound in the polls." Other optimistic projections surfaced in the White House. Vice President Mondale sent the president an analysis by pollster Peter Hart, who anticipated a "comeback" in Carter's popularity. By late summer this expectation became much more common. On August 14, 1978, for example, the vice president sent Stu Eizenstat an editorial from the *Milwaukee Journal* that welcomed a report of a "public backlash against criticism of President Carter."[21] The article no doubt bolstered their optimistic bias.

Carter's success in dealing with Egypt and Israel at the Camp David Summit also invited optimism. One memo to the president from Assistant to the President for Congressional Liaison Frank Moore and Stu Eizenstat reports on Delaware Senator Joseph Biden's calling with poll numbers purporting to show that "positive movement in your direction was occurring prior to the Camp David announcement." Carter passed the memo to his wife, who passed it to their son Chip. On September 29, a memo from Hamilton Jordan to Carter said that the "post Camp David euphoria" could be used to inspire trust in Carter's economic leadership. On October 13, Jody Powell informed the president that the *New York Daily News* was about to run a story on the "The Remarkable Comeback of Jimmy Carter."[22]

On February 22, 1979, Gerald Rafshoon sent an article, titled, "Carter may win in 1980 despite low rating—pollster," to several of Carter's top aides. Perhaps the height of administration optimism occurred after Carter's Crisis of Confidence speech. The immediate public reaction to the speech was favorable. Carter himself passed along a stack of supportive letters to Hamilton Jordan with the handwritten note, "Ham, glance at these. We should have 25,00 [*sic*] Americans eager to help us. J."[23] In November, soon after Americans working in the embassy in Iran were taken hostage by followers of the Ayatollah Khomeini, Jody Powell's office received an ABC-Harris Survey that spoke of the political comeback in public support that Carter had made as a result of his handling of the crisis and posited its possible permanence.[24] The rally-around-the-flag support that Carter received after the taking of American hostages gave the White House hope for a longer resurgence for Carter in the polls. All of the good words notwithstanding, the Iranian hostage situation slowly eroded Carter's support.

Belief in the Need for Better Communication

A striking pattern of public opinion interpretation occurred in all three administrations right after their popularity began to decline: an omnipresent belief that the drop in approval was due to problems in White House communications. Officials consistently agreed during these times that "the message isn't getting out," or "our story isn't being told." Essentially, these administrations acted on the tacit assumption that the people *would* support the president if they more clearly understood what he was doing. The situation was thus dismissible as not really serious; after all, support would come as the people were educated.

Truman

The Truman administration's reaction to the decline in popularity followed a pattern that we will see again in the Johnson and Carter terms. The White

House consensus was that the lack of public support was primarily due to poor communication. The archival record indicates that the administration believed that its difficulties with the public could be resolved if only it could produce better speeches and get its message out. Indeed, the phenomenon continued late into 1951, as approval polls revealed a sustained lack of public support for Truman.

Of course to some extent the administration leaders were right. No doubt some of their problems were due to poor communications. Truman was not a gifted public speaker like Roosevelt, nor did he demonstrate his predecessor's charm in dealing with the press. However, the administration relied on the poor communication explanation too extensively. As this discussion will show, the Truman administration became increasingly unwilling to acknowledge the public's judgment of its actions, relying instead on the belief that it was failing to communicate clearly enough for the public to understand.

One feature about this phenomenon is unique to the Truman administration. An examination of White House documents suggests that the Truman administration actually had two time periods when it believed its problems could be addressed by better public relations. The first of these began in mid-1947 and lasted into the early days of the 1948 campaign season. The second began in late 1950 and lasted through 1951. Interestingly, both of these periods occurred during major slides in public approval; Truman's Gallup approval rating slid from 60 percent in March, 1947, to 36 percent in April, 1948, and from 46 percent in July, 1950, to 23 percent in November, 1951. Even if they ignored polls, as Truman claimed they did, administration leaders were certainly aware of their lowered public standing. They believed that they could address the problem through better communications.

Two incidents in June, 1947, nicely illustrate the faith of Truman and others associated with the administration that presidential explanations alone could sway the public to support Truman. First, DNC Executive Director Gael Sullivan responded to worries about former cabinet member Henry Wallace, who had become vocal in his opposition to Truman's domestic and foreign policies. Sullivan's memo advises that because Wallace would be a candidate in 1948, Truman should counter Wallace with presidential fireside chats explaining the president's position.[25] In this instance, Truman did not follow the advice. Later that month, however, at a cabinet meeting on June 20, 1947—the day Truman vetoed the Taft-Hartley labor bill—Secretary of Agriculture Clinton P. Anderson told Truman, "The people of the country do not understand the mistakes in the bill." Truman responded, "I am going on the radio tonight—to explain what this bill would do."[26] He did. Truman seems to have concurred with Anderson's suggestion that an explanation to the public could solve their problems.

There was also a belief that Truman could sway the public's concerns about the cold war by giving good speeches. One example occurred after Czechoslovakia fell to Soviet subjugation in February, 1948. Soviet-American relations had become severely strained, and Henry Wallace called for Truman and Stalin to meet and address the tension. In response to these events, George

Elsey advised Clark Clifford that the president should give a speech "strong both in content and delivery." Elsey wanted Truman to address relations with Russia, because Truman had spoken best "when he has been 'mad.' . . . His poorest deliveries have been when he is merely *for* 'good things.'" Truman appears to have accepted the advice. On March 17, he gave a St. Patrick's Day speech in New York City that spoke of the need for Congress to speed its work on the Marshall Plan, support universal military training, and "enact temporary selective service legislation." In explaining his policies, Truman referred transparently to the "one nation" that was dominating its neighbors and obstructing international cooperation. The speech went on to denounce Communism and Henry Wallace. "I do not want and will not accept the political support of Henry Wallace and his Communists. If joining them or permitting them to join me is the price of victory, I recommend defeat. These are days of high prices for everything, but any price for Wallace and his Communists is too much for me to pay. I'm not buying." The speech was nationally broadcast on the radio.[27] Communication was also seen as the remedy to a worried public a month later, when James Davis, a director at the Department of the Interior, wrote to Clark Clifford that Truman needed to give "a simple restatement of fundamental American principles" to address the "bewildered, frightened and baffled" average American.[28]

Clark Clifford believed that Truman's poor speaking ability was a cause of the administration's public relations problems. A 1948 campaign report, "Progress of the Campaign," in Clark Clifford's files states that "the whole problem of the President's speeches is a separate one and not reported herein."[29]

Comments suggesting that the administration could communicate itself out of its problems with the public increase noticeably in documents written starting in late 1950, after the second slide in Truman's approval. Eleven days before the 1950 elections, for example, Ken Hechler suggested to George Elsey that the president should respond to Republican charges concerning "softness on communism." Hechler wrote, "If a devastating answer is delivered to this charge, it would give a specific lift in close states where it is a leading issue." Truman did address the issue of Communism three days before the election in a political speech, broadcast on radio and television and paid for by the Democratic National Committee. The speech spoke of many policy issues, including the dangers of isolationism and "the threat of communist aggression." Two days later, speaking from Independence, Missouri, he spoke out again about the threat of Communism in the world.[30] The concern with communication continued after the 1950 election. At a cabinet meeting on December 22, for example, while talking about German re-armament after World War II, the president called for emphasizing the administration's position against those who wanted a return to isolationism. Meeting notes detail the president's comments: "This policy is approved by the Security Council and the President. It is important that this position is made clear to the republic and to the rest of the world."[31] Truman seemed to be relying on the belief that the drive toward isolationism could be conquered simply by presenting rational facts to the public. Political allies thought similarly. Congressman Richard Bolling of

Missouri wrote a letter to the president in early 1951 suggesting various ways that the administration could effectively disseminate information to the public; the president agreed and indicated that he would act on the congressman's suggestions.[32]

Notes of the cabinet meeting on February 2, 1951, also show the concern with communication, this time over the administration's Korean policy. Truman says that the question of "Why are we in Korea?" is a "pertinent" one and indicates that he is "planning to get the answer to the people." Vice President Alben Barkley responds, "The exposé must be handled in a dramatic way—maybe in a speech by the President. We must maintain the morale of our own people." Charles E. Wilson, director of the Office of Defense Mobilization, adds, "We must all make a contribution to re-assure the people of the rightness of our position." To this, Barkley responds, "There is an eagerness on the part of the public to know the facts."[33]

The administration was extremely focused on communication during the spring of 1951, a time during which Truman had a March–April approval rating of 28 percent and a May approval rating of 24 percent. Implicit in all of their discussions was the notion that the public was not adequately apprized of the administration's understanding of political events. On March 19, George Elsey proposed to Ken Hechler that certain people on the staff of the White House and the DNC get together on a regular basis "to discuss ways of producing more and better publicity for the administration." Four days later, Kenneth Hechler informed another official of his feelings about the activities of the Bureau of the Budget: "I am shocked at the complacency of those responsible for explaining our budgetary and fiscal policy to Congress and the people. I am also disturbed by the fact that this situation looks like it will get worse before it will get better." On April 2 he sent a somewhat petulant memo to an official at the Bureau of the Budget expressing his belief that they could get "better information on budget policy out to the people . . . if one or two staff members could devote more uninterrupted time to this task."[34]

Assistant Press Secretary Joseph Short, on the president's orders, prepared a memorandum discussing the administration's need to communicate its policies more effectively. Short wrote the memo immediately after an April 2 meeting with several of the administration's key advisors present, including assistants Matthew Connelly, George Elsey, Averell Harriman, Charles Murphy, Short, and the DNC's publicity director, Charles Van Devander.

> It was recommended by this group that there be launched a nationwide speaking campaign in which Cabinet officers and sub-Cabinet officers would carry the message of the administration's policies and objectives to the 48 states.
>
> Those attending the meeting felt that the administration's "story" was not reaching the American public. . . . The speaking campaign would take directly to the people the tremendous foreign and domestic programs of the administration which now are being obscured by issues of much less importance.

The next two paragraphs reveal, however, the extent to which the administration was assigning its problems to the failure to communicate a message. Note the number of issues involved.

> For instance, the reasons for our fighting in Korea cannot be told too often. Re-explanation of NATO and of what has been, and is being, accomplished through ECA and Point Four, one of the most imaginative programs ever conceived, badly needs selling to the American people.
>
> When our emergency Domestic Policy (price control, etc.) is nearer to crystallization, the speeches on foreign policy should be intermingled with those explaining what is being done to hold the country together internally during this period of a larger military build-up. The story of the progress of the build-up, within security limits, should also figure in the speeches.[35]

The administration's concern with communication continued. On April 20, 1951, George Elsey prepared a letter that he ultimately did not send. Nonetheless, it is an interesting example of the mindset of administration officials. Elsey addressed the letter to pollster Hadley Cantril at Princeton and included eight speeches given by the president between October, 1950, and April, 1951. Elsey was going to take up Cantril's offer to "go over them and make suggestions so as to improve the identification and understanding by the people of the President's problems." In late May, 1951, the administration was undertaking the production of a publication concerning its foreign policy going back to the Yalta conference at the end of World War II. A memo about the publication notes, "it is vital that we get together something for publication and wide distribution, not only for speakers, but for the hundreds of thousands of people throughout this country."[36] In October, a lengthy memo was circulated in the White House that discussed communication problems. The memo states that the "Republican National Committee has been skillfully pouring a steady stream of poison into the minds of the American people for four years. We have a lot of work to do to offset this poison and to get our own story before the people." Again, note the firm belief that their problems stem from an inability to tell their "story." Other comments in the memo are similar: the DNC's need to create a speechwriting division "is so obvious that it need not be argued here"; "since we do not have most of the press and radio with us, we must blanket the country with speakers from Cabinet rank on down"; "the information officers in the Executive Agencies should be needled . . . some of them are not doing a good job in telling their story to the people." The memo concludes, "The National Committee must devote itself single-heartedly to telling our story and must be staffed with people who believe that this is the most important function in the world for the next twelve months."[37]

Despite the efforts at communication, Truman's Gallup approval rating never rose above 33 percent after distribution of this memo.

Johnson

The Johnson administration was also convinced that its problems stemmed from its inability to explain policies to the public. This attitude is startling pervasive. On May 17, Robert E. Kintner distributed a memo to Johnson and his chief assistants indicating his displeasure with the president's speeches. "The material that is being developed for his [the president's] consideration is not adequate, fresh enough or sufficiently significant." The memo arranges plans for future speechwriting and concludes, "It is the desire of the President to . . . concentrate more on major addresses in an important setting, in order that he will have the opportunity to explain more fully and more carefully his domestic and foreign policies and his future plans and their execution." Johnson wrote on his copy, "Bob—good. L." The staff met May 20 to discuss the problem. Kintner and Moyers observed that the president was "not being adequately serviced" in his speeches and that those involved in the speechwriting process had become "embarrassed by the methods of procedure and the results."[38]

Curiously, several memos written in various offices on June 9, 1966, also reiterated this theme. Hayes Redmon, assistant to Bill Moyers, wrote two memos to his superior that day discussing Johnson's falling public approval. One memo reports that Redmon's discussions that morning with pollsters Gallup, Harris, and Quayle led him to conclude that the president must "offer 'some ray of hope' that the situation will improve." A later memo that day indicates Redmon's reflections:

> The memorandum I sent you earlier today pointed out that the pollsters feel Vietnam and inflation are the primary causes for the President's slump in the polls. While I agree that these are certainly no good, I have the strong impression that our problems go beyond a mere statistical read-out on some worrisome issues. I feel that the President is simply not getting through to the people. I fear that his regionalism, accent and his press reputation for cantankerousness and willfulness are creating an atmosphere of unpopularity for him. I believe there is a serious need to freshen his image.

Redmon further notes that discussions with Democratic Party operative Fred Dutton were confirming his own beliefs: "He [Dutton] said that the Great Society is simply not being sold. He feels the fact that the President achieved the greatest legislative program in our country's history has not gotten across to the public." Moyers relayed the information of the memo to President Johnson, including the need "to offer some ray of hope."[39]

A June 9 memo to Special Assistant to the President Marvin Watson from assistant Sherman Markman expresses a similar theme. Markman's concern about a negative Iowa poll resulted in conversations with Iowa Governor Harold E. Hughes and his chief political advisor. The Iowans discussed the problem that Johnson was having in their agricultural state. "Both agreed that the problem is image rather than substance, but the bad image has struck home." They recommended that Johnson take advantage of a scheduled June 30 speech in Iowa by giving a "strong presentation" explaining the importance of the Midwest. "It should be extremely down to earth." Markman continues, "The Governor is strong in his suggestion that the President throw away the script and talk straight to the people as he can do so magnificently."[40] Note the pervasive belief that speeches, communication, and correction of "image" problems are the solution to the administration's difficulties.

A final, June 9, image-problem memo to the president deals with the subject of inflation. Kintner writes, "I have been trying to figure out how to get over nationally the story that while prices are higher, people earn more, their living standards are higher, and theoretically at least, they should be able to save more." Kintner asks Johnson for permission to talk to Treasury Secretary Henry Fowler and CEA Chairman Gardiner Ackley about "the assembling of some real information, in a simple form that people can understand." Johnson approved.[41] The memo surmises that inflation would not be a political problem if the White House could only communicate its "story" more effectively.

Various memos that summer before the midterm election indicate the continued White House obsession with speechmaking. A memo from Moyers to Johnson was attached to a survey of members of Congress about issues of concern in their districts. The members were also asked about "the most important subjects for speeches" in their area; that information was carefully tabulated according to region of the country. A June 27 memo from Redmon to Moyers relays information to various individuals about Johnson's deteriorating support among farmers: "all are agreed that what's needed is a 'tub thumping' farm speech . . . . What we really need is some good quotable material on the farm situation from the President." In early August, assistant Harry McPherson returned from a trip and discussed with Moyers the opinions of people he met in Rhode Island, making some suggestions. Moyers passed the list of suggestions along to the president, including this one: "As much outright candor, even to the point of risk, about what the President is doing or not doing in every major crisis situation. Honest mistakes of judgment sometimes sit better with the public than success won by sleight-of-hand. If he could be seen to stumble, occasionally, while trying to do the best he could for the public, it would help."[42] Similarly, staff aide Will Sparks wrote to Cabinet Secretary Robert Kintner on August 26 about Johnson's "speech-writing problems."

> The President is not getting enough credit for being the kind of man he is, and for the ideas he supports.
>
> One reason is that neither his personality nor his true concerns are being projected adequately in his formal appearances . . . .
>
> It might help, I believe, if more attention were paid to what I call . . . the purely rhetorical aspects of the President's appearances.[43]

Numerous other examples portray the administration's faith that it could talk its way out of problems if it could only be more clear, more open, more forceful. But one document illustrates this idea more than any other. Staff Assistant Charles Maguire typed twenty-seven pages of notes from a meeting on November 3, 1966, between the president and his speechwriters. Archival researchers will find these notes remarkable for several reasons. The notes are very detailed and include long quotes of comments from those in attendance. Furthermore, the notes reveal the earthy, home-spun side of Johnson that is often missing in the bland memoirs and histories of his administration. The memo includes colorful language, analogies to his "uncle Ezra," comparison of his desire for peace with sexual urges, and chides to his aides about their wives' physical statures.

Most striking for the purposes here, however, is the firmly expressed blame on speechwriting for poor dealings with the public. The president's comments demonstrate this point:

> He saw two deficiencies in present speeches: (1) "Sex 'em up more." (2) "Make them Presidential.". . .
>
> The President discussed the speeches he had delivered on his Asian-Pacific trip. He felt they did not communicate his goals. They were not simple enough, sharp enough to get the message across . . . .
>
> The President referred to the Manila communiqué as a case in point of bad communications. It was much too long. It was not at all quotable. . . .
>
> The President's general impression of the Manila communiqué: "It constipated me. I vomited twice.". . .
>
> He elaborated on the one-sided Liberal arguments, referring to . . . criticism about U.S. bombing "of steel plants and oil refineries.". . .
>
> "We've got to get this point over . . . it isn't fair and we're not doing the job . . . we can use the White House and all the Government to put these points over . . . but we are not doing it . . . we are too damn soft and puddin-headed.". . .
>
> As an example of an area where we have failed repeatedly to communicate a true and meaningful story, the President instanced "higher prices and inflation." "Folks just don't know that they can pay those high prices and still have more left over."
>
> The same is true of the Vietnam story. The same is true of so many signing statements; "no one listens, no one remembers."

Johnson perhaps clung to his belief that "the message isn't getting out" longer than his speechwriters. The meeting notes reveal that, in Johnson's absence, which occurred in the middle of the meeting, the speechwriters agreed that a major problem was Johnson's insistence on headline-grabbing features (called "grabbers" by the president) in all his speeches. When Johnson returned, he said that he wanted in every speech "one good lead . . . even if you have to say 'my wife is ten months pregnant.'"[44] While others were shying away from sensational presentations, Johnson was still holding on to the belief that dramatic statements could get public attention and support. These repeated references to communication technique and image presentation illustrate the administration's premise that the American people *would* support it if they knew what it was doing.[45]

Of course, many have noted that Johnson communicated poorly in large, staged settings.[46] But the administration's problems amounted to more than simply style. This was the same Lyndon Johnson who had won 61.1 percent of the popular vote in 1964, and the same Lyndon Johnson who had at least two years of strong support. Johnson's public speaking technique left much to be desired, but it was clearly not the cause of all of the administration's troubles.

In fact, the administration faced serious problems with its programs. As noted earlier, inflation rose dramatically in 1966, perhaps stemming from the added spending in Vietnam and on the Great Society. Many of the problems associated with the War on Poverty were leading to urban and racial unrest, and the administration had few answers for the resulting problems.[47] Poor image alone did not account for the Gallup Poll's report that only 32 percent of the population held a favorable opinion of the Great Society.[48] By the end of 1966, nearly 400,000 American troops were stationed in Vietnam, 6,377 Americans had been killed, and leaders could see no obvious solution to the conflict. When Gallup Polls revealed in November, 1966, that a third of the public declared that American involvement in the Vietnam conflict was a mistake and 40 percent disapproved of Johnson's handling of the situation in Vietnam, the administration inexplicably persisted in blaming image problems. Many people may have had serious questions about administration policies, but the administration chose not to address that possibility seriously. As Altschuler observes, "Polls were not . . . able to provide the scientific evidence that would convince Johnson that his policies had lost public support."[49]

Carter

The Carter administration was especially convinced that its problems stemmed from poor communication. Indeed, this phenomenon can be seen earlier and lasts longer in the Carter administration than in the other two administrations. Carter's slide in approval began quite early, as did the conviction that communication was the cause of the slide. As with the Truman administration, the Carter administration would continue its focus on communication even into its unpopular times.

The first suggestion that Carter needed to communicate better occurred in the summer of 1977, right at the end of his short honeymoon. In June, Carter received a letter from pollster David Yankelovich, which analyzed Carter's public standing. The letter was passed to several people in the White House—including the president—and was summarized for Carter. Yankelovich's letter asserts, "Our conclusion is that communication with the public—effectively launched by your speeches several months ago—has now badly stalled, and the momentum of public support needs to be built up again." Cabinet Secretary

Jack Watson concurs in a memo but tells the president, "I also think that we cannot put the whole burden of communication on you." Watson's memo asks other members of Carter's senior staff to comment on better ways to communicate Carter's positions about energy. Later that month, Jody Powell also voiced his concern about communication. His memo advises the administration to develop "and constantly reinforce three or four themes to give meaning to what is now to the public a confusing and unfocused series of actions and statements."[50]

The focus on communication as a source of Carter's problems became even more pronounced as his first year in office ended. On December 27, 1977, Stu Eizenstat sent Carter a memo, which Carter labeled "excellent" and forwarded to the vice president, Hamilton Jordan, and Jody Powell. In the memo, Eizenstat calls for Carter to combat the public's confusion from a "blizzard of legislation" by a "public education process under which you are seen to focus on only a few key items." Hamilton Jordan's comments, three weeks later, on the upcoming State of the Union Address, reinforce the idea that good speaking is a solution to Carter's problems with the public. "For a lot of the wrong reasons, the American people have incorrect impressions today about your ability to lead this country and manage the government. This speech offers a good opportunity to correct some of these impressions. Nothing is more important than your strong delivery of this speech and I would encourage you to take as much time as necessary away from the office to prepare for the speech."[51]

A memo from the vice president's chief of staff, Dick Moe, to Mondale, Jordan, Powell, and Deputy Assistant to the President Landon Butler on April 3, 1978, also exemplifies the administration's belief that it was not making its efforts clear to the public. "The problem is that we are not getting much credit for having reduced unemployment nearly two points in the last year, and even where we do it is largely wiped out by increasing apprehension over inflation. . . . All this together . . . has . . . led many people to conclude that a) we don't share their deep concerns about the economy, b) we have no policies to deal with them, or c) if we do have such policies, we're somehow unable to make them effective. There's no other way to account for a 72 percent disapproval rating on the President's handling of the economy." Moe suggests that Carter give a nationally televised "Economic Report to the Nation."[52] Although a direct link to this memo is not clear, the president did give a speech concerning the administration's inflation policies to the American Society of Newspaper Editors on April 11.[53]

At least one journalist at the time observed that the administration was fixated on communication as its central problem. Dom Bonafede of the *National Journal* wrote that members of the administration were "convinced that the problem was not the President's performance or the substance of his policies but the inability of the White House to get its message across to the public."[54]

In May, 1978, Executive Associate Director for Budget Bowan Cutter sent a memo to Hamilton Jordan suggesting that the administration's declining public support stemmed from "public concerns about our competence." Cutter's proposed remedy was to "have a unified political/policy strategy and theme. We've not really had one to date; and 'getting control' could be such a theme. But if it is, it must be expressed in every way we can—in speeches, public statements, backgrounders, etc." A Gerald Rafshoon July memo to the president details "the tone, themes, and priorities" that Carter should communicate. "The tone projected by you over the next ninety days should be one of competence. You should be serious, methodical, purposeful—working hard."[55]

Mrs. Carter may have shared in the belief that communication was at the core of the administration's problems. The First Lady passed to the president a copy of a memo written by essayist Norman Cousins to a source outside the White House known to the First Lady. She advised Carter to read it and send it to Gerald Rafshoon. The memo encourages the president to make more upbeat statements about the energy crisis and to "picture it as a chance for Americans to move on to a new and higher plateau where they can fulfill their potentialities as individuals."[56]

Those in the administration, of course, were proud of their achievements and were always concerned when they believed they were not getting enough credit. Stu Eizenstat was clearly upset at a Harris Poll in July, 1978, that showed that the public disapproved of the president's handling of cutting the rate of unemployment, despite the gains in employment during his time in office. Eizenstat forwarded the poll to Communications Director Gerald Rafshoon with a note, "This is incredible. Can we do something to correct this?"[57]

In August, 1978, the administration began looking for a "theme" for the Carter presidency. Discussion in an August meeting indicates that although the staff would not "remake Carter's 'image,'" they would "help clarify and focus public perception of Carter." Later that month, Stu Eizenstat also wrote about the idea of finding an "administration theme"; he suggested "peace and prosperity." Around this time, Gerald Rafshoon was concerned about projecting a theme for the upcoming Camp David Summit. In late August, he said that they should emphasize "*CARTER IN CONTROL* . . . In control of the meeting . . . in control of his staff . . . in control of the coverage." On September 1, he sent Carter another memo reemphasizing the need for that theme. Hoping for successes in September, he told Carter that the "over-all sense of purpose which has been clear to you from the beginning . . . is only now emerging into public view."[58]

The administration also focused on getting out its economic policy message. Hamilton Jordan wrote to Carter in early September, "I believe that we have got to convince the American people that you are *serious* about inflation and are *continually working* on inflation." That note was attached to a memo to the president from staff member Joe Aragon in which he writes, "The public needs to know that the government is, in fact, making an effort to . . . bring inflation under control." Carter annotated the memo with a message to "coordinate with major inflation announcements." The theme of communication continued. In late September, Jordan advised Carter to use a group of senior advisors to "advise you how to present your program to the American people." In the same memo, Jordan identifies one of the administration's biggest weak-

nesses as "the *perception* that we don't have our act together on economic policy matters."[59] The administration was convinced that the public disfavor was
due to misperception; it stood to reason that better communication was the
solution.

Gerald Rafshoon was also involved in discussions about the administration's inability to deliver a clear message. An October 11 memo to him from
Labor Secretary Ray Marshall presents an example of this. Marshall tells Rafshoon, "One of the Administration's biggest domestic success stories has been
the reduction on [*sic*] unemployment. . . . Yet, as you know, the Administration
has *not* gotten anything like the credit it deserves for this major accomplish-
ment." Rafshoon replied favorably to Marshall. In October, Rafshoon's assistant, Greg Schneiders, responded positively to a report that pollster Peter Hart
had stated that the Carter presidency needed a theme that the public could easily understand. By December, Rafshoon had enlisted Jody Powell to join him in
emphasizing the administration's need to tell its story. On December 1, the two
wrote a joint memo to Carter urging him to give a speech on waste and fraud
in government, stressing that it was "important to demonstrate leadership on
this issue—*to send the message* to the public, the press and the bureaucracy
that you have a *personal* interest in it." An undated 1978 note from Powell to
Rafshoon after a presidential trip reinforces the importance of better communications: "Although coverage on the trip was good, it was despite rather than
because of the President's speeches. He needs to spend more time working on
these rally speeches."[60]

The failed-message theme continued into 1979. In March, Secretary of
the Treasury Michael Blumenthal met with Hamilton Jordan and Gerald Rafshoon and presented a memo to discuss this idea. The memo notes the successes
the Carter administration had had in the economic realm but concludes,
"Nevertheless, we get little or no credit for any of the positive developments,
while being loudly blamed for every conceivable economic problem in the land,
real or imagined. . . . Like it or not, we have failed to convince the public that
the President is a strong economic chief, leading and influencing events rather
than reacting to them." Jordan passed the memo to the president.[61]

In April, Dom Bonafede of the *National Journal* returned to his observation about the White House's obsession with broadcasting its message. An
article about Gerald Rafshoon notes, "Efforts to articulate presidential objectives and priorities, normally referred to in the White House as 'getting our
message across,' have been refined but still remain a problem. 'We have to do a
better job of educating the public,' remarked a White House aide, repeating a
familiar refrain."[62]

Indeed, the administration at this time was wrestling what it perceived to
be a communication problem. In June, Carter approved a Powell plan that required White House officials to register with him any contact with the press and
required cabinet officials to get prior approval from Rafshoon. Powell reported
that the result of such a move would be positive, because, "People long to see
you crack the whip a little and impose some order on what they see as chaos in
the Administration." Similarly, a memo by Jack Watson on June 21 advises the

president to get control of the federal government's "contradictory, inconsistent and hopelessly confusing statements on the energy situation." Advice even came from outside the administration. A July memo from Jesse Jackson to Carter laments that Carter's accomplishments "go largely unnoticed," partly because of "hostile" media. Jackson recommended that Carter appear on the Phil Donahue show![63]

Vice President Mondale and Hamilton Jordan were also similarly concerned about improving the public's view of the president. Together they wrote to Carter that he should focus his schedule on inflation and energy, because these were chief issues of concern to the nation. "The overall image should be of you working with your advisors to make progress in these areas." Sometimes the fixation on image could be amusing. One memo from Rafshoon and Powell tells the president how to give a message about increased oil prices: "It should be done with force and a little anger. Dark suit." Some staff members believed that the administration needed to overcome past failings. A mid-June memo from Rafshoon to Carter advises, "In the month of July, we should thoughtfully conduct an 'operation repair.' During this month I propose that we have a three-network interview (or [CBS anchor Walter] Cronkite alone) that encompasses domestic as well as foreign issues."[64]

The administration's obsession with how to communicate culminated in a major public relations gambit—the Crisis of Confidence speech or "malaise" speech to its detractors—in which Carter spoke to the American people about the need for the country to reunite and about how he would overcome his own shortcomings as president. Administration leaders consulted many people on how to proceed with this, and unsigned notes from a Jody Powell file labeled "Dinner with Bill Moyers, et al." indicate that plans were formulating as early as May for a dramatic speech "to connect in [the] most basic way to the public concerns." Notes of the dinner meeting suggest the effect the administration was hoping to achieve: "'making conscious what lies unconscious' must strike deep to trigger response. Mea Culpa." The speech was to be part of a dramatic event to "make [a] deep psychological connection to the public."[65]

The administration had planned for the president to speak about the country's energy problems on Thursday, July 5. On July 3, Hamilton Jordan wrote to the president, informing him that he still favored giving the energy speech but that Pat Caddell wanted Carter to give the Crisis of Confidence speech. Jordan notes scornfully that Caddell "continues to argue that we need first to make our 'America is going to hell speech' to grab the attention of the American people and then to focus their attention on the energy problem. . . . Pat is right that we are not in an ideal posture at the present time to rally the American people. We are low in the polls and a lot of people have turned us off and given up on this. *But we cannot not speak out and not attempt to lead just because people may not listen to us and may not follow.* We have no choice but to try." His five-page memo concludes with the line, "The [energy] speech is badly needed."[66]

Despite Jordan's plea, the energy speech was canceled, and the administration decided to give the Crisis of Confidence speech on July 15. By all indications, this speech resulted from extensive planning and discussion in the White House. As noted earlier in this chapter, Carter initially received a positive response to his speech. However, his public approval rating would remain low after he dismissed his cabinet and left the impression that his administration was in crisis.

The speech did not mark the end of the administration's attention to "getting out the message." In fact, unlike Truman or Johnson, this theme would continue for the remainder of Carter's term. Carter's staff seemed anxious to act immediately after the Crisis of Confidence speech because they felt that they had the public's attention. On July 27, staff aide Chris Matthews sent Jody Powell a message, saying that the public needed the rationale behind Carter's thinking, adding, "It seems to me that neither set speeches nor press conferences allow the President to get this kind of coherent message across." Matthews advised on-air television interviews. This idea seems to have been popular. On August 2, Gerald Rafshoon sent Carter a memo of "proposed media events": "During the next six weeks, I think it is crucial that we take advantage of opportunities to get our message out about the energy crisis." The memo suggests, among other things, that the president appear on a special primetime edition of *Meet the Press* and that he appear on a National Public Radio call-in show.[67] (Although there were no national broadcasts, the president did conduct a call-in show in Davenport, Iowa, on August 21. The president opened the show with remarks about removing the "threat to our Nation's energy security."[68])

In the aftermath of the Crisis of Confidence speech, the administration hoped to use the television networks as allies. In August, Gerald Rafshoon suggested that they should work with network executives to shape public opinion about energy. Rafshoon's memo contends that "we are faced with a basic public misunderstanding about the nature and severity of our energy problems." Focusing again on countering the public's confusion, the memo further notes, "Network television is the most powerful communications system in the world and can play an important role in attacking our energy problems by increasing public understanding." The memo was circulated to Jody Powell and others. Powell responded by writing, "Let's do it."[69]

Curiously, the idea of needing better communication then seemed to be ignored until November when Pat Caddell sent a memo to Carter about his public standing in a primary challenge from Senator Edward Kennedy. Caddell's memo argues: "we are *not* simply the victim of 'not getting our story out,' we are hostage to *real* events and to the *appearance* of how we respond to those events." Was this a change of heart? Hardly, for Caddell then places the blame squarely on the administration's failure to communicate effectively, discussing how the administration has failed with the public because of "the signals we send; frankly we respond too much and appear to initiate too little; hence, we appear to dominate too little." Caddell then provides examples, including Carter's having had only one "inflation event" since early September: "While not suggesting an answer to inflation, it appears to me that certainly we could have done more, sent more signals, been more in the thick of this major issue than we have." Note that the Caddell memo is still asserting that the sending of "signals" is at the root of Carter's low standing in the polls. Caddell, in an exasperated tone, then faults Carter's staff for not recognizing the need to take the initiative in the sending of signals. "It seems that three years of failure to send those signals or *understand* the process of synthesizing substance, boldness, signal, drama, and communication has led your principal advisors to simply walk away from it. . . . Without question, [sending signals] is the road that will yield the most results—force up the job ratings—provide rationale for voters to move toward you. I have totally and abysmally failed to move anyone on this subject. Therefore I am prepared to remove myself from the debate."[70] Given the record, however, Caddell's assertion, that the administration had failed to emphasize communication, falls flat. Caddell's text essentially argues that the administration was not communicating *effectively* despite the fact that it was plagued by "real events."

Caddell's fear that the administration had "walked away" from concern about communication also seems unfounded. In November, White House staff director Alonzo McDonald wrote to Jody Powell concerning the need to "'merchandise' the President's record," arguing, "we are not obtaining the depth [*sic*] appreciation of the President's programs, an understanding of the concepts underlying his actions and recognition of the thoughtful reasons for his positions." McDonald's memo suggests that they should "try several approaches in parallel to get our basic message across . . . The President is obviously on top of the substance with an amazing mastery of detail and a clear view of what he is trying to do, an impression the public does not have."[71]

Other undated 1979 memos identify Carter's speaking style as a cause for many of his difficulties. A memo written by Gerald Rafshoon asserts that Carter's speeches were too "gloomy" and advises more positive statements. Also in 1979, someone wrote to Greg Schneiders, commenting on a draft memo to the president about campaign themes. The author recommends adding a section that states, "Your speaking style is a serious problem. I know that you don't want to talk to a speech coach about it (though I wish you'd reconsider, because there are purely technical hints—proper use of breath and so on—that could help substantially). You should practice more."[72] A draft memo on the same topic by Rafshoon also advises Carter to speak only to small groups, because, with larger groups, "you tend to lose your voice, yell at the audience, appear strident, and lose that all important rapport." Rafshoon wrote that Carter should use his rhetoric to "overcome the misimpression that you're not tough enough for the job."[73]

A memo from Assistant to the President Anne Wexler and Al From on January 9, 1980, suggests that Carter should use the State of the Union to "get his themes across." In April, the issue of inflation was also a cause for promoting public communication. Three advisors assert in a memo to Carter that, despite the administration's implementation of an anti-inflation program, "we are headed for the classical trap—although significant activity is going on and people are working, public perception often seems to be that nothing is happening if you are not visibly involved." As a result, the three recommend that

Carter engage in a series of "anti-inflation" activities including speeches and briefings. Carter approved the proposal. In June, Stu Eizenstat recommended that Carter give more speeches about the budget, because "very few people actually know about the merits of and purposes behind your budget proposals." Eizenstat's text explains, "The particular value of speeches has been raised to me by several members of Congress recently, but also yesterday by Haynes Johnson of the *Washington Post*. . . . Johnson admitted that on the merits we really had not been inconsistent. But the public perception was otherwise—a fact he attributed to not having sufficient public and detailed explanations of our actions. He recommended more public speeches by you as a remedy." Perhaps pathetically, in December, 1980, after Carter had already lost his reelection bid, Jody Powell and Jack Watson were advised that the president should communicate with the public during his remaining time to overcome "unfair public perceptions about his record." Anne Wexler relayed her concerns to Powell that Ronald Reagan would get credit for Carter's accomplishments. A series of presidential trips was advised.[74]

As their popularity declined, these administrations began to subtly close themselves off to public opinion. When they were popular, they were afraid of losing that popularity and were thus motivated to pay attention to public opinion. The opposite occurred after their popularity declined. They fostered an optimistic belief that their popularity would soon return. The attempt to return to cognitive consonance between public support and administration actions is one explanation for the optimism. This may have resulted in the new belief that popularity was returning. This belief allowed these administrations to allay their concerns about additional support loss. As a result they could comfortably be less attentive to public opinion.

Perhaps most significantly, each of the three administrations presumptuously dismissed their problems with the public by blaming communications and style. Cognitive dissonance theory contributes an explanation for this. The declining congruence between administration actions and public support motivated these administrations to seek the consonance of their popular times; indeed, with the Truman administration this belief began again after their second slide in approval. In the minds of administration leaders, an efficient, dissonance-reducing technique involved blaming style and not substance. Style, after all, is more easily changed and potentially less serious.[75] These administrations did not entertain the notion that the public had good reasons not to like what they were doing.

This focus on communication and the belief in an imminent rise in popularity limited the extent to which these administrations were able to be responsive to the public. While Geer's expectation that modern politicians would be responsive to the public seemed possible in the previous chapter's analysis of the popular times, it seems less so in the times analyzed in this chapter. Instead, the three administrations studied here behaved in a manner more analogous to Jacobs and Shapiro's discussion of recent politicians who, they assert, look to public opinion to determine the best way to "craft" their messages and acquire support for previously determined policies. Although the Truman, Johnson, and Carter administrations were not overtly looking to the public simply to determine the most likely way to get a positive response, their obsession with communication had the same effect. That is, the administrations began to see the public more as an audience for their message and ceased to see the public as a guide for their actions.

The Truman, Johnson, and Carter administrations all began to grow out of touch as their popularity declined. Unlike earlier times when high public approval served as a source of self-worth and a cause for self-congratulation, later times were marked by a discrepancy between the administrations' beliefs about their actions and their information about public opinion. By creating a belief in a deficient communication technique, they were able to act as if the public would support them if only it understood their perspective more.[76] They further believed that public support would return as soon as the people heard the right message and caught on to what they were trying to do.

They were growing out of touch.

Chapter 3

Interpretation in Unpopular Times
Dismissive and Distrustful

Few presidents have the fortune of seeing their public approval rise back to the levels at their inauguration for any sustained period of time. For the three presidents studied here, the approval levels would drop and generally remain low. Truman and Carter each saw their approval levels drop into the 20 percent range. In fact, Truman's approval rating never climbed above 36 percent in his last two years in office, and Carter's was seldom above 45 percent. While Johnson's approval never dipped into the 20s like Truman's and Carter's, his approval rating would remain frustratingly low for a long time, below 45 percent more often than not in his last two and a half years in office.

This chapter will examine the interpretation of public opinion during the nadir of presidential popularity. In chapter 1, presidential interpretation during times of popularity was likened to a winning candidate on Kingdon's congratulation-rationalization continuum, with presidents' acting in a self-congratulatory manner. In this chapter, we will see that the loss of popularity resulted in their acting like Kingdon's losing candidates. They were losing in the perpetual campaign for public approval that characterizes the modern plebiscitary presidency. As with the rationalization of Kingdon's losing candidates, these administrations tended to blame their low level of approval on external causes. They were no longer convinced that stylistic changes alone would enhance public standing. Instead, they dismissed indications of public disapproval either as outright fabrications and misrepresentations or as indications of how the political opposition had manipulated public opinion against them.

The low levels of popularity resulted in these administrations' exhibiting classic signs of cognitive dissonance. Fiske and Taylor's *Social Cognition* notes that selective interpretation occurs when an individual translates ambiguous information in such a manner as to make it consistent.[1] As their approval levels further declined, individuals in these administrations became susceptible to interpreting negative information in such a way as to allow them to continue to believe that they had public support. This selective interpretation can be seen in three ways: (1) they frequently blamed their problems on the unfair manipulation of political opponents; (2) they developed beliefs that allowed them to dismiss the dissenting portion of the population as an atypical minority, even when evidence suggested otherwise; (3) for Truman and Johnson, they and their administrations developed a deep distrust of polls and pollsters. By cognitively creating enemies against their administration and the nation, they began to see opposition as unrepresentative of the American people. In addition to the selective interpretation, all three of these administrations began to patronize the public, perhaps as a way of dismissing public opinion. While these phenomena would sometimes occur at moments of frustration during popular times, the archival evidence suggests that the occurrence was much more common during unpopular times.

Ultimately, the ability of these administrations to dismiss public dissent interfered with their ability to be responsive to the public in any meaningful way. The phenomena observed in this chapter occurred twice for the Truman administration, first as the 1948 election approached with the expectation of a Truman loss and again as the slumping public support of the second term persisted. This chapter provides evidence that Lyndon Johnson went a step further than Truman or Carter in closing off public opinion. Johnson and his staff began publicizing even the most trivial instances of public support as a substitute for getting real support. As illustrated by Bruce Altschuler and discussed further below, the Johnson administration also attempted to manipulate the sources of public polling data.[2]

The Unpopular Days of Harry Truman's Presidency

Truman's public support had badly deteriorated by 1951, as shown in figure 3.1. Of the twelve Gallup public approval ratings that year, only three were above 30 percent. In November, Truman's approval had fallen to 23 percent. In February, 1952, the number fell to 22 percent, a record low to this day for presidents since public approval ratings were first taken during the Roosevelt administration. His approval rating did not rise above 33 percent again.

Truman had to deal with a wide variety of issues during the remainder of his term. The war continued to rage in Korea. A series of financial scandals involving prominent Democrats marred the administration's reputation. Truman's decision in April, 1951, to fire the popular General Douglas MacArthur for insubordination drew widespread condemnation—though the public slowly came around to Truman's point of view. In April, 1952, frustrated by the implacability of a strike at the nation's steel mills, Truman seized the mills and operated them under the auspices of the federal government, only to have the Supreme Court rule his actions unconstitutional two months later.

In November, 1952, the Democratic nominee for president, Adlai Stevenson, lost his bid to Republican Dwight Eisenhower. The Republicans won a narrow majority in both houses of Congress.

The Unpopular Days of Lyndon Johnson's Presidency

Figure 3.2 traces the drop in Johnson's popularity. His approval rating had fallen significantly by the autumn of 1967. Previously, the administration's levels of public approval were frequently good enough to maintain the hope that they would again rise. But the second half of 1967 was marked by a series of events that permanently scarred the Johnson administration: race riots in

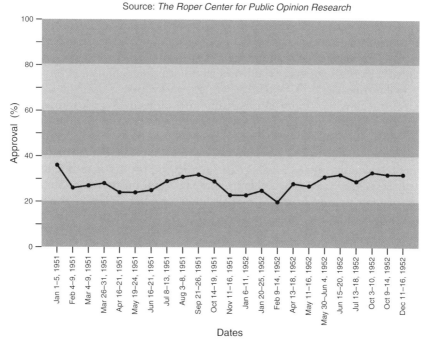

Figure 3.1
TRUMAN (LATE — LOW APPROVAL)
Source: *The Roper Center for Public Opinion Research*

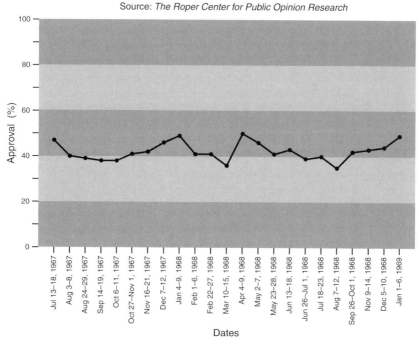

Figure 3.2
JOHNSON (LATE — LOW APPROVAL)
Source: *The Roper Center for Public Opinion Research*

Detroit in late July; a massive antiwar march on the Pentagon in October; and a decision in November by Minnesota Senator Eugene McCarthy to challenge Johnson for the Democratic nomination. Gallup's approval ratings for Johnson reflected the administration's difficulties, remaining below 40 percent from August through October.

By November, 1967, however, the administration had begun a brief respite from bad news. Johnson's approval rating crept up slowly to 42 percent in November, 46 percent in December, and even to 49 percent by January, 1968. This may have stemmed from a pro-Vietnam blitz orchestrated by the administration including optimistic speeches by the U.S. commander in Vietnam, General William Westmoreland, and U.S. ambassador to South Vietnam, Ellsworth Bunker. However, Johnson's political fortunes were lost with the optimism when, in late January, 1968, the Vietcong coordinated a surprisingly strong attack during the Vietnamese Tet holidays. Public opinion turned almost immediately against the war. In February, CBS News anchor Walter Cronkite summarized the situation for the American people like this:

> It seems now more certain than ever that the bloody experience in Vietnam is to end in a stalemate. This summer's almost certain standoff will either end in real give-and-take negotiations or terrible escalation . . .
>
> To say that we are closer to victory is to believe, in the face of evidence, the optimists who have been wrong in the past . . . to say that we are mired in stalemate seems the only realistic, yet unsatisfactory, conclusion.[3]

In early March, Johnson won a surprisingly narrow victory over Senator Eugene McCarthy in the New Hampshire primary, beating him by less than 7 percent. That same month, the Gallup public approval rating for Johnson was a mere 36 percent, with 26 percent of the public approving of his handling of the Vietnam War, and 49 percent thinking that the U.S. fighting in Vietnam was a mistake, according to Gallup Polls.[4] On March 31, Johnson withdrew his candidacy from the 1968 presidential election. The immediate public response was supportive, with Johnson's Gallup approval rating climbing to 50 percent; encouraging telegrams and letters flooded the White House.[5] Even so, his standing with the public never fully recovered. By August, it had fallen again to 35 percent, and it would range between 42 percent and 49 percent for the remaining months of his term.

The Unpopular Days of Jimmy Carter's Presidency

The last year and a half of Carter's presidency were troubled by a series of events, and Carter's relationship with the public remained strained.

After his cabinet shake-up in July, 1979, his approval rating remained under 33 percent until November, 1979, as figure 3.3 shows. On November 4, 1979, Iranian students took over the American embassy in Teheran—to protest

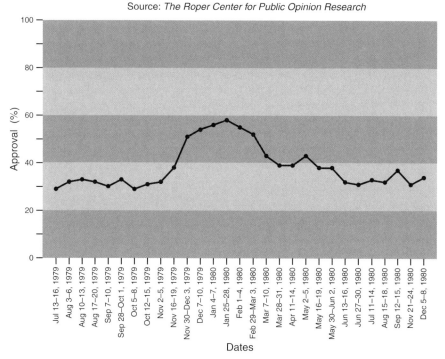

Figure 3.3
CARTER (LATE — LOW APPROVAL)
Source: *The Roper Center for Public Opinion Research*

the U.S. decision to admit the former Shah of Iran to the United States to seek cancer treatments—and took the embassy personnel hostage. The Americans would remain hostages for over fourteen months. On December 27, the Soviet Union invaded Afghanistan and put in place a government more to their liking. As is typical in such instances, the public supported the president during this time; his approval rating rose to 58 percent by the end of January. From there, his approval rating began a slow, downward drift. By late March, it had fallen to 39 percent. In June, it was 31 percent, and it would not climb above 37 percent for the remainder of his term.

The events of 1980 had made it difficult for Carter to regain ground with the public. Because of the invasion of Afghanistan, Carter announced in January that the United States would not attend the Olympics that summer in Moscow and urged American allies to do the same; the decision proved controversial. In late April, a military attempt to rescue the hostages in Iran went bad before it started—due to helicopter problems—and eight Americans were killed in the Iranian desert during the aborted attempt. In an unfortunate fate for Carter, election day was the one-year anniversary of the taking of hostages in Iran. He lost his bid for reelection, gathering only 41 percent of the popular vote.

Defining and Dismissing the Manipulative Opposition

Frustrated politicians often blame their problems on the unfair acts of political enemies. During the Watergate crisis it was revealed that the Nixon White House had an official list of enemies, and some of the names on the list included people whom casual observers would hardly consider dangerous. During the peak of the controversy surrounding President Clinton's scandals involving Monica Lewinsky and Whitewater, his wife publicly asserted that the problems were caused by a "vast right-wing conspiracy."[6]

The administrations studied here are no different. Each of them, frustrated by the problems caused by the lack of public support, found enemies to blame. Like most politicians, they sometimes blamed the press. They targeted the unfair behavior of political opponents. They blamed members of their own party or the party establishment. They even identified specific individuals as the cause of their problems. At other times they dismissed criticism as the manipulation or manifestation of socially undesirable elements. By assigning blame, these administrations avoided a more careful examination of the causes of public discontent. This became particularly noticeable when their public approval had persisted in serious decline.

Truman

The Truman administration had an early occasion to blame its problems on enemies. In 1946, the administration's domestic agenda faltered before an uncooperative Congress, and the president's staff looked for the source of the troubles. Lobbyists captured their attention. In March, Robert Hannegan, then postmaster general, wrote to Truman about the "lobby lice" that he believed were dominating Congress: "The lobbies do not voice the popular will," and he advised Truman to launch a "vigorous offensive . . . against these selfish 'me first' lobbies that are promoting disunity and disrespect for sound Administration proposals." Hannegan's letter suggests that such an attack "on these legislative vultures would provoke a healthy response from the people and help to unify their support of vital national legislation." Truman concurred, replying that someone should deal with the "pain in the neck" lobbyists.[7]

Truman and Hannegan also soon targeted journalists. A September correspondence between these two shows the president blowing off some steam at two newspaper columnists. Hannegan wrote to Truman to assure him that a columnist's assertion that Hannegan would not support Truman in 1948 was false. Truman responded by calling two columnists "sphere heads" and stating, "If either of them ever tell the truth, it is by accident and not intent."[8]

By mid-1947, the attacks on enemies sharpened. Two people emerged as targets of administration distrust: Henry Wallace and James Roosevelt. Wallace, who not only had served as Franklin Roosevelt's second vice president but also in the cabinets of both FDR and Truman, was increasingly seen at the time as a radical. (He would run for president against Truman in 1948 on the Progressive Party ticket.) On June 6, George Elsey sent Clark Clifford three "items

relating to Mr. Wallace's activities and their affect upon Administration decisions." A memo prepared by Democratic National Committee Executive Director Gael Sullivan reads, "There is no doubt that Wallace has captured the
imagination of a strong segment of the American public. His meetings have
been well attended. Much of the enthusiasm has been stage managed by Communists. The chanting and the cheering have all the appearance of staged
events." Sullivan continued that many in the crowd were "rabid left-wingers"
but feared that there were others drawn to Wallace. He also noted that a resolution sponsored by James Roosevelt, son of Franklin Roosevelt and a member of congress from California, to "greet Wallace with open arms" to a meeting of the California state Democratic committee had narrowly been defeated.[9]
The following April, Truman received a letter from a supporter in California,
reporting on the activities of a Democratic dinner in Los Angeles. It noted that
the event was "dominated" by James Roosevelt, who planned it such that it
"would not be in any sense a Truman dinner."[10]

As the 1948 election approached, speculation was high that Truman
would not be reelected, and the behavior of the administration was consistent
with that of the other administrations during their unpopular times. Truman's
prospects looked bleak, and his staff frequently attacked the press as a mis-
chievous group that was deliberately causing problems for the president. An
August memo from William Batt, director of the research division of the DNC,
notes, "Our biggest issue, high prices, is being fouled up by a concentrated campaign from Republican (i.e., all) newspapers and radio commentators."
Another memo a few days later finds press complicity in attacks on the administration: "The American people are being saturated with propaganda in the
press and on the radio to the effect that the Truman administration has done a
poor job in dealing with Communism. . . . The false impression now existing
in the minds of millions of voters about the supposed relationship between the
Democratic administration and Communists must be erased."[11] Truman's
friend and former senate aide Max Lowenthal lodged a similar complaint in
October, when he wrote to Clark Clifford that the president's campaign needed
to emphasize that "the widespread propaganda, through the press, the radio
and independent commentators, to the effect that the result of the election is a
foregone conclusion is part of a highly organized and richly financed campaign
against the President. This campaign is underhanded vicious and effective." An
unsigned report in Clifford's files, which seems to be written around October
15, also suggests repeatedly that the media has been spreading "unfair propaganda." The report finds a particularly sinister reason for the "propaganda of
the radio broadcasters": "The news broadcast programs are for the most part
sponsored only by the wealthiest corporations. These sponsors pay many millions of dollars each year to the broadcast companies for the radio chains to
broadcast through their newscasters. . . . But, by using their news broadcasters
to further political propaganda favorable to them, they are in reality making
contributions running into millions of dollars to the Republican Party. And . . .
these wealthy corporations . . . have been greatly benefitted by the last income
tax law that was passed." The memo then goes on to discuss particular broad-

casters and the sponsors of their programs, pointing out how the broadcasts do the bidding of the companies that sponsor them.[12] The source of the memo is unclear, and it may have come from outside the White House. Nonetheless, it is consistent with the White House attitudes about the press, and its presence in Clark Clifford's files suggests that the author may have been an ally prominent enough to come to Clifford's attention.

Sometimes the Republicans could be singled out, as in one memo about the 1948 special session of Congress that referred to the Republican leadership as "Neanderthal men" and "reactionaries."[13] Paranoia and griping about the opposition during a tough campaign is not unusual, but the administration's tendency to find enemies continued as it grew more unpopular after the election.

Sometimes the attacks could be amusing. Truman, to vent his anger, had a habit of writing letters that he did not send. Fortunately, many of these letters survive. One of these, written in September, 1949, shows Truman's feelings about the dishonesty of the press. Offended by an editorial in *Editor and Publisher* that criticized him for his disparagement of the press, Truman's letter proclaims, "If ever an organization needed searching criticism in the public interest, it is a press that turns out to be ninety percent wrong, both in politics and in public policy. I expect to crusade for an honest, free press and sometime or other we will get just that sort."[14]

The complaints grew harsher and more frequent in 1950 and 1951 as the administration's popularity was steadily declining. A memo by Ken Hechler— dated June 19, 1950, but which does not have an addressee and may have been a memorandum for the record—records observations about a television program sponsored by a group calling itself the "Citizen's Committee for the Hoover Report." Hechler documented the television program like a crime event, reporting on the time it was broadcast, and the name and address of the narrator. The memo seems to be a simple disputation of the facts of the broadcast, which was introduced by the author as "ninety-eight percent anti-Administration propaganda and two percent discussion of the Hoover Commission." There were other sources of irritation, too. Some in the cabinet, for example, thought that the press was having a damaging impact on the people. At a December 12 cabinet meeting, Secretary of Labor Maurice Tobin reported that he was concerned about public morale. Notes of the meeting report that after blaming the press for being "ruthless and damaging," he "suggested that [the] publishers of [the] U.S. be brought to Washington and told of their responsibility to encourage American patriotism and morale." To this, Secretary of Commerce Charles Sawyer agreed, and added that "broadcasters are also a vital force in such a program." One sees the extent of Sawyer's concern: "One of our real problems today is whether we are going to save the Bill of Rights. Commentators and columnists have a right to say anything they please about the Govt and its officers—which they see fit to abuse."[15] Apparently members of the press cleaned up their act with amazing speed. A week later, Tobin reported to the cabinet that his concern "has evaporated into thin air" because the "press seems to have had [a] change."[16]

The administration was quick to see the media as a presidential enemy in the aftermath of Truman's controversial firing of General Douglas MacArthur. A memorandum in George Elsey's files reads, "The President has probably noticed that the Scripps-Howard newspapers, in recent weeks, have been sharpening their attacks against the Administration. There is good reason to believe that this is the opening campaign in a real journalistic war against the Truman program." A comment by Charles E. Wilson, director of Defense Mobilization, at an April 20 cabinet meeting suggests that he believed the press was acting unfairly. Wilson said that he had spoken to a group of "news editors" after MacArthur's farewell address to Congress and "was shocked to learn of their emotional surrender to MacArthur's speech."[17]

Truman himself was quite annoyed at the press. In late April, he sent Clark Clifford a copy of a memo that discusses whether he should sue the *Chicago Daily Tribune* for libel over an editorial calling him "crooked as well as incompetent." Truman's cover letter to Clifford indicates the extent to which he believed the press was mistreating him.

> There have been only two or three Presidents who have been as roundly abused and misrepresented in certain sections of the press as I have. I call your attention to Washington, Jefferson, Jackson, Lincoln and particularly to Grover Cleveland. I have just finished going through McElroy's life of Cleveland and I don't think there ever was a President as thoroughly misrepresented by the press as he was, and I don't think there ever was a more honorable man in the Presidency, although he followed the program of going straight ahead with his policies when they were as unpopular as they could be.[18]

The desire to shoot the messenger is an understandable one. But note Truman's conviction that his problems stemmed from his "misrepresentation" in the press rather than any genuine disapproval by the public.

The administration blamed irresponsible actions by other political actors as the cause for public misconceptions about it. Sometimes comments were simply attempts to lash out at actions by the political opposition. For example, when Secretary of the Air Force Stuart Symington said at an August, 1950, cabinet meeting that budget cuts to regulatory agencies were "impeding the war effort" in Korea, Truman responded that the cuts were a "deliberate and planned program of the Right Wing Democrats and the Republicans." As the 1950 election season approached, the frustration increased. In September, former Secretary of the Interior Harold Ickes wrote to Truman that he had never "seen politics played so foully" as they were in the 1950 campaign.[19]

In the 1950 election, the Democrats lost seats in both the House and Senate. The administration responded by singling out individuals who supposedly caused the problem. Ken Hechler identified their losses as due to the red scare tactics of Senator Joseph McCarthy, writing that the election results "represented a temporary triumph for the smear campaign of character assassination." Cabinet meeting minutes from March 30, 1951, show Truman agreeing with the secretary of agriculture that Allan Kline (president of the American Farm Bureau Federation) is "still doing everything he can to embarrass the administration." At a cabinet meeting three days later, Truman said, "We must take initiative to offset the current campaign to discredit the President and this administration" and that he planned "to form a strategy committee to implement this drive."[20]

Truman's staff even deemed the Democratic National Committee unsupportive of the president. In April, 1951, George Elsey routed to several people a newspaper article that discussed the "lack of guts" in the Democratic Party. Handwriting at the bottom of the routing slip, which appears to belong to speechwriter David Lloyd, picks up on the theme. "We are indeed observing the wheezes of a gutless Democratic Party, the tired old horse is being pulled backward by the State Department, the Budget Bureau, and the National Committee."[21] A short time later the administration had reason to see the Democratic National Committee as opposition, because the Committee was not forthcoming in supporting Truman after the firing of MacArthur. Indeed, White House memoranda suggest that the DNC was attempting to be nonpartisan about the issue! One memorandum in the files of Kenneth Hechler illustrates this point. The memorandum does not have an addressee, so it appears to be "for the record," but the content indicates the extent to which administration leaders believed that the DNC was being uncooperative. The memo is a non-verbatim summary of three conversations that Hechler had with the DNC's public relations director Charlie Van Devander, which Hechler describes as varying between "the exploratory, the explanatory, and the hortatory." The memo asserts that Van Devander told Hechler: "There's some difference of opinion over what the National Committee should do in this case. This is a national issue, and should not be made a partisan football." Van Devander told Hechler that he didn't want it to seem that the DNC was "spreading propaganda." A similar memo by Hechler four days later reemphasizes this point: "The National Committee says it is reluctant to take an aggressive role in this matter, lest it lend an air of partisanship to the affair."[22]

Of course, Republicans were always on the list of people working against the administration. At a cabinet meeting May 4, 1951, Vice President Alben Barkley accused the Republicans of "cheap politics" for attempting to have an open meeting of the Armed Services and Foreign Affairs committees about MacArthur's dismissal. As the 1952 elections approached, the administration became increasingly wary of Republican practices. An October, 1951, memo, in George Elsey's files, looks ahead to how the DNC should prepare for the 1952 election. The memo states in part, "Our basic problem arises from the fact that the Republican National Committee has been skillfully pouring a steady stream of poison into the minds of the American people for four years." The president shared these fears. At the final cabinet meeting of 1951, Truman told the cabinet that they could not allow Congress to "sabotage" their achievements.[23]

Sometimes Truman condemned foes personally, as when he informed Secretary of the Interior Oscar Chapman that the former secretary, Harold Ickes, had "decided to join the opposition," adding that "he can't stay in one man's corner very long—especially if there is a headline in attacking that man." (A column Ickes wrote in *The New Republic* had angered Truman.) In a May 1952 memo, Truman directed his wrath at columnist Drew Pearson, whom he accused of following a usual pattern of neglecting "to find out the facts" but instead interviewing "some disgruntled Government employee or some pathological liar" to get his story. Truman added that he wished there were a way to "really make a liar out of him, worse than he is—but that is something that is hard to do." Truman's letter responded to words from the DNC Chairman Frank McKinney, who had characterized a Pearson article as a "malicious attack" and an example "of the end to which our enemies are going to detract us" in the fall campaign.[24]

Truman and his staff were, of course, able to find scapegoats for their failing fortunes in the 1952 campaign. In September, the president told his cabinet, "81 percent of the press is supporting Eisenhower. 15 percent supporting Stevenson." After the election, Truman pronounced the election result due to "hero worship" and the "McCarthy-Jenner-Nixon poison."[25]

Johnson

The Johnson administration also believed that others were manipulating public opinion against them. As with Truman, this occasionally manifested itself in the form of hostility to members of the press. Panzer, for example, countered a series of articles by columnist Walter Lippmann that criticized Johnson's lack of credibility by noting,

> Lippmann has to be taken in context and that would include these forgotten facts:
> * He supported Alf Landon in 1936.
> * He supported Tom Dewey in 1948.
> * He supported Eisenhower in 1952.[26]

Unmentioned was the fact that he also supported Johnson in 1964 and Kennedy in 1960. Johnson and Panzer were annoyed in late October, 1967, about press reactions to a "misleading" Gallup Poll. *Time, Newsweek,* and *The New Republic* were all considered guilty of overstating Gallup's published report of American objection to involvement in the war in Vietnam. Among their agreed remedies was a backgrounder to columnist Robert Spivack, who occasionally wrote about the "unfairness of the press."[27] A more biting example is this comment: "To find out what the public is thinking on Vietnam . . . turn to columnist Joseph Kraft. He will contemplate his navel and tell you the U.S. mood . . . Kraft's interpretation of the national mood is palpable bunk based on the fuzziest wishful thinking."[28]

Often the administration accused other political actors of deliberately distorting the truth. Robert Kintner believed that political manipulation by the opposition was leading people astray: "I believe that many people think there is not the 'will for peace' within the administration. This is nonsense, of course, but it is getting wide currency through Kennedy, McCarthy, and etc."[29] Democratic opposition was considered especially contemptible and, correspondingly, dishonest.

The Johnson administration frequently took to defining its detractors as socially undesirable, thus allowing them to be dismissed. A particularly poignant example of the Johnson administration's dismissing the opposition for its social undesirability can be seen in an unsigned "memorandum for the record" in the files of Marvin Watson:

> The assortment of clippings which follow traces in capsule-like form the results of a political guerrilla force outside the major political parties that has crystallized during the past two years. Its influence is far-reaching. It has become a potential threat to our democratic institutions as well as to the Democratic election success in the presidential and congressional elections in 1968. It goes by many names and its seemingly loose organizational ties include a broad range of groups and individuals—from known and avowed communists such as Herbert Aptheker, to the Stokely Carmichaels of the militant black power movement, to the peace demonstrators, the draft-card burners, LSD disciples, to the campus agitators such as Paul Booth, to the alienated intellectuals, community organizers, well-meaning clergy, and others who are unhappy, bewildered, and confused by the complexity of the national and international problems with which we must cope.
>
> . . . this proliferation of groups is exerting influence and political power out of all proportion to its actual strength because its appeal is to a narrow segment of our total electorate. However, it is well-organized and financed, vocal, aggressive, and uses effective infiltration and propaganda techniques as well as violence when necessary to carry out its purpose. Its activities are reminiscent of those of similar groups during the 1930's and 1940's. Its targets are similar: students and faculty, social welfare and other politically naive individuals, the clergy, labor unions, minority groups, the poor, the ignorant, and many Federally-financed programs dealing with these people. Many of the leaders of these groups are the same individuals who received their basic training in the depression years.
>
> The fruits of this activity are seen every day and are illustrated in the attached clippings: riots, demonstrations, civil disobedience, anti-Vietnam agitation, campus uprisings, bloodshed and property destruction—all of which weaken our national unity at a time when we must be united before the world.[30]

Note that this memorandum completes the rationalization not only by putting down the leaders of the opposition but also by dismissing those members of it who do not fall into such categories as "LSD disciples" as "unhappy, bewildered, and confused" or "well-meaning" or "politically naive individuals." The allegedly atypical opposition is said to be targeting a "narrow segment" of society, but in fact its total size is quite large, including: students, labor unions, minorities, and the poor.

Similarly, a memo to Johnson on March 8, 1968, explains Eugene McCarthy's political assets as "the organizational talents of the Communists and the hemi-demi-semi-Communists, who have been out of circulation (and making money) since Henry Wallace."[31] Not only were they communists, they were not even good communists!

The administration clearly showed signs of frustration with dissenters. Records indicate that the opposition was considered to be unfair, unpatriotic, overly vocal, and even subversive. Campus protestors, for example, were considered by Vice President Hubert Humphrey to be part of a "well-planned" organizational effort. In fact, Humphrey's belief that he recognized the same people at various demonstrations resulted in a request to the Justice Department to examine the possibility.[32] A memo to Johnson relays excerpts from a speech by White House reporter Merriman Smith who thought Johnson the "object of some of the worst vilification" that he had seen covering the White House. The excerpt notes Smith's suggestion: "It is time for the 'squares who raise kids, mow their lawns, and pay their taxes (to) decide to involve themselves by getting off their patios and telling the dirty mouths to shut the hell up.'" Smith reportedly had to print "several thousand" copies of the speech to satisfy requests for copies. (The memo notes that Smith was ill-received by the press because of the remarks: "He was snubbed by some of his colleagues and accused of apple-polishing."[33]) The White House staff developed a siege mentality, evident in the battle analogy used in this excerpt from an unused speech prepared for floor use by a member of Congress:

Mr. Speaker,

The fire directed at the White House in the past few weeks rivals in sheer volume the incoming shells that landed on Con Thiem a short time ago.

The volleys come from batteries on the left and on the right. There are big Republican B-52 raids on the President's policy in Vietnam. There are waspish attacks by ADA raiders. There are salvos of scorn and a drumfire of distrust.

The Gallups and the Harrises are booming too with their pseudo-scientific O-bombs. ("O" for opinion, that is).

Mr. Speaker, the air is thick with the sulphur and brimstone of these American fulminations. Even the *Wall Street Journal* has made a low-level strafing run at the President. Its reporters shot up the White House with a burst of interviews with 12 people who were unhappy with the President . . . .

Mr. Speaker, I think something should be done about it.

I propose a thirty-day halt in the bombing—of LBJ, that is.

> I propose a de-escalation of the dissent being directed at our President.
>
> I propose a halt to the flock from the fringes which is now being aimed at the White House.[34]

Note the degree to which the administration had selectively interpreted dissent as unpatriotic or unfair; this allowed the Johnson staff to dismiss dissent more readily. They no longer expected to win over opposition with better speeches or changed style. They now discounted criticism and disagreement as coming from society's "fringes." Therefore, administration leaders no longer needed to concern themselves with it.

Carter

The Carter administration also saw some of its problems being caused by people out to get the administration. Before Carter's term even began, Pat Caddell wrote the president that he was worried that the press seemed "determined to portray your administration as one that's not going to keep its campaign promises." In only the administration's second month in office, leaders were already considering the possibility of a primary challenge in 1980 from California Governor Jerry Brown who "will try to find encouragement for his effort in the public opinion polls and among the party elite and elected officials who have never been close to us." A memo the same month, about how to mobilize support for the SALT II treaty, suggests that some in the administration believed that "the effectiveness of the right-wing effort" could stifle their success.[35]

Not until the second half of 1979, when the Carter administration's public standing was very low, did references to enemies or outside sources of problems become particularly pronounced. The administration's suspicions were often targeted at Massachusetts Senator Ted Kennedy, who announced his candidacy for the presidency on November 7. Many in the administration questioned Kennedy's character. President Carter sent Jody Powell an article from the University of Virginia campus paper, *The Cavalier Daily*, which accused Senator Kennedy of having stolen two horses while attending the University of Virginia Law School.[36] A memo from Powell to Carter that same day returns the allusion to Kennedy, talking about the consequences of a failed Carter presidency: "Unless we deal with this problem, this country will be headed by a not-too-bright rich kid who has shown no inclination to face up to the need for maintaining a strong defense, or a Connally/Reagan type who will use the public sentiment for stronger defense as an excuse for abandoning domestic social goals and possibly embarking on ill-considered adventures to prove how tough we are." In December, Powell had to advise Carter not to "go after EMK [Edward M. Kennedy] on anything no matter how provoked or irritated you may be with his irresponsible behavior. That irresponsibility is apparent throughout the country." The same day the president received a note from appointments secretary Phil Wise informing him that former DNC Chairman and Special Trade Representative Robert Strauss and former Secretary of State Dean Rusk were going to make a speech against Kennedy. The note says that the speech "will contrast him with his two brothers. Try to prove that Rose didn't have triplets." On the top of the message, Carter wrote "good."[37]

Another perceived enemy was the media. Attacks on the media intensified after the middle of 1979, as Carter's popularity remained consistently low. A document written a few weeks after the Crisis of Confidence speech typifies the administration's attitude. Counsel to the President Robert Lipshutz forwarded to Jordan, Powell, and Rafshoon a letter he received from a television personality in Arkansas who reported feeling that the media was "out to destroy any political leader who isn't a darling of the left-wing elite." Lipshutz's attached memo says that the letter "relates directly to the conversation which Jerry [Rafshoon] and [presidential advisor] Charles Kirbo and I had in Ham [Jordan]'s office on Wednesday morning." After the failed attempt by the military to rescue American diplomats held hostage in Iran, Carter penned the following note to National Security Advisor Zbigniev Brzezinski: "Zbig—Jack Anderson (and others) maintains that I slashed DoD [Department of Defense] recommendations in rescue force levels and caused failure. He's a liar, but should be answered. Check with Harold, Jody."[38] Carter did not simply assert that Anderson was misinformed but called him a *liar*.

The administration held particular scorn for *Newsweek*. As early as November, 1977, a handwritten note from Carter to Milwaukee Mayor Henry Maier states, "Newsweek is the worst violator of the self-initiated story, quoting 'sources' which may or may not exist." In May, 1979, Jody Powell sent the president a memo, noting that they had problems with *Newsweek's* Washington Bureau "from the start" and suggesting that Carter talk to the magazine's New York editorial staff instead. Carter agreed with the plan, writing in response, "Newsweek is one of the worst now. They have little regard for accuracy."[39]

In August, 1979, Jody Powell suggested that the president give a one-on-one interview with NBC television reporter Marvin Kalb, because, "Given the hypercritical attitude of the press in general, we should take advantage of the opportunities to have the President speak directly to the public." Staff sometimes lumped the media in with other groups. An Alonzo McDonald memo in late August about campaign themes suggests the need for the president to counter "the avalanche of criticism and ridicule heaped upon him by the elite, the effete, the press and those aristocratic foreigners." Carter himself seemed focused on media criticism. In October, he told Jody Powell, Stu Eizenstat, and Charlie Kirbo to release an "accurate" transcript of a statement he made about the Federal Reserve Board: "The [Washington] Post interpretation is erroneous—predictably."[40]

Patronizing the Public

One possible outcome of the frustration caused by an unsupportive public would be to patronize it. Indeed, these administrations all partook in some form of patronizing the public, usually through statements that the public was uninformed or confused. On very rare occasions, the comments could be more disparaging. The most patronizing comments took place during times when the public was least supportive of the administrations. This patronizing attitude led directly to the process of growing out of touch. By dismissing public opinion, the administrations no longer needed to take it seriously.

Truman

Truman staffers often asserted that the public was uninformed about issues of importance to the administration. Of course, the public is frequently uninformed, but the administration only seemed to find this problem in public responses to their *unpopular* actions.

Early patronizing comments by the administration took the form of statements that the public was confused. For example, in March, 1946, as concerns about the future of Europe loomed large, Robert Hannegan wrote to the president about a survey of newly registered Democratic voters in Chicago that was taken by precinct captains. Hannegan's memo reports that the survey "spells out some of the war fatigue, confusion of thought, and fears now gripping the people that can lead to snap judgements against the administration." He added that an upcoming presidential address "could serve to blanket the hysteria churned up from current headlines and accent our strivings for a workable peace." Another example of the administration's dismissal of public opinion occurred in April of 1948, when James Davis, an official in the Department of the Interior, wrote to Clark Clifford with this view of the public: "The average person at the present time is bewildered, frightened and baffled because he cannot understand what is going on all around him. Economics, nuclear physics, electronics, and the war of ideologies have got him. In desperation he will turn to whatever person or creed he thinks can restore his lost sense of security and well-being." Davis's memo adds a ray of hope, which also reveals an image of a simplistic public, stating that the average American "will joyfully turn to a simple restatement of fundamental American principles backed by American power."[41] This image, of the American people as lost in a confusing world that they need explained to them, gave the administration the freedom to disregard public attitudes.

Frustration with the public can be seen in the 1948 election season. The pollsters had mistakenly predicted a loss for Truman. In October, after attacking pollsters for partisan bias, Democratic National Committee Chairman Joseph Keenan lashed out at the public who followed the polls. Fearing a depressed turnout, Keenan wrote that polls had induced "the already shamefully slothful American public from protecting and exercising their birthright of voting once every four years." A mild rebuke of the public can even be seen after the election, when the administration was otherwise attentive to public opinion. A memo prepared December 30, 1948, for James Webb, director of the Bureau of the Budget, examines Truman's labor policy options. Webb passed the lengthy memo to Clark Clifford. One statement in the memo reveals consternation with the public: "the people of the United States need to learn, and the

President needs to serve as educator here, that there is no magic formula which will bar major interruptions of essential services in a free society."[42] The statement implicitly suggests that the public, which had just reelected Truman, was uninformed and at fault for being annoyed with strikes.

The administration patronized the public again after the 1950 congressional elections in which the Democratic Party lost five Senate seats and twenty-eight House seats. A Kenneth Hechler memo analyzing the election results observes the successes of Senator Joseph McCarthy's "red scare" tactics and portrays the American public as confused and taken with hysteria. "People were worried by the terrible complexity of the international situation, and it looked so simple and easy to accept the scapegoat suggested by McCarthy and his smear crew. That was the simple-minded answer to all the troubles of war in Korea, the draft, rising prices, and uncertainty about the future." Noting that the effects were strongest in urban areas, Hechler comments, "The hysteria seemed to grip the city population like a strange disease." Hechler's observations about the public may have been correct, and this example of patronizing is mild. However, the administration's relationship with the public continued to deteriorate, and Hechler's patronizing attitude intensified. In March of 1951, he sent George Elsey a memorandum discussing the country's inattention to foreign policy. Hechler contrasted the public's attitudes with the intense interest during the debate in 1950 about crossing the Thirty-eighth parallel in Korea. Blaming the apathy on the country's obsession with some of the Truman administration's scandals, Hechler wrote, "I think this type of discussion has more or less fizzled out. People have their eyes riveted on the crime investigation telecasts, and make up new jokes about mink coats and anything else to divert their attention from what's the clear and present danger. This is sort of like the farmer who was interested in finding out what's going on between the hired hand and the maid up in the haymow while the river is overflowing its banks and destroying his crops. Somehow what's happening in the haymow seems to be more interesting at the time."[43]

It is important to note that, with a few exceptions, these patronizing attitudes occurred at times when the administration's relationship with the public was strained. By adopting a patronizing attitude, the administration was able to alleviate its worries about the public. Because Truman and his staff found it far easier to dismiss the public as confused or apathetic than to deal with the public's concerns, the consequence was an administration content to be out of touch.

Johnson

The Johnson administration occasionally patronized the American people, especially after mid-1967, as the administration's Gallup public approval rating was usually below 45 percent and sometimes below 40 percent. For example, in September, 1967, Fred Panzer prepared for Marvin Watson a "brief summary of the fevers which have coursed through the American body politic." The twelve-page document recounts various occurrences of vocal opposition back to the time of the Articles of Confederation. The research implies that the Vietnam protesters were part of a long tradition of opposition starting with Shay's Rebellion and the Whiskey Rebellion. By making this comparison, Panzer was able to downplay the importance of the opposition by comparing it to 180 years of American history. Panzer said that the report "may bear out Thomas Jefferson's cool observation that 'a little rebellion now and then . . . is a medicine necessary for the sound health of the government.'" Special Assistant Ernest Goldstein added another patronizing comment in late 1967, describing his speech to students at Amherst College to President Johnson this way: "I was pleasantly surprised to find that dialogue is still possible. There was only one rude incident."[44]

Some memoranda indicate an air of intellectual superiority within the White House, allowing the White House to discount public discontent as unreasonable. On one occasion Panzer notified the president that the public was not accepting his call for an income tax surtax to control inflationary pressures. "Apparently the public has learned only half the lesson of the 'new economics'—the part about cutting taxes and increasing federal spending to stimulate the economy. They don't buy lesson number two—the steps necessary to control inflation." Three weeks later Panzer informed the president that, according to Gallup, while 58 percent disapproved of Johnson's handling of the war, 63 percent backed the continued bombing of North Vietnam. "In other words, a majority disapproves of the very same policy it approves. This is nonsense. The contradiction means, as I see it, that while people favor bombing versus stopping the bombing they just don't like the war."[45] By so dismissing the public's "nonsense," administration leaders could maintain the conviction that they were acting wisely.

Carter

The Carter administration also participated in some patronizing of the public. Most of it occurred in the last year and a half of its term. Carter's detractors, of course, claim that his entire Crisis of Confidence speech was essentially a disparagement of the public, because it suggested that there was something wrong with the American people. In addition to observing the "crisis of confidence" in the country, the speech noted "the growing disrespect for government and for churches and for schools" and that "too many of us now tend to worship self-indulgence and consumption."[46] Although Carter did not actually blame the public in the speech, the documented planning for the speech indicates that the administration did believe that the country's problems had led citizens to the point where they no longer had faith in public institutions. As Pat Caddell told Carter a few days before the speech, his organization found "major shifts in structural attitudes that signaled a rapid disintegration of optimism and efficacy in the country. Because they began before the heavy impact of this year's inflation/gas crunch the increasing malaise has been deepened, not caused, by those occurrences."[47] As a result, the speech called on the country to "commit ourselves together to a rebirth of the American spirit."[48]

Prior to the Crisis of Confidence speech, Carter's speechwriters were already preparing speeches suggesting that Americans needed to unite to solve their problems. One speechwriter told Jody Powell that closing remarks of a draft speech "make your point that our problems will be solved only if Americans have the will to face them and make sacrifices where needed." Note the subtle suggestion that the fault is with the public. A similar message passed through the White House in July: "Ambassador Walter Annenberg called for the President this afternoon with the following fervent plea: That the President get on television and issue a call for patriotism during this troubling time—remind the people of their freedom and the corresponding responsibilities of their freedom." Annenberg added that the public was "hungry" to hear this message. While the administration characterized Americans as flawed, they are not here seen as fundamentally flawed; rather, they need to be reminded of their duty. Alfred Kahn, the president's advisor on inflation, adopted an angrier tone on July 11, when he wrote to Carter that the nation's energy problems could have been addressed earlier "had the country begun what it should have begun five years ago, or what you urged it to do two years ago—when you called for the moral equivalent of war, only to have that call ridiculed by cheap cynics and ignored by people of little vision." Kahn noted that the public was looking for a "quick solution" to the problems.[49]

Occasionally, the administration mildly patronized the public by labeling it as confused, insecure, or uninformed. In August, for example, Rafshoon advised Carter that the public did not understand the nature of the nation's energy problems. The president passed the memo to several key people in the administration, including the vice president. In January, 1980, White House staff members Anne Wexler and Al From reported to Carter that "Americans want desperately to feel secure again." In April, Al McDonald told Jody Powell, "The public is confused. It does not know how to react in the face of the many complexities now facing our nation."[50] The public's dissent was thus subtly dismissed.

Distrust of Polls and Pollsters

Frustration over bad poll results might result in politicians' blaming the pollsters. Indeed, the Truman and Johnson administrations were deeply suspicious of polls, believing that they were either poorly done or deliberately biased against them.[51]

Truman

As could be expected from a trustee-style president, Truman largely dismissed polls as tools of governing. Truman was also highly distrustful of the pollsters themselves. His staff reflected these attitudes as well.

Polls in 1948 showing that Truman would lose that year's election certainly triggered much of the wariness. For example, in October, 1948, a letter from DNC Chairman Joseph Keenan to Clark Clifford expresses great suspicion of the partisanship of pollsters:

An analysis of the pollsters in 1932, 1936, 1940 and 1944 show a single consistent pattern. Starting with the disastrous LITERARY DIGEST deception a more cautious approach of propaganda ensued. The record will show, I am quite sure, that the contest between Roosevelt and Landon up to the last week of the campaign—according to a claim made by Gallup—was anyone's choice. In 1940 the Gallup results up to the eve of election and including the Saturday before Tuesday, saw a perilously close race with the edge pointing toward Wilkie. In 1944 the same technique was followed . . . . It will be noted that where mistakes have been made every year from 1932 inclusive, in every instance they have been made in favor of one party—the Republicans—with never an overestimate of the Democratic figures and prospects.

Keenan later referred to pollsters as "propagandists."[52]

Still, Truman was able to overcome the concern about pollsters long enough to meet Louis Bean, a pollster and an advisor to the agriculture department during the Roosevelt administration, in the Oval Office on December 2, 1948, a month after the election.[53] The meeting was arranged by Senator-elect Clinton Anderson of New Mexico, who hoped to give the president "a more balanced viewpoint of the election outcome." Despite the meeting, other references to pollsters remained negative. In February, 1949, publisher Alfred Knopf sent Truman a letter thanking him for his reference in a speech to a Knopf publication called *The Pollsters*, by Lindsay Rogers. Knopf also forwarded Truman a critical letter he had received about the book from George Gallup.[54]

As its popularity again declined, the administration relied on its suspicions of the pollsters to alleviate concerns about public opinion. A telegram to Truman's friend and military aide General Harry Vaughan, dated May 6, 1950, expresses great suspicion of pollsters.

> GALLUP AGAIN FOOLING PUBLIC WITH POLL DESPITE LAST EXPOSE STOP MANY PAPERS THREW HIM OUT INCLUDING ATLANTA BUT STILL HAS CONSIDERABLE LIST STOP HIS LAST PRESIDENTIAL POPU-LARITY POLL ABSOLUTELY INCREDIBLE STOP IF HE CONTINUES HIS PROPAGANDA MAY WELL RESULT LOSS OF DEMOCRATIC STATES COMING CONGRESSIONAL ELECTION GRADUALLY HURTING ADMIN-ISTRATION STOP CONGRESS SHOULD IMMEDIATELY INVESTIGATE HIM AND OTHER CUNNING POLITICAL POLLSTERS PARTICULARLY DURING PRESIDENTIAL TOUR STOP[55]

In February, 1952, Frank McKinney, chairman of the DNC, informed George Elsey that the DNC would be tracking polls. The letter nicely illustrates how the Democratic leadership approached polls with suspicion, and how they learned to ignore bad news. "We Democrats have had a lot of reasons to think about opinion surveys . . . . I have, therefore, asked our Research Division to prepare each month a report on what opinion polls are saying. It will help us decide which polls to take seriously and which to disregard." (They were not entirely dismissive, however. McKinney affirmed that he had instructed the research division not to "pull any punches . . . . The Republicans in 1948 showed what happens to people who attend only to those aspects of opinion surveys which make them feel good!")[56]

In August, 1952, the president's press secretary, Joseph Short, wrote to DNC Chairman Stephen Mitchell. Short indicated that the president was distrustful of Gallup's analysis of public opinion and suggested that members of Congress may need to respond: "I am sending you an interesting analysis of the Gallup Poll. It shows that Gallup apparently is again crediting the GOP with more support than they really have, and the Democrats with less. The President has read it and hopes that the public's attention may be called to what is going on . . . .I suggest that this might be done by someone on the Hill like [Kentucky Senator Earl] Clements, [Oklahoma Senator Mike] Monroney, [Oklahoma Senator Robert] Kerr, [New Mexico Senator Clinton] Anderson or [Ohio Representative] Mike Kirwan."[57] By the end of Truman's term, when popularity was low, suspicion had transformed into an outright belief that pollsters were undermining American democracy.

Johnson

The Johnson administration followed a similar pattern. The same administration that so carefully read and analyzed polls suddenly changed its opinion of them when public approval declined. Instead of attempting to analyze polls, Johnson and his staff tended to find fault with them, particularly when the polls disrupted their carefully constructed view of the public. Louis Harris, who bore the brunt of some of Johnson's criticism, has noted that Johnson only believed in polls "when they tended to support what he was doing."[58]

The administration complained not about polls per se but the "inept" or "biased" way in which they were conducted.[59] Often this tendency manifested itself in examinations of contradictions between Gallup and Harris. On February 17, 1967, Panzer completed a report requested by Johnson on this topic. The report begins:

> For two weeks running, the two giants of the polling industry have collided head on. The result: they have sprung a Gallup-Harris "credibility gap."
>
> But while they have been hurt in the collision, you, an innocent bystander, have also been injured.
>
> Looking at the two polling "accidents" in detail . . . we can place the blame on "driver error." There was either an error of omission or commission.
>
> But beyond this, there is reason to believe that their vehicles— the polls—are unsafe.

Panzer proceeds to explain how the contradiction occurred, pointing out that Gallup and Harris failed to report the conditions under which their polls were taken, asked bad questions, or faultily reported their results. Despite the problems, Panzer notes that Johnson was gaining more favorable press coverage. He then asks, "Will the polls show the change?"

> Possibly, but there are several hurdles.
> 1) The pollsters have a built in bias which they may or may not be able to keep out of their interpretations.
> • Gallup is a Republican and very conservative.
> • Harris was very close to the Kennedy camp in 1960.
> 2) The newspapers can slant the polls . . .
> 3) Polling is still a crude tool that is not as foolproof as it is reported by the pollsters.
> 4) The news releases put out by Gallup and Harris do not give all the data and background that every trained person needs to make sense of them.[60]

On September 8, 1967, Panzer informed the president that the forthcoming Gallup release would show him losing in a hypothetical election against Michigan Governor George Romney by 50 percent to 44 percent. Harris polled at the same time but claimed a Johnson "victory" of 52 percent to 48 percent. Panzer's advice: "The best thing to do is to let the pollsters explain it. If it casts doubt on their credibility this will also cast doubt on the accuracy of their presidential popularity ratings too." Note that Panzer not only seemed to doubt the quality of the polls but also sought to protect the administration by discrediting them. The following month Panzer gave Johnson a letter from a Gallup surveyor who perceived problems with the survey technique: "Mr. President: I thought you would like to read this letter from a Gallup Poll interviewer who disapproves of the way Gallup is handling his job as a pollster."[61]

The administration frequently speculated that the poll write-ups expressed political leanings of the pollsters themselves. As just shown, Panzer was suspicious about Gallup's Republican affiliation and Harris's attachment to the Kennedys. On October 3, 1967, Panzer reported to LBJ that a recent Gallup Poll showed that a Nelson Rockefeller/Ronald Reagan ticket would have a substantial lead over a Johnson/Humphrey ticket. Panzer correctly noted that Gallup transgressed from his usual practice by also giving the percentages without the undecideds, which seemingly raised New York Governor Rockefeller's popularity. "Note: It is unusual for Gallup to distribute the undecided vote as he has in this release. It looks like he wants to show the Rockefeller-Reagan ticket in the best possible light. In fact, his story is almost a plea for Rockefeller to run." Panzer's distrust of the pollsters continued through the Johnson administration. Document suggesting this include a memo to LBJ on October 24, 1967, in which Panzer writes that Gallup's claim that he was conducting "interviews in depth" was "highly questionable" because of "loaded" questions designed to bias the answer. On November 3, Panzer reported that he was investigating why Gallup's published figures had not changed in two weeks. It appeared that Gallup merely reused the same data. Panzer concluded, "If this holds up—and I think it will—the story of what looks like a shady practice should be broken." On December 1, Panzer was displeased that Gallup had "buried" the fact that a trial heat showed LBJ defeating Nixon. Panzer's explanation: "To me it is an example of Gallup's shenanigans."[62] Panzer even took to ridiculing Gallup Polls that did not cover topics of interest to the administration. On December 21, Panzer sent the following telegram to Marvin Watson who was with the president's party in Canberra, Australia:

> Gallup's Sunday Release shows that a ten year drop in church attendance has been halted. Pass it along to the Pope.
> Coming Wednesday in the Gallup Poll: "Is God Dead? The Public's Answer."
> If this keeps up, Gallup may next ask: "Do you approve or disapprove of the way God is handling his job?"

This telegram must have been warmly received in Canberra, because it was passed along for the president to read.[63]

Johnson shared the suspicion of polls and pollsters, despite his continuous obsession with them. As early as late 1966, for example, Johnson informed his aides, "We're up eight percent on women and you can't find it—it's buried. The Kennedys have always owned Harris . . . . [T]hey can always get a Bobby poll among the liberal Democrats in California." In February, 1967, he assigned Jim Jones to examine "'Why polls are downgrading us.' Survey of what Harris and Gallup are up to."[64] On October 6, 1967, Johnson asked Panzer to prepare a set of five critical letters to George Gallup, which were apparently designed to appear as if they had come from ordinary citizens. These letters countered Gallup's "plea" to Rockefeller to run for president. One reads as follows:

> Dear Mr. Gallup,
> A Rockefeller-Reagan ticket is ridiculous.
> I can appreciate how much you would like the New York Governor to win the Republican nomination. And I don't even have to read between the lines of your story.
> But teaming him up with Reagan is too much.
> How about a George Wallace-Martin Luther King ticket? It would get all the Negro votes plus the backlash votes. Or maybe a George Wallace–Bobby Kennedy ticket to combine the conservative and liberal votes.
> Sincerely,[65]

It is not clear from the record what Johnson did with these letters. Later in the year, Johnson attached a note requesting speeches to a 1951 Gallup Poll that had shown 66 percent of the people polled wanting to pull U.S. troops out of Korea. "People can't follow Dr. Gallup, Harris. If we had followed him [*sic*] we would have been in a big mess."[66] Johnson ostensibly blamed Gallup, not the people he polled, as the source of bad advice about Korea.

The president and his administration may have had serious gripes with the actions of pollsters and the way their polls were conducted. In fact, many of the administration's complaints about pollsters were true: Gallup was Republican; Harris was closer to the Kennedys; newspapers and pollsters can and do slant polls. Yet the administration did not attend to these concerns until its nadir of popularity. This selective interpretation of information allowed the administration to dismiss more readily the unpleasant news relayed in the polls. Furthermore, as Altschuler has observed, pollsters were often exceedingly ingratiating to President Johnson, a fact that makes the president's paranoia about pollsters seem even more extreme.[67] (A message from Press Secretary George Christian on December 1, 1967, to Marvin Watson reads: "[VISTA Director] Bill Crook advises that Dr. Gallup has been hinting that he would like to have a private meeting with the President. Crook claims Gallup feels bad about polls reflecting badly on the President."[68]) The distrust of polls allowed the administration to block an avenue of information from the American public.

Two Johnson Reactions

Two reactions to the decline in public approval seem to be peculiar to the Johnson administration. Rather than attempting to acquire accurate information about public attitudes, Johnson frequently focused his concern on creating the *appearance* of public approval. Public support is crucial to the operations of the modern presidency. Because indices of public support were not available when dealing with other crucial political actors, the semblance of support was created to fill the need. This manifested itself in two ways. The administration tried to (1) publicize any indications it could find of pockets of support and (2) manipulate the indicators of public support.[69] The administration had finished the process of closing itself off to careful analysis and interpretation of public opinion. Instead, it tacitly had deemed the appearance of popularity to be a sufficient substitute for any real understanding of public opinion.

Speaking of Popularity

During the second half of the Johnson administration, the White House began to attempt to curry public favor by informing the public of how popular Johnson and his policies were. That is to say, they resorted to telling the public how popular Johnson was with them. Johnson clearly needed the appearance of popular legitimacy in order to operate effectively.

The president himself seldom actually spoke to citizens about their opinions. Usually, he would ask his subordinates to coax others to reveal positive indicators of public opinion. For example, on May 7, 1967, while retreating to his Central Texas ranch, Johnson was informed that his popularity and the support for his Vietnam policies were increasing. Johnson had the following message relayed to Press Secretary George Christian, "George: call a backgrounder on this. Just visit with them and show them this—AP, UPI, and two of the networks."[70] Other evidence shows Johnson asking subordinates to spread good news. On October 17, 1967, Fred Panzer informed Johnson,

> I spoke to William J. Eaton of the *Chicago Daily News* as you requested. I gave him the data on recent Harris polls which showed you beating four GOP rivals nationally. I also gave him more on the New York poll.
>
> He was very happy to get the information because he said he was puzzled by hearing so much about your low popularity. I think I helped clear this up for him.[71]

Later that month, Johnson took note of a favorable article by journalist Roscoe Drummond placed in the *Congressional Record* by New York Congressman Leonard Farbstein. The article demonstrated Johnson's lead in presidential pairings in New York state against Republicans Richard Nixon, Charles Percy, Ronald Reagan, and George Romney. Attached to a copy of the page from the *Congressional Record* was a note from Johnson to his press secretary, "George Christian: have Bill White and Drew Pearson write columns like this." On November 16, 1967, Panzer forwarded some favorable poll results to George Christian with the message, "The President asked me to get to you some of the favorable polls and election results for backgrounding columnists. Roscoe Drummond for one." Sometimes the requests were to members of the Congress rather than the press. On February 4, 1968, Johnson sent a memo to an unidentified recipient, "ask them to be sure to get the Gallup poll of last Saturday and this Sunday and have a good speech written for somebody to put in the record—[Oklahoma Senator Fred] Harris or [Wyoming Senator Gale] McGee. [Oklahoma Representative Edmond] Edmondson put [it] in [the] House side, but I want it in on the Senate."[72]

Occasionally Johnson's attempts to spread the good news bordered on the silly, as he would try to make national news out of trivial local indicators of support. This occurred primarily during the second half of his administration, when the low approval level was cause for concern. On March 29, 1967, for example, Johnson suggested that George Christian give columnists Roscoe Drummond or Richard Wilson poll results from *Valley Times*, a weekly paper in southern Worcester County, Massachusetts. The poll showed that of the sixty-eight people who cast opinion ballots, fifty-eight preferred Johnson over Massachusetts native Robert F. Kennedy. A memo from Marvin Watson in October, 1967, informs Johnson that eight high schools in Illinois chose Johnson as their "person most admired in the world": "Some of the reasons why President Johnson was most admired were stated to be 'because he faces a lot of responsibility and seems to handle it well.' And, 'because he is a very brilliant man.' Another boy said that Johnson was admired because he 'can evade all criticism and quiet all opposition.'" Handwriting on the memo indicates that Johnson told aide Jim Jones, "Find [a] way to get this out—Drew Pearson or somehow." Another notation indicates that George Christian sent Drew Pearson a note, "Can you make something of this? Regards."[73]

Playing the Numbers

One phenomenon particularly noticeable in the latter years of the Johnson administration is the degree to which it concerned itself with the numbers in polls rather than the opinions reflected in the numbers.

Administration concern with poll numbers can be seen in its intensified attention to poll questions and survey techniques. In October, 1967, Panzer forwarded to Johnson a letter from a Gallup interviewer who was disturbed by the fact that the approval question, "Do you approve or disapprove of the job President Johnson is doing as president?" did not allow respondents to qualify their answers. Panzer discussed the matter with statistician Richard Scammon, who suggested taking a poll with a substitute question, "Do you approve, disapprove, or partly approve and partly disapprove of the job President Johnson is doing?" Panzer explained, "Then we show [Gallup] the results of [our] question . . . which presumably would reveal a high proportion having mixed feelings and try to get Gallup to change his question." Johnson approved of the idea, scrawling on the memo a note to Marvin Watson, "M–, OK. What do we do about this?" Watson forwarded the memo back to Panzer with a note, "Fred, can we get this done?" A later memo indicates that Panzer unsuccessfully attempted to convince Gallup to change the question.[74]

Another example of the concern with the numbers can be seen in the administration's attempts to manipulate short-term public attitudes to create positive poll results. On July 28, 1967, for example, in the wake of race riots in Detroit and following a presidential address to the nation about the situation, Fred Panzer informed Johnson that the Gallup Poll would be conducting a survey on August 3 on Johnson's approval rating and the reaction to his efforts to ease racial tension. Panzer's memo advises quick action to appeal to the public, "since at critical times the public responds favorably to Presidential action." Note that Panzer was not concerned about understanding public opinion but rather about affecting the poll. Similarly, on December 13, 1967, President Johnson responded to a Gallup Poll of the country's GOP county chairs by suggesting a similar poll for the Democratic Party. Johnson told Jim Jones, "Get something each week to all county chairmen and committeemen boosting us. Then take a quiet poll."[75] Again, the fact that Johnson wished to blitz the Democrats with favorable information before surveying them is an indication that his concern was not so much with their opinions as with the poll numbers he could manipulate out of them.[76]

As the Truman, Johnson, and Carter administrations faced the nadir of their popularity, they no longer were open to the public. In fact, they had developed ways to dismiss negative indicators of public opinion. All three administrations became convinced that part of their problem was the unfair manipulation of the public by political enemies, the media, and socially undesirable elements of society. Two of the three administrations became extremely distrustful of the polls themselves. All three presidential administrations engaged in some patronizing of the public, sometimes by dismissing public disapproval on the basis that the public was uninformed, confused, or inconsistent in its opinion. Such reactions allowed them to distrust reports that showed a lack of support by the public. After all, they could dismiss signs of disapproval as partial fabrications or reason that citizens would be supportive if they were not being manipulated by the administration's enemies.

For the Truman administration, these phenomena were also noticeable during 1948, when expectations were high that Truman would not be reelected. Perhaps Johnson lost touch the most. Johnson's efforts to manipulate poll results and to spread the news about even the most insignificant indicators of public approval suggest that he gave up even trying to assuage the public's fears, preferring instead to mask any indications that the public was unsupportive of him. Altschuler, observing the way that the Johnson administration used poll data, writes, "Polls were not enough to break the isolation of the president."[77]

There are several ways to explain the phenomena observed in this chapter. The behavior of these presidents and their associates are classic examples of the rationalization of Kingdon's losing candidates. As Kingdon observes, "losers are inclined very strongly to believe that voters are not informed about the issues." He notes that they tend to blame uncontrollable factors for their loss.[78] Similarly, these administrations, which were losing in the perpetual campaign for favorable poll ratings, saw all of their problems stemming from either a poorly informed electorate or *external* factors: polls were wrong; pollsters were biased; the opposition was manipulative, unfair, and ill-equipped to understand what these presidents were up against.[79]

Meaningful political responsiveness to the public was impossible under these circumstances. Despite Geer's belief that public opinion polls reduce the ability of today's politicians to rationalize their beliefs about the public, the evidence here shows three administrations who were quite able to deny the extent of their problems. Cognitive dissonance between these administrations' beliefs about the competence of their actions and the negative indicators of public prestige led them to become suspicious of public opinion polls or to dismiss dissent as the coordinated machinations of various detractors. The *selective attention* to optimistic information during the times of moderate approval had given way to *selective interpretation* of otherwise negative information.[80] These presidents, in effect, were dealing with postulated publics believed to be unable to communicate amidst all the vocal detraction. The administrations only heard the voices of increasingly scarce supporters—though they doubted their scarcity.

The role of public opinion at the low point of popularity is noteworthy because it is counter-intuitive. One might have expected that the Truman, Johnson, and Carter administrations would have sharpened their attention to public opinion as public approval dropped, so that they could have adjusted their actions or their public presentations accordingly. Instead, in all three cases we see that attention to public opinion was diminished through the avoidance of unacceptable information. Their behavior made it extremely unlikely that these administrations would be responsive to public opinion.

They had grown out of touch.

Chapter 4

The Narrowing Public
Changing the Strategic Motivations for Looking to Public Opinion

The administrations' pattern of interpretation did not solely lead them to grow out of touch. They also grew out of touch because they changed the questions they asked about the public as their popularity declined. This was quite rational. Because public support is critical to the modern presidency, their strategic motivation for examining public opinion changed along with their public standing.

What motivates presidential attention to public opinion? For one, a presidential administration may desire to be politically responsive. That is, it may hold a genuine desire to serve the public interest and to reflect the public will. For another, it is probably aware that public opinion can serve as a valuable resource for dealing with people in positions of power. So too, individual presidents may find themselves worried about the next election, either their own or the congressional midterm election. They may also look to public opinion to fulfill their psychological needs; popularity, for example, could be an important reaffirmation for the chief executive.

This chapter will examine what motivated the Truman, Johnson, and Carter administrations to look to public opinion. The nature and degree of their concern with public opinion changed with their political fortunes.

Each of the administrations studied went through a similar pattern of asking questions about the public. When they were popular, usually during the earliest days of their tenures, they asked questions about the public's *issue agenda*. Knowing the power of public support, they also asked questions that would help them use public opinion as a resource when dealing with other political elites. They sought to *maintain and expand* their public support base.

As it became clear that public support was declining, each administration shifted its focus. Staff members reacted immediately by asking *What's going wrong?* and attempting to find a reason for the decline. The answer proved elusive. Consequently, the questions they asked about the public revealed their concern for *defining and stabilizing* support from their base coalitions.

When these administrations were unpopular, their motivations shifted again. Their remaining public support bases were critical, and they sought public opinion information to *consolidate and protect* the coalitions they had.

The changing motivation for examining public opinion is important, because when an administration changes the questions it asks about public opinion, it also changes the answers it gets. Furthermore, for the Truman, Johnson, and Carter presidencies, these changes facilitated their growing out of touch, as the questions they asked narrowed the scope of the public to which they were attentive.

What Does the Public Think About Issues?

One striking similarity among these administrations is that their early days were marked by attentiveness to the public's stance on issues. As they began their terms, all three acted with the public in mind when discussing their administration's agenda, though their particular motivations were somewhat different. Truman and Carter wanted to engage the public in dialogue about policy issues. Truman was attentive to information about the issues of concern to the public and always wanted to make sure that public opinion was ready for the administration's objectives. Carter was extremely focused on maintaining dialogue between the White House and the people on various issues. Johnson was also attentive to the public's issue agenda, but he sought to curry public favor by advancing popular concerns. All three were seeking to maintain or even expand their support base.

John Geer's expectation that modern politicians would be responsive to public opinion seems to have held true when these administrations were popular. Public support was matched with a high degree of openness to the public's issue agenda.

Truman

The Truman administration's attention to the public's policy agenda was no doubt tempered by the fact that Truman began his term during the thirteenth year of Roosevelt's time in office. The New Deal had already been implemented, and Truman had not yet formulated his own Fair Deal. Furthermore, the war in Europe and the Pacific was preoccupying the country and the administration. This was not a time for the creation of new policies as much as it was a time to finish old business.

Even so, the administration did begin with some concern for the public's policy agenda. The State Department, for example, was sending Truman regular memos about public opinion polls regarding foreign policy.[1] Cabinet discussions on this topic also took note of the public. At a cabinet meeting November 16, 1945, the cabinet discussed an international agreement on the use of atomic weapons. Even on such a crucial matter, several members of the cabinet referred to the public's preferences. Secretary of War Robert Patterson stated his belief that the public would support the proposal. Secretary of the Navy James Forrestal added that people would "want assurances that Russia will play ball." Postmaster General Robert Hannegan agreed.[2]

The administration kept the public's opinion in mind when making domestic policy as well. For example, the administration's discussions on the

n ignored Elsey's advice and gave the speech to Congress on March 12,
s memo reveals his concern for public input into an "All-out" policy an-
ement.

> The public is not prepared. Public acceptance and support—the
> unity of all the people—must come after the "All-out" speech.
> Nothing would be more disastrous than to have such a speech divide
> the country. I believe an "All-out" speech will have a divisive effect
> if delivered too soon. A series of Presidential and Cabinet speeches
> and Executive department actions will be necessary to educate and
> inform the public to the point where the "All-out" message can be
> delivered and have the desired effect. The time to begin this educa-
> tion is now, and the forthcoming speech should be one of a series,
> building as rapidly as possible to the great climax—the "All-out
> speech."[5]

As the 1948 election approached, the administration heightened its inter-
in the public's foreign policy opinions. Leaders particularly noticed reaction
U.S. policy toward Israel/Palestine. At a cabinet meeting on April 9, 1948,
der Secretary of State Robert Lovett reported the results of a public opinion
ll about American policy toward Palestine. In July, Lovett had a poll for-
rded to Clark Clifford about the same topic. Some staff members expressed
ncern about the public fallout of Truman's recognition of the state of Israel
October. A memo for the record (which got passed to Clark Clifford) noted
at some politicians were being booed for supporting a plan that limited the
ze of Israel's borders.[6]

An examination of the archival evidence reveals that Truman and his staff
eldom discussed the public's issue agenda after 1948. The drop in attention
orresponds with a decline in public approval ratings; although Truman's pop-
larity reached 69 percent when he was re-inaugurated in January, 1949, it fell
o 51 percent by the end of that year. After that, it would not hit 50 percent
gain and stayed in a range between 22 percent and 36 percent during 1951 and
1952. As will be shown, this decline in attention to the public's issue agenda after a popularity drop is consistent with the pattern of Presidents Johnson and
Carter.

Johnson

Like Truman, Lyndon Johnson began his presidency with a strong interest in
determining the public's stance on issues. Johnson's historical reputation as
someone who understood power politics would suggest that a desire to broaden
his base of public support and enhance his ability to deal effectively with other
political actors motivated his interest in public opinion.

Johnson began his term using the public as a source for determining the
administration's agenda. In 1963 Johnson asked Princeton professor Eric Goldman to contact scholars and other intellectuals to acquire new ideas for the ad-

precarious post–World War II labor situation focuse
lic attitudes. At a September 28 cabinet meeting, FDIC
advised the president against supporting legislation th
sory arbitration with labor unions "at least until publi
tallized." Minutes of the November 23 cabinet meeting
with public opinion regarding the need for legislation
that were occurring throughout the country. Secretary (
lenbach argued that it was time for the administration to
legislation because neither labor nor management "real
file are ready to go through with things." Secretary of t
Vinson reasoned that if they created an impartial board t
the public would support it. Indeed, the cabinet was qui
litical benefits to be accrued from public support. Secr
Harold Ickes favored using a "fact finding board" to exan
relations, because such an approach would "cause the pres
ion to be effective."[3]

Schwellenbach's comments at the November 23 cabi
score another phenomenon of the way the administration
opinion in the early days. Not only did the administration b
for the public's issue agenda, its leaders also had great co
that they understood the public's agenda better than others d
ing the Labor Situation"—a document dated November 30,
ably prepared for that day's cabinet meeting—reports that "ii
of mind the Congress, if left to its own initiative, will probal
tion which may well be resented by both management and la
ment instead proposes a two-phased approach to creating a l;
"would undoubtedly be fully condoned by public opinion an
whole probably not meet with too intense antagonism on the
management or labor." The administration was also confiden
would allow them to ignore the business elite. At a cabinet mee
1946, focusing on the continuation of wartime price controls,
negan noted that he was "convinced that the rank and file of [t
people want price controls continued" despite the "vocal" oppos
ness leaders.[4]

When the administration's popularity was up, it kept the pu
while making policy decisions. In 1946, Truman's Gallup approva
from 63 percent in January to 35 percent in December. But in 1947
lic approval was again increasing, the administration looked to
for some guidance. One interesting example occurred in March, wl
Elsey advised Clark Clifford that Truman should not give his Truma
speech to Congress. The speech declared it to be the American poli
port actively "free peoples who are resisting attempted subjugation.
tion to calling for massive aid to Greece and Turkey, it implicitly estab
American cold war policy of resisting communist expansion. It was
the most important policy announcement of the president's tenure. /

ministration. Yet the administration paid attention to more than just university elite. In October, 1964, Douglas Cater prepared an analysis of surveys in ten states, commissioned by the White House from pollster Oliver Quayle. The memo ranks public issue concerns in the various states and notes a high degree of public concern about waste in government spending. Johnson requested that his speechwriters take this survey information into account while preparing speeches.[7]

Much of this concern could have stemmed from the pending presidential election. The archival evidence, however, suggests that Johnson continued to be willing to use polls to help formulate his agenda even after the election.[8] In June, 1965, the White House commissioned a Gallup Poll to ascertain public attitudes about immigration policies.[9] Later, in August of 1965, Douglas Cater would use a Gallup Poll to advise Johnson "to set ambitious but realistic goals" in various areas of interest to the public; Johnson approved of the formation of a task force to pursue the idea. Memoranda about the 1966 State of the Union message also reflect the administration's attention to public opinion when establishing legislative objectives; Special Assistant to the President Joseph Califano, for example, asked Hayes Redmon for information from polls on a wide variety of topics.[10] Johnson himself was interested in acquiring information concerning public opinion about his domestic program; a memo from Redmon to the president in November, 1965, reads, "Mr. President: Louis Harris has agreed to do the poll you asked for on the Great Society."[11]

The administration's interest continued into the following year. At the beginning of the 1966 congressional session Bill Moyers received a memo from Redmon discussing issues of importance to the public that Congress had dealt with in the previous session. Redmon concluded that, politically, there was "a lot of mileage left" in the administration's programs.[12] During the early years of Johnson's term, when the president was popular, he and his administration continuously monitored the public's attitude about specific issues.

Carter

Of the three administrations studied, Carter's began with the most focus on ascertaining the public's issue agenda. This may have stemmed from the fact that his inauguration gave his party the White House for the first time in eight years. Conversely, it may be because Truman and Johnson each *inherited* an agenda. Whatever the reason, the early days of the Carter administration were especially marked by this attention. Even before the inauguration, pollster Pat Caddell told President-elect Carter that "most Americans have little faith that the government really represents the people." Caddell advised Carter to "substantially and symbolically produce an accommodation between leaders of government, business, the consumer movement, labor, the environmental movement, farmers, and, of course, ordinary citizens. The goal would be to produce a national agenda with clear goals and a definition of responsibilities. A national group, picked by the president, could be formed to begin talking about the problems." Caddell further recommended,

We would have a kind of national "town meeting" providing a "dialogue" on problems and hopefully some answers.

I don't believe the idea is as crazy as it seems. There's a national
yearning for some kind of effort to bring us together. A success
would strike a deep and significant chord in the country.[13]

In a follow-up memo drafted January 10, 1977, Caddell asked Carter
whether his idea of developing a group "for an accommodation process between the people, the government, and various groups" was a "viable point that
ought to be pursued." The president-elect wrote "yes" in the margins.[14]

The early days of the Carter administration involved much discussion
of ways for the public to contact the administration. Some of this took the
form of what was labeled the "People Program." On February 8, 1977, Greg
Schneiders, director of White House projects, updated the president on the
"Status of the People Program": "Our goal is to develop step-by-step a comprehensive and institutionalized program which enables you to reach the
people and the people to reach you." The memo outlines several ideas, including a "White House Visitors Program" that would involve "bringing randomly
selected private citizens to Washington for meetings with you and your family
and to participate in various White House functions"; development of live two-
way broadcasts between the president and citizens or groups; a radio call-in
show; town meetings followed by the president's staying in private homes; and
a system whereby the president would be given "occasional recommendations
of private citizens to be called by you." Perhaps the volume of input was too
much. Two days later Schneiders asked the president not to tell people to communicate with him directly, because some people would be disappointed not
to speak with the president, and the White House was unable to handle *all*
the problems mentioned by the people.[15]

Much of the impetus for following public attitudes came from the
president himself. For example, Carter asked Schneiders to prepare for him
a "status report each Friday until further notice" on how the mail room was
handling its mail volume. In early March, Carter informed staff member (and
cousin) Hugh Carter that he would be interested in "pro and con figures" on
issues that resulted in numerous calls to the White House.[16]

On March 8, Schneiders informed Carter that, after several successful
events, the People Program was ready to be dismantled and turned over to other
government agencies. He recommended that the related "People Committee"
continue to meet monthly. He also warned the president not to "wear out our
welcome in the American home." However, immediately after saying that, he
advised Carter that they should limit themselves to "two press conferences each
month . . . two or three fireside chats each year, two radio call-in shows each
year, three trips to the people each year."[17] This "limit" still left thirty-two
events between the president and the general public each year.

The president and top administration officials were attentive to the public opinion information presented to them. One illustration of the degree of

Carter's attentiveness occurred on July 5, 1977, when he criticized a summary of that week's mail to the White House by noting in its margins that the opinions reported on the second and third pages were inconsistent with each other. In June, Margaret Costanza, assistant to the president for public liaison, informed the president that Ohio Lieutenant Governor Richard Celeste was requesting the help of her office in gathering the comments of citizens at state fairs around the country. Costanza thought it was "an excellent idea similar in tone and effect . . . to your March radio call-in show and other 'People Program' efforts." Perhaps indicative of the sincerity of the administration's desire to seek out the views of the public, Staff Secretary Rick Hutcheson advised the president that Deputy Assistant to the President Landon Butler "does not think that the 'people program' should be politicized or partisan." Inexplicably, Butler then recommended that the state fair poll be done through the DNC instead. The president responded to this by noting that the program would be "ok for Ohio only." An October memo from pollster Pat Caddell also reveals the administration's attention. Caddell forwarded to the president some data on foreign policy that National Security Advisor Zbigniev Brzezinski "wanted you to have immediately."[18]

Vice President Walter Mondale contributed to the administration's interest in ascertaining the public's policy preferences. In September, 1977, Mondale wrote a memo to the president assessing his role as vice president. The memo is fascinating not only for its introspective and reflective tone, but also for the way it speaks of public opinion. At one point, Mondale advises, "I think it might be useful to undertake a 7 to 10 day domestic tour later this year to try to determine how we are really doing in certain areas. Basically, it would be a learning and listening tour which might include visits to successful housing, educational and other kinds of projects, meetings with community leaders, tours of depressed urban areas, etc." The president responded to this idea by writing "good" in the margins.[19]

The administration's attention to the public's issue agenda trailed off after Carter's popularity declined. There are a few exceptions to this, but the Carter administration's motives for looking to the public changed. Never would they be as open to the issue agenda of the entire public as they were in the popular early days of Carter's term.

How Can We Use the Public as a Political Resource?

Attention to public opinion does not occur entirely out of concern for political responsiveness. Presidents are well aware that public opinion can be used as a *political resource*. When they are popular, their popularity can help them to achieve their objectives. Certainly one of the reasons that presidents look to the public is to find information about public support that can be used when dealing with other political elites. Yet in seeking out supportive information, presidents subtly narrow the segment of the population to which they are paying attention and to which they could be responsive. Furthermore, they no longer receive advice from or maintain a dialogue with the public, preferring instead to use information about the public to gain the upper hand.

Truman

Truman was well aware of the ability to use favorable public opinion to push policies that he sought. This occurred while his popularity was high, right after the end of World War II. Truman wanted to continue conscription and universal military training and to prevent the country from returning to a policy of isolationism. At a September, 1945, cabinet meeting, the president told his cabinet members that they needed to act quickly "in order to take advantage of public opinion." Notes of the meeting indicate that Truman believed that a delay would strengthen the isolationists' position. At a cabinet meeting on November 30, 1945, the president again identified the potential use of public opinion, this time to push labor legislation, commenting to the cabinet that "public opinion must be built up before this could be done effectively."[20]

Others in the administration shared the notion that they could use the public as an effective resource. In early January, 1946, Truman gave a nationally broadcast radio address, calling on Congress to take action on several domestic policy bills stalled in the legislative process. Postmaster General Robert Hannegan advised at a January cabinet meeting that the administration should take two months to "followup" and "take advantage of current public opinion." The cabinet also saw public opinion as a potential resource in May, 1946, when discussing how to deal with a coal strike. Truman was contemplating a government-proposed settlement accompanied by a threat that the administration would seize the coal mines unless they abided by the proposal. The secretary of the interior, Julius Krug, believed that this approach might work if the president went to the public and told them "what was proposed and refused."[21]

In 1947, Truman was also hoping to use public opinion to push the Marshall Plan, although he knew the risks. At a March 7 cabinet meeting, he said that this would be "the greatest selling job ever facing a President." He believed that he needed to "get the facts to the country to get the support necessary. We can't afford to revive the isolationists and wreck the United Nations."[22] Note that he deemed public opinion as a necessary resource to achieving his objectives.

Johnson

President Lyndon Johnson was particularly attuned to the ability to wield the mandate of public support in such a way as to ensure continuous success. Indeed, the legendary stories of Johnson carrying poll results in his pocket during the early years of his administration illustrate the nature of his concern—the president would use these polls to prod refractory elite political actors. The archival evidence also shows this attention to the administration's bargaining position. Soon after the 1964 election, the White House was aware that John-

son's landslide could be used effectively when dealing with Congress. For example, administrative assistant Henry Wilson informed Special Assistant to the
President Larry O'Brien of the status of North Carolina election results.

> The President carried the state by 174,000 votes or 56 percent.
> [Democratic Gubernatorial Candidate Dan K.] Moore carried
> by 172,000 . . .
> So the Moore people can make no pitch that the president
> rode Moore's coattails.[23]

Similarly, Eric Goldman writes about Johnson's edginess in 1964 on the night
of his election. Despite the certainty of the outcome, Johnson was concerned
with the margin of victory. The fears were unwarranted: Johnson's 61.1 percent
of the popular vote was (and still is) a record. Yet, Johnson's focus that night is
telling: "All election evening Lyndon Johnson closely watched one particular
instance of ticket splitting. A Kennedy was running in 1964, Robert Kennedy,
candidate for United States Senator from New York. LBJ carried the state by a
plurality of approximately 2,600,000 votes, RFK by 720,000. The President
was particularly interested in the Senator-elect's victory statement on television.
Robert Kennedy said that his win represented an 'overwhelming mandate for
the policies of John F. Kennedy and of course Lyndon Johnson.'"[24] Johnson was
aware that his landslide victory carried with it political clout.

The administration continued to wield public opinion as a tool after
the election of 1964. For example, on April 1, 1966, Marvin Watson informed
the president that White House staffer Ralph Harding showed Idaho Senator
Frank Church a poll indicating that 88 percent of the people of Idaho supported Johnson's Vietnam policy. "Ralph stated that he had discussed this
with and explained it to Senator Church, and that this information had a very
sobering effect on Senator Church."[25] The strategic use of information about
public opinion curbed another political actor's recalcitrance in supporting
Johnson's policies.

Furthermore, the administration was always attentive to information that
indicated the president's potential strength over other politicians. In April,
1966, Johnson's staff commissioned a New York poll from Oliver Quayle,
whom Johnson used regularly as a pollster. The poll measured the impact on
public opinion of critical public hearings held by Arkansas Senator William
Fulbright on Johnson's Vietnam policies. The poll showed that Johnson's approval rating in New York was 67 percent versus 53 percent for New York Senator Robert Kennedy, who opposed the Johnson Vietnam policies; Kennedy's
approval rating dropped after the hearings. A Bill Moyers memo to Johnson
about the poll indicates that Johnson may have actually gained support from
the hearings, and notes the "increased vote of confidence" for Johnson. Similarly, legislative aide Michael Manatos alerted the president that "without exception" all of the senators seeking reelection in 1966 "expressed unanimous
support of their constituents and themselves for your policies in Vietnam."[26]
Members of the administration knew that support for Johnson could translate

to presidential leverage, especially when Johnson had the support of another politician's constituents.

Carter

The Carter administration also understood the usefulness of using public opinion as a tool for achieving its policy goals. An April, 1977, memo, for example, discusses a "national computerized questionnaire process" as a way for the president to "gain support for his programs." Later the same month, Carter distributed a Harris Poll to his top administration officials that showed strong public support for his energy policies. He instructed Frank Moore, assistant to the president for congressional liaison, to distribute the poll to all members of Congress.[27]

The pressure of public opinion was even sought on matters of foreign policy. For example, a March, 1977, memorandum to Hamilton Jordan discusses ways to mobilize public support for the SALT II Treaty. Similarly, a May memo indicates that National Security Advisor Zbigniev Brzezinski and his deputy assistant, David Aaron, met to discuss "the politics of SALT" and agreed that the president should start "reaching out to the public at large" to gain support for the treaty. The memo suggests ways to go about doing this. Foreign policy was also Hamilton Jordan's concern when, in June, he prepared an eight-page memorandum to the president on "winning public and Congressional support for specific foreign policy initiatives."[28]

A memorandum sent September 19, 1977, to presidential aide Hamilton Jordan from Assistant Secretary of State Hodding Carter III typifies the way the administration thought about public opinion as a resource. Hodding Carter noted that those in Congress who were tentative about supporting the Panama Canal Treaty needed to know that the issue was "palatable politically." He added that recent poll results were showing more public favor toward the treaty and that this could be used to "build on the current momentum and to accelerate the shifts." President Carter did exactly that in a November 5 letter that he sent to every member of the Senate seeking support for the Panama Canal Treaty. A letter in Carter's handwriting informed the senators that a recent poll had indicated that the public supported the treaty by a two-to-one margin.[29]

The energy issue brought about similar action. The president was advised in October that unless the administration made "an all out effort over the next four to six weeks to arouse public support for our energy plan . . . it will be difficult for the House to stand firm on these issues." Hamilton Jordan responded to this, noting in one memo the importance of refocusing the public on the energy issue. Jordan asserted that success on the energy issue would allow them to "begin 1978 with considerable momentum in the Congress."[30]

Through 1978 the administration continued to view the public as a helpful resource in dealing with Congress. In April, Vice President Mondale's chief of staff Richard Moe sent a thoughtful memorandum to the vice president and to other key figures in the Carter administration about how the SALT Treaty was faring with the Senate. What makes the memo interesting is the subtle way that discussions about the treaty's prospects in the Senate are constantly tied to discussions about how the public perceives the issue. Moe introduces the body of the memorandum by saying, "Let me lay out some of the reasons why I believe we're in such bad shape both on the Hill and with the public." At one point in the eight-page document, Moe states that "the current public atmosphere could not be less conducive to selling a new SALT agreement." Moe, and others in the administration, saw the public as critical for the sale. Moe advised that the president "should get his side of the story to the country first" and that the administration should use a "citizens committee" and send out speakers throughout the country. He also advised the creation of a "high level White House task force . . . to design and implement the necessary public and congressional strategies."[31] At this point in the Carter administration, dealings with the public are extensions of dealings with the Congress. A letter from National Security Advisor Zbigniev Brzezinski to Pat Caddell similarly illustrates the link between Congress and the public: "When the President set the direction for the U.S. foreign assistance programs he also suggested that we undertake public affairs activities that would inform the Congress and the public of our objectives in this area."[32]

Sometimes the administration focused on the public less subtly and more specifically. One instance involves Greg Schneiders's writing about how to pass the president's energy program. He advised the "development of public support" on particulars of the president's energy bill "targeted to specific members of the Conference Committee."[33] A "strategy memo" prepared by communications director Gerald Rafshoon about "Developing Public Support for the President's Energy Program" also illustrates this tack. Rafshoon clearly defines his position about the role of the public: "This is not an *educational campaign*. We are not trying to teach the American people about the energy problem or the President's plan. Our goal doesn't require this and time doesn't allow for it. The focus should be generally on passage of a plan so that our nation will finally have a national energy policy." At one point he does write, "The target of our exhortation should be Congress directly—not the people." Nevertheless, he and the White House staff see the public as instrumental to pressuring Congress. He continues, "We are, before the American people, calling on Congress to stop talking and to produce an energy plan."[34]

What's the Reason for the Support Loss?

Public approval for the president and support for administration policies are critical to an administration's ability to achieve its objectives. Therein lies a crucial factor in losing touch with public opinion. While these case studies show how attentive the administrations were to public opinion early in their terms, they also reveal how the process of losing touch began. All of these presidents, for various reasons, faced serious slides in public approval. Hoping to arrest the decline, their administrations tried to define and stabilize their political base. As a result, the nature of the information they sought about public opinion changed. By necessity, the issue of popularity would gain in importance as other notions of public opinion—such as the public's issue agenda or the public's support for specific administration policies—would become less important. Consequently, questions about *public approval* slowly drowned out some wider questions about *public opinion.*

The following discussion will illustrate that as the openness of these administrations to the opinions of the general public waned, so did their ability |to be responsive to public opinion.

Truman

Despite Truman's reputation for being a trustee-style leader, his administration was not impervious to concerns about popularity. Truman was enough of a veteran of Washington politics to know the importance of public support. As his popularity declined, the Truman White House looked to the public to determine the cause. This was especially true in the election years of 1946, 1948, and 1950. By the second half of 1951, his public approval was staying low, and the archival record suggests that he and his staff ceased to worry about the cause of their problems with the public.

The first signs of trouble occurred in late 1945 but went virtually unnoticed. Truman's staff attributed public dissatisfaction to issues pertaining to the end of World War II and the return of American soldiers. For example, a memo to Truman from Matthew Connelly on October 2, 1945, suggests that the president receive a daily update of releases from military service and let the press know he was doing this. Connelly rationalized that this would "be helpful in the present dissatisfaction concerning release of the boys in the Armed Service." Truman wrote on the bottom, "Mentioned at cabinet and agreed to." With time, the complaints from the war-weary public became more serious. Robert Hannegan reported to Truman in March, 1946, that Chicago Democratic precinct captains were "alarmed by many complaints seeming to indict the Democratic Party as a war party." Hannegan said that this was an indication of "the war fatigue, confusion of thought, and fears now gripping the people that can lead to snap judgments against the Administration." Hannegan suggested that an upcoming speech would "serve to blanket the hysteria churned up from current headlines and accent our strivings for a workable peace."[35] (Truman spoke of an urgent need for world peace at a March 23 Democratic "Jackson Day" dinner.) The administration was beginning to realize that problems existed with the public, though it exhibited no sense that the problems were serious.

The administration became more aware of their problems over time. In October, 1946, Matthew Connelly was told by the president's administrative assistant, David Niles, that one of his friends in the Gallup polling organization had told him "that never since they have been taking polls has there been such a swing away from the Administration as has been taking place the past six weeks. In their opinion, the Senate and House will both go Republican." A few days later, Hannegan acknowledged the problem at a cabinet meeting, noting that there were "no glowing reports" about the "political situation" in the country.[36]

Some in the administration believed that their problems stemmed from the disaffection of southern Democrats over the race and states' rights issues. An analysis prepared during the 1948 campaign, for example, reports "anti-Truman" sentiment in the South based on race, conservativism, a "boundless enthusiasm for 'free enterprise,'" and "a real, deep-seated adherence to states rights and a violent antagonism to centralization and collectivist movements." The document warns of the possibility of a "new party alignment in the United States and a two-party system in the South."[37]

After the 1948 election and through 1949, the administration's relationship with the public remained relatively placid, with Gallup approval ratings above 50 percent. The administration's approval began to slide again in 1950, however, and once again it looked for possible causes of public disfavor. In July, White House staff aide Kenneth Hechler had lunch with Milton Stewart, an aide to Congressman Franklin Roosevelt, Jr., and wrote down Stewart's points afterward. Among other things, Stewart reported "that people were very much worried about skyrocketing prices," "farm surpluses," inadequate expansion of large industrial plants, and a sense that the administration was not working enough on civil defense.[38]

The Democrats' loss of twenty-nine House and six Senate seats in the 1950 election also invited questions about their declining situation, but the answers would elude them. The president immediately blamed the loss of seats primarily on "local situations" and denied that it was part of a trend. A Hechler analysis the day after the election suggested that the total number of losses was less than the historical average. Still, the memo analyzes the cause for the loss. Hechler notes that problems in urban areas were being caused by "McCarthyism, worry about the war and the draft, the high cost of living, and the tremendous propaganda of the A.M.A." A memo by speechwriter David Lloyd the following day agrees with Hechler's assessment that the Democrats were having problems primarily in the cities.[39] Another election analysis, in staff assistant George Elsey's files, placed blame on the effects of Senator Joseph McCarthy's red scare tactics and denied that the public was dissatisfied with the administration's Korean War policy and foreign policy. One other explanation was more ethereal; at a cabinet meeting December 12, 1950, Secretary of Labor Maurice Tobin reported being disturbed by the "morale" of the public.[40]

Speculation about the reasons for public disapproval continued through the first half of 1951. One theory circulated that the public believed that the administration was too closely linked to special interests. An April, 1951, Kenneth Hechler memo to George Elsey states that the public was criticizing the administration's anti-inflation, price-stabilization program because "most people feel the Administration has catered too much to group interests" and that the public would "applaud" a presidential statement that was "in the national interest." Later, Hechler would identify citizens' education level as the culprit. In July, he passed to other staff members a poll that indicated that highly educated independents were more likely to support the president's foreign policy than those with less education.[41] The Truman administration's loss of public support obviously shifted its attention from the public's issue agenda to the cause of the support loss. This shift contributed to the process of growing out of touch.

Johnson

For the Johnson administration, the tone of White House memoranda changes noticeably when the strategic focus became *What's going wrong?* Hayes Redmon's memos to Bill Moyers, for example, illustrate the new-found concern with identifying the president's supporters and detractors. On May 27, 1966, Redmon informed Moyers of the results of a poll conducted by Oliver Quayle: "The President's loss is among Republicans. Some moderates are returning to their party and very few Goldwaterites are coming over to the President. At the same time the President holds the Democratic vote very well." In June, Redmon's conversations with Gallup, Harris, and Quayle provided this explanation of declining support: "All agree that the primary cause is the Vietnam situation. Also a major secondary factor is the rising cost of living. There is general agreement with Lou Harris' comment that people are in a 'foul mood' regarding Vietnam." Moyers passed the bad news to the president in a memo.[42]

The administration was growing more attentive to finding the cause of the problem. The same day that Moyers wrote his memo to Johnson, Sherman Markman wrote a memo to Marvin Watson that was subsequently passed to the president. Markman asked Iowa Governor Harold Hughes three questions about a negative Iowa poll: "1. Do you think the poll accurately reflects the facts . . . ? 2. If so, what are the causes of the disaffection? 3. What can be done about it?" The discussions continued. A White House staff meeting on June 24, 1966, determined that there were three sources of the decline: Vietnam, inflation, and relations with farmers. A July memo from Hayes Redmon to Bill Moyers contained a lengthy quote from George Gallup about the causes of sharp drops in presidential popularity. The memo, which expresses Gallup's assertion that inaction frequently results in such declines, circulated through various offices and was ultimately passed to staff members Jake Jacobsen, Marvin Watson, Joseph Califano, Douglas Cater, Harry McPherson, Robert Kintner, Walt Rostow, and to the president.[43] Clearly, the administration was cognizant that it had a problem.

As public approval began to drop, the administration was forced to examine the public's attitude on the administration's record to date. It no longer had cause for rejoicing. While Johnson's Gallup approval rating stayed near 50 percent through the summer of 1966 and remained above 44 percent through the first half of 1967, the public evaluation of Johnson's record on certain issues was bleak. In August, 1966, for example, pollster Louis Harris informed the White House that 90 percent of the public gave Johnson an unfavorable rating on controlling inflation. In late September, Bill Moyers was informed of poll results indicating that only 18 percent of the country wanted to continue fighting in Vietnam at the current levels; 18 percent wanted to withdraw entirely and 55 percent wanted to escalate further (9 percent were undecided).[44]

The administration would continue to seek the causes of their erosion of public support. However, by focusing on approval levels, they were distracted from the wider attention to public opinion that marked their more popular days in office.[45]

Carter

The Carter administration also found itself having to evaluate why its popularity was dropping. One of the first occasions of this came not from the White House but from the Democratic National Committee, which, in May, 1977, analyzed an assortment of polls in an attempt to determine the cause of Carter's early popularity decline. A similar report was conducted in October, but neither report was conclusive as to the cause of Carter's falling public approval.[46]

In 1978, the White House itself began to be more concerned. In May, Vice President Mondale sent Carter a report by pollster Peter Hart that indicated that Carter's problem may have been caused by a lack of "tangible accomplishments" during his first months in office; the pollster anticipated a number of accomplishments and a return of Carter's favorable ratings.[47] In May, Jack Valenti (a member of Lyndon Johnson's staff who by this time had become the president of the Motion Picture Association of America) sent a ten-page letter to trade representative Robert Strauss. Strauss passed the memo, which he labeled "a bit dramatic but interesting" to Hamilton Jordan and Jody Powell, and told them they could decide whether or not to send it to Carter. Valenti began by stating that he was basing his thoughts on "recollections of similar torments endured by another President." Valenti reported that the economy was the "key, crucial issue." In concluding the memo, Valenti—echoing a popular refrain of Lyndon Johnson's—reported that he wanted Carter to succeed because "he is the only president I've got."[48]

In May, W. Bowman [Bo] Cutter, executive associate director for budget, informed Hamilton Jordan that he believed that the president's "badly deteriorated" public standing was related to "concerns about our competence." In July, Stu Eizenstat received a memo from Al Stern that stated the belief that "unforeseen inter-related factors" were at work, including bad relations with Congress. Stern believed that their predicament "should not be approached with a sense of crisis."[49]

How Can We Consolidate the Coalition?

As time progressed and their popularity waned, these administrations all shifted their foci. Because public support is necessary for presidents, they needed to consolidate and protect their support bases, no matter what their problems were with the public.

This can be seen in two ways. First, the Truman and Carter administrations focused attention on their degree of support from *groups* within their traditional coalition; for example, as Democrats, both presidents began to worry about their support among labor unions, urban dwellers, minorities, etc. This is consistent with Jacobs and Shapiro's observation of politicians in the 1980s and 1990s subverting attention to the general public to the policy goals of their supporters.[50] Second, all three administrations began to look to public opinion with attention to winning the next election, either for themselves or for the Democrats in Congress.

This shift in attention from the public at large to the coalition is significant, for it signifies another narrowing of the size of the public with which the administrations were concerned. Political realities no longer allowed the luxury of examining the whole public or its problems. By diminishing the number of citizens to which they were attentive, these administrations continued on the journey of growing out of touch.

Truman

Truman's need to focus on the Democratic coalition began very early in his term. When the postwar euphoria wore off, the country wanted to return rapidly to normal and quieter times; Truman's popularity slid as expectations rose. Worse still, because Truman became president during the fourth term of a Democratic administration, he did not have the enthusiastic support of the public at-large that often marks a new administration. The situation demanded—even during his early days as president—that he look to the Democratic coalition for support.

The Truman administration worried about one of the main parts of the Democratic coalition: labor. A memo to the president from his close friend and press secretary, Charlie Ross, illustrates this concern. On January 3, 1946, Ross sent Truman an advance copy of an article by George Gallup. The article contained some good news for the president: Truman's problems with labor unions, Gallup said, did not extend to the rank-and-file members. Still, it was not until the Republican-controlled Congress passed the Taft-Hartley Act in 1947 that Truman had the real opportunity to focus on the labor coalition. The Taft-Hartley bill put a number of restrictions on labor unions, and because of the administration's difficulty with strikes, the majority of the cabinet urged Truman to sign the bill. But according to Truman biographer David McCullough, Truman was personally opposed to the bill, and he saw it as an opportunity to "bring labor back into Democratic politics."[51] A poll of 163 Democratic representatives by the Democratic National Committee showed that 95 of them believed the president should veto the bill.[52] The sample may have been too small. On June 20, Truman vetoed the bill, and a majority of Democratic representatives joined the Republicans in overriding the veto.[53] The repercussions, however, proved favorable to Truman. His action strengthen his support among unions and helped him in his 1948 reelection bid.[54]

The approaching 1948 election kept the administration focused on groups within the coalition. The best evidence of this can be seen in the

"Clifford-Rowe memorandum," a campaign strategy memo presented to the president in November, 1947. Washington attorney and Democratic Party insider James Rowe originally drafted the memo for the president in September. Instead of reading it—perhaps because of his distaste for Rowe's law partner, Thomas Corcoran—Truman forwarded it to his assistant, Clark Clifford. Clifford was impressed by Rowe's analysis and rewrote the memo under his own name, borrowing extensively from Rowe's language. He sent the memo to the president on November 19. The prescient analysis correctly predicts that Dewey would be the Republican candidate. The memo also reviews Truman's coalition, breaking it into component groups. The Clifford-Rowe memorandum says that it was "very true" that the "Democratic Party is an unhappy alliance of Southern Conservatives, Western progressives and Big City labor." The memo notes that the South could be "safely ignored," but that the president "*must* . . . get along with the Westerners and with labor if he is to be re-elected."[55] The memorandum continues by analyzing the impact of independent and progressive voters, farmers, union members, liberals, blacks, Jews, Catholics, and Italians.[56] Clearly, Clifford and Rowe were preoccupied with Truman's ability to shore up his support from groups and preserve his political base.

Of course, the archival record is full of discussions about parts of the coalition during the late summer and fall of 1948, as the campaign was at its peak and Truman was concerned about attracting voters. The concern with groups within the coalition continued after the 1948 election, too. For example, four days after the election, Philleo Nash notified Truman that he had received sizable percentages of the votes of African Americans. A more detailed chart was also produced later that month, which analyzed the black vote in twenty states.[57]

A November 30 letter to Truman from Senator-elect Clinton Anderson of New Mexico analyzed the impact of the farm vote on Truman's election. Anderson's letter observes that farmers are strongly for the president, but so is labor, and that Truman should be ready to balance the claims of farmers who "may want everything that they think your victory entitles them to." Labor, as always, remained a focus. A memo from Bureau of the Budget director Jim Webb to Clark Clifford on December 30, 1948, discusses the political and policy implications of Truman's calling for repeal of the Taft-Hartley Act now that he had a Democratic majority again in Congress.[58]

Two years later, after the 1950 elections and after their public support declined again, administration leaders refocused on their coalition groups. For example, Ken Hechler wrote a memo on November 15, 1950, refuting an assertion that the Democrats lost seats in Congress due to the defection of farmer support. Hechler believed that switches in the voting patterns of urban voters caused the losses. Consequently, David Lloyd suggested to administrative assistant Charlie Murphy that Hechler take "a field trip" to major cities in order to talk with "party leaders and the leaders of the labor political organizations, going over their figures, interviewing precinct workers, etc."[59]

From its first days in office, the Truman administration was forced to pay attention to support from within the traditional Democratic constituency. It is significant that after a few years in office, this became the only part of the public examined. No longer were Truman staff members discussing the policy preferences of the general public, nor were they even seeking out the reasons for their overall declining support. Instead, the public with which they concerned themselves had narrowed to include only the group necessary for Truman to function in office.

Johnson

Unlike the Truman administration, as the Johnson administration's popularity declined, it did not focus so much on the groups within its public coalition. Rather, its staff members concentrated on the potential electoral consequences of their support loss. The administration's attention to their base electoral coalition became particularly evident after May, 1966, when its Gallup public approval rating had first fallen below 50 percent. By the summer of 1966 the administration's concern with public opinion seemed to stem primarily from the need to galvanize support for the Democratic Party before the 1966 midterm election. For example, Bill Moyers, press secretary, asked staff assistant Fred Panzer to prepare a report on the issues that Democratic members of Congress believed were of the greatest concern in their districts; the report was forwarded to Johnson in June.[60] In mid-July, Moyers made several suggestions to Johnson to help the Democratic cause in the 1966 election.

> 1) Before the Freshman democrats go home . . . you should have all the first-termers down for a meeting, pictures with you, etc.
> 2) I would like to see you ease into an occasional television press conference now rather than wait until the fall and have it charged that we are doing it only because of the campaign. If you have one in July and another in August, you can go on to have one in September and October, as well. There is no question that you are good at this game, and I think it is important—as November approaches—for us to have silenced the charges of "lack of information," "what is the Administration hiding?," "inaccessibility," etc. Furthermore, the Republicans have a hard time demanding equal time for your televised press conferences.
> 3) Your schedule in September seems to be getting filled . . . but I hope you could save a two-week period just in case you decide to (a) return to Honolulu, or (b) tour the Far East to visit our allies supporting us in Vietnam. A successful trip of this kind could have considerable impact in November . . . and the American people like nothing better than seeing their President well-received abroad.[61]

Johnson accepted the advice. The Democratic candidates for Congress visited Johnson eleven days after the Moyers memo. One hundred Democratic freshmen met with the president on September 6, and photographs were taken of

Johnson shaking hands. On October 7, Johnson again met with congressional candidates.[62] Furthermore, Johnson held televised news conferences on July 20 (three days after the memo), August 27, October 6 and 13, and November 4; Johnson had only had one televised news conference in 1966 before the Moyers memo.[63] Johnson visited the Far East in late October and early November, returning six days before the November 8 election. As could be expected, Democratic successes in the midterm elections were becoming an increasingly salient strategic concern with public opinion as the elections approached.

The 1966 midterm election brought Johnson a loss of forty-seven Democratic members of the House and two Democratic senators. Not surprisingly, the administration then became concerned about the implications of the loss for its own future in 1968. For example, in January of 1967, James Rowe forwarded to Johnson a 1966 election analysis: "an attempt to be as objective as possible about what happened on November 8 and to learn what happened, looking forward to a national Democratic victory in 1968." Concerns about reelection preoccupied Johnson until his March, 1968, decision to withdraw from the campaign. (See the appendix for a discussion of whether Johnson considered himself a candidate in 1968.) The slide in public approval resulted in Johnson's continued attempt to consolidate his base of public support. For example, Johnson began 1967 by attempting to appease and win back those who were opposing him. According to a letter from Bill Moyers to Johnson, which Moyers wrote in late 1967 after leaving the White House, the January, 1967, State of the Union Address had been designed to reestablish a base of support for LBJ. "Last year's State of the Union message was deliberately designed, as you suggested, to appeal to our opponents. The polls had turned downward. We had just lost 47 seats in Congress and found a more obstinate House . . . . The speech, in response, struck the role of underdog. It was an appeal for understanding and sympathy for patience and moderation."[64] Johnson's attention to his electoral coalition was clearly justified. Not only would it become more difficult to pursue his programs and policies, but his 1968 reelection chances were in doubt.

The 1968 election would serve as the prime motivator for attention to public opinion in Johnson's last years in office. [The appendix suggests that if Johnson truly were not a candidate for reelection, he was nonetheless keeping his options open so that he could choose to run.] Indeed, one feature characteristic of the remainder of Johnson's term was the ever-present attention to polls showing whom the public would prefer as the Democratic Party's candidate or who would win an election if it were held that day. These polls, called "presidential pairings," played an important role as indicators of Johnson's base coalition of public support.

Administration attention to such sources of public opinion increased drastically in 1967, as declining approval ratings and the 1966 midterm election results made it clear that Johnson could face a serious challenge from within the Democratic Party. Johnson's staff most feared a challenge by Robert F. Kennedy. Yet 1967 began with White House knowledge that Kennedy's appeal had begun to fade. Part of the reason for the drop in Kennedy's popularity was a controversy between the Kennedy family and biographer William Manchester. Although Manchester claimed to have been given complete rights to the Kennedy family's story of their reaction to the assassination of President Kennedy, the Kennedy family sued Manchester over parts of his book *The Death of a President,* claiming that he had breached an agreement and had violated the Kennedy family's privacy. According to Harris Polls that Cabinet Secretary Robert Kintner and staff member Fred Panzer examined and passed on to the president, the negative publicity for the Kennedy family resulting from the suit adversely affected Robert Kennedy. An advance release of a Harris Poll given to the White House reads, "Senator Robert Kennedy's standing with the American people has taken a tumble downward. By 56–44 percent, the public now prefers President Johnson to Kennedy as the Democratic candidate for President in 1968. Only two months ago, Kennedy was the choice over Mr. Johnson by 54–46 percent." The survey also indicated that support for a Kennedy vice presidency was also slipping, with Vice President Hubert Humphrey only narrowly behind the New York senator as the public's preference.[65]

Despite Senator Kennedy's drop in public appeal, the White House remained attentive to this potential challenge from within the Democratic Party In early March, Robert Kintner reported to the president with poll results showing RFK's losing an election to Michigan Governor George Romney and tying the former vice president, Richard Nixon; Kintner suggested that these findings could be attributed to Kennedy's increasingly intense stance against U.S. policies in Vietnam. Yet the White House concern continued. On March 23, Panzer informed the president that a Gallup Poll completed March 15 showed a preference for LBJ over RFK.[66] The president again received assurance in May:

> On Wednesday, May 10, 1967, Gallup will release a poll showing your pairing with RFK. It will show
> • LBJ now has a decisive edge over RFK.
> • RFK has lost much of his support.[67]

The president was particularly interested in this and requested more information. Panzer informed Johnson that the public had undergone "a complete turnaround in preference between LBJ and RFK since January 1967." At the beginning of 1967, Kennedy was preferred over Johnson 48 percent to 39 percent, but by late April Johnson was preferred 49 percent to 37 percent. According to Gallup, Kennedy's losses came largely from Democrats, with Johnson leading 52 percent to 39 percent among Democrats. Gallup cited the Manchester book controversy, a rise in LBJ's popularity, and Kennedy's dissent on Vietnam policy as the reasons for the changed preference.[68] For a while, fears of a Kennedy challenge were quieted.

The Johnson administration demonstrated attention to Democratic coalition support in other ways, too. In February, 1967, White House officials anticipated the early endorsement of LBJ from Iowa Governor Harold E. Hughes and became anxious when it seemed slow in coming. On April 19, Johnson discovered that the Gallup Poll had surveyed Republican county chairmen nationwide, and wished to know if a similar poll had been conducted within the Democratic Party; White House aide Jim Jones considered this an "urgent matter." When Marvin Watson responded to the president with a memo from Fred Panzer explaining that the last poll of Democratic county chairmen was in June, 1964, the president wrote on the bottom, "M—Can't some editor we know get Dem. chairmen views? L."[69]

As the political horizon became increasingly negative, the challenges came both from the Republican and Democratic Parties. The Johnson administration, by that point, was no longer building or defining a public support base. It was playing defense—and losing.

Johnson's continued success in presidential pairings with various opponents was mixed, and then it steadily declined. The late fall and early winter of 1967 increasingly showed Johnson to be in trouble. One chart filed in the White House Central Files on November 22, 1967, listed Gallup and Harris "trial heats" for the first eleven months of 1967, with Johnson losing all the mock elections listed in October and November.

Curiously, Gallup Polls indicated a slight rise in Johnson's approval rating during the same time period. The rise in approval may have resulted from some optimistic reports of the Vietnam War's progress made during the U.S. visits of General William Westmoreland and Ambassador Ellsworth Bunker. By December Johnson staffers saw some positive impact on the presidential pairings. On December 1, 1967, Panzer reported that Gallup now listed Johnson leading Nixon by four percent. By late January, Panzer would report that Johnson led all Republicans except Nelson Rockefeller, whom he was slightly behind.[70]

January, 1968, was a time of self-assurance for the administration about Johnson's renomination by the Democratic Party. On January 10, 1968, a poll by Oliver Quayle of likely voters in the New Hampshire Democratic primary revealed that Johnson was rated favorably by 73 percent and unfavorably by 27 percent, versus a 56 percent to 44 percent ratio for Eugene McCarthy. Quayle's analysis also showed LBJ leading, with 82 percent, while McCarthy and RFK held 9 percent and 8 percent of the decided voters, respectively.[71] Again, on January 18, in a New Hampshire poll conducted by Napolitan, registered voters showed Johnson leading McCarthy, 76 percent to 6 percent, and Kennedy, 67 percent to 22 percent. Similarly, when Johnson asked Panzer for information about his support among 1964 Democratic national delegates, Panzer reported that 87.1 percent of respondents would support Johnson's reelection.[72]

In late January, however, the already topsy-turvy political environment changed drastically for Johnson, for the worse. Despite the administration's successes in convincing Americans during late 1967 that the United States was making progress in Vietnam, the Vietcong launched a major offensive—the Tet offensive—on January 30, 1968. Although the American and South Vietnamese forces were considered victorious over the Vietcong on the battlefield, reaction to the Vietcong's surprise show of force signified a turning point in American public opinion about the war, particularly because it followed on the heels of the optimism created by Westmoreland and Bunker. It profoundly affected Johnson's 1968 reelection aspirations.

The administration was soon forced to divide the focus of its electoral concerns between some rather strong Republican opposition and the newly emerging Democratic opposition. By early February, Senator Eugene McCarthy was attracting supporters in his bid for the Democratic nomination, and rumblings continued about a possible challenge from Robert Kennedy, particularly after the Tet offensive. Furthermore, Johnson's public approval rating declined markedly in the first six weeks after the Tet offensive, from 48 percent to 36 percent.[73] Clearly, LBJ again had to concern himself with Democratic Party politics.

By March, Johnson and his staff accepted that reelection would be a struggle. Even so, the New Hampshire primary surprised all political observers, including the president.[74] Although Johnson's name was not on the ballot, most pundits expected he would far out-distance McCarthy, even as a write-in candidate. As it turned out, Johnson only narrowly defeated McCarthy, 49.5 percent to 42.7 percent, and McCarthy claimed a "victory" because of his surprise showing. Four days later, no doubt inspired by Johnson's politically crippled status, Robert Kennedy announced his decision to seek the nomination. Johnson's ability to gain his party's nomination was in doubt.

While Johnson's political fortunes were crumbling, he and his staff had come to a crucial decision to stop most of the bombing of North Vietnamese territory as an overture to encourage peace talks. This was a decisive moment in the administration's policies in Vietnam, and the president was scheduled to announce his decision in a nationwide broadcast on March 31, 1968. Yet the conclusion of the speech stunned even the most astute political observers.

> With America's sons in the fields far away, with America's future under challenge right here at home, with our hopes and the world's hopes for peace in the balance every day, I do not believe that I should devote an hour or a day of my time to any partisan causes or to any duties other than the awesome duties of this office—the presidency of your country.
>
> Accordingly, I shall not seek, and I will not accept, the nomination of my party for another term as your president.[75]

With that, the Johnson administration began to come to a close.

Curiously, the attention that the administration paid to its reelection efforts did not help and may have even hindered its understanding of public opinion. Earlier, the administration contracted the range of its attention to public opinion by narrowly focusing on the cause of their decline in public approval. Here, we see that the problem may have worsened: the administration became concerned with maintaining its support base and its standing relative to other candidates rather than with maintaining its public approval. After all, lowered public approval was less relevant if potential opponents could be defeated.

Carter

Like Truman, Carter focused his attention more on the groups within his coalition than on the Democratic Party as a whole. Because the Carter administration's popularity decline began fairly early in its term, it only stands to reason that its concern for the base coalition occurred early, too. In fact, even before Carter took the oath of office, Pat Caddell warned him that his "political situation is precarious for a Democrat," adding that the "Democratic party is in serious national trouble—with a shrinking and ill-defined coalition."[76] Concerns about the coalition did not begin in earnest, however, until the summer of 1977. Ted Van Dyk of the Agency for International Development, for example, cautioned Carter that he lacked a "strong political base" in the country. Another memo, about Carter's Middle East policy, notes that there was "widespread concern in the American Jewish community over the President's positions on Israel" and that their "political position" with that community was "fluid." Carter himself must have had his coalition in mind when he told Hamilton Jordan, "Ham—We need some PR on Spanish speaking appointments. Get it. JC."[77]

Attention to the base coalition continued through 1977. In September, Carter hand wrote a response to a memo from Vice President Mondale, suggesting that Mondale could help the administration "defuse some of the problems with women, blacks, urban groups, etc." Others thought that Carter needed to do this too. Hamilton Jordan, Richard Moe, and staff member Timothy Kraft advised Mondale in November that the president needed to budget time for "constituency groups." A lengthy December report that appears to be written by Mondale notes, "We took office last January with a large amount of public goodwill but with the enthusiastic support of few of the traditional or institutional Democratic constituencies—labor, teachers, farmers, Jews, minorities, party activists, liberals, etc." The report notes that these groups were "skeptical and deliberately withheld their judgement and, more importantly, their commitment." The report recommends that they spend "the first six or eight months of 1978 to consolidate our relations with these groups."[78]

Apparently, the advice took hold. In early January, 1978, Jody Powell advised Carter to give an interview with editors of black news organizations, saying that such an interview "would fit in with our plans to deal more effectively with constituency groups this year."[79] Carter followed the advice and gave an interview to "Representatives of Black Media Associations" on February 16.[80]

In February, Mondale and Eizenstat responded to a request from Carter to evaluate the "political status" of a plan to reorganize the government's civil rights enforcement mechanisms. The document analyzes reaction to the plan according to Democratic constituencies, noting that minorities, women, and "age groups" supported the plan, and that organized labor would not oppose the plan. The memo advises announcing the plan "at a major ceremony attended by representatives of civil rights, women's business, and labor groups." Carter concurred.[81] On February 23, Carter announced the plan in the East

Room of the White House and specifically mentioned by name the organizations represented at the announcement ceremony. With a few exceptions, most were traditional Democratic constituency groups.

> We have with us officials of a wide range of organizations, some of which I would just like to mention so that you'll know how broad is the interest and support for the action that we will introduce this afternoon: the Urban League, the National Urban Coalition, the NAACP, the Leadership Conference on Civil Rights, the National Organization of Women, the American GI Forum, the Mexican-American Legal Defense and Education Fund, the American Association of Retired Persons, the American Federation of Government Employees, the National Federation of Federal Employees, the National Association of Government Employees, the Chamber of Commerce of the United States, the Business Roundtable, the National Association of Manufacturers, the National Governor's Conference; representatives from other groups like the United Automobile Workers; major corporations, NBC, General Motors. And we are particularly honored to have with us two women who represent leaders who were great and courageous innovators in equality of opportunity and civil rights in our country, Mrs. Martin Luther King, Jr., on my left, and Mrs. Lynda Robb, the daughter of President Lyndon Johnson.[82]

Carter was aware of his problems with the traditional Democratic groups and may have even been defensive about his standing with them, as can be seen in this note he wrote in February to Secretary of Housing and Urban Development Patricia Harris and Stu Eizenstat: "Be sure to get written suggestions re urban policy from black leaders and other groups so as to derive good ideas and to minimize the inevitable criticisms later on. J.C."[83] Perhaps he was defensive because of pressure from his own staff. In March, 1978, Hamilton Jordan sent Carter a harsh memo on this theme, arguing against an urban policy proposal that Jordan saw as underfunded. Jordan wrote, *"If you propose an urban policy that only contains $600 million new Federal dollars, I will predict that it will be the single biggest political mistake we have made since being elected. . . .* Mr. President, I do not see how we can continue to alienate key groups of people who were responsible for your election and still maintain our political base. The groups that make up the urban coalition—blacks, Hispanics, labor, Democratic mayors, etc.—have been waiting all year for the 'comprehensive, major program' that we promised them." The same day, Jordan himself was advised about the coalition when a staff member wrote to him that the administration should take actions to appease state Democratic Party chairs.[84]

The Carter administration's concern for groups within the political base began to diminish after mid-1978. There were rare exceptions. In May, 1979, Jody Powell responded to a memo from Frank Moore by noting that the administration needed "to consolidate support among middle-of-the-road Democrats." Later that year, a series of memos led up to an October, 1979, proposal to Hamilton Jordan and Jody Powell to get the emerging Christian evangelical political movement behind the president. In response, Carter met with leading evangelical Christians in January, 1980. Similarly, a January, 1980, memo to Jody Powell discusses support for Carter's renomination among African-Americans.[85]

A concern with maintaining an election coalition for the president slowly replaced the former attention to groups within the Democratic coalition. Of course even in the earliest days of their term the Carter administration addressed how it would fare in 1980. In March, 1977, Hamilton Jordan wrote Carter a general memorandum discussing, among other things, the Democratic nomination in 1980. A December, 1977, report in Hamilton Jordan's files discusses the likelihood of a challenge from California Governor Jerry Brown and the type of campaign he would run. The report also advises that the administration "begin developing [a] 1980 political strategy for each state, particularly the key primary states." In 1978, staff members referred occasionally to Carter's 1980 election prospects. A July memo notes that they had eighteen months "to raise the approval rating 13 percent," presumably by the time of the first Democratic primary. In another memo that year, Hamilton Jordan emphasized the importance of the SALT II Treaty to Carter by writing "if we ratify a SALT II Agreement in 1979, and the economy is in reasonably good shape, I believe that it will insure your re-election in 1980."[86]

Attention to Carter's reelection heightened in 1979. In February, for example, Jerry Rafshoon passed to several of Carter's senior level staff a *Chicago Sun-Times* article about the president's odds in 1980. A March memo in Jody Powell's files shows Carter with a strong lead in the presidential preference of delegates to the Democratic midterm conference. A May memorandum by Pat Caddell analyzes the results of a national survey that focused on Carter's reelection chances.[87]

The real test came in early November of 1979 when Senator Edward Kennedy announced that he would challenge Carter for the Democratic nomination. The administration had anticipated the announcement by the time Kennedy made it official, forcing Carter's staff to pay attention to his reelection coalition. At times, they found themselves grasping for anything showing support, as in a poll of 122 Democrats at a county fair in Wisconsin that got passed from the vice president's office to Jody Powell through Hamilton Jordan's office.[88] By December, with the New Hampshire primary fast approaching, the White House was keenly aware of how their actions would affect their support in the primary election. A December 7 memo from Jody Powell to the president about an upcoming meeting with reporters advises the president to avoid attacks on Kennedy. The same day, James Free, special assistant for congressional liaison, informed the president of a Tennessee straw poll showing Carter's lead over Kennedy. Carter asked Jody Powell to publicize the poll.[89]

The concern with Kennedy continued. A December 31 memo in Jody Powell's files (and probably written by him) prepares the president for an interview with ABC News and advises him on how to answer questions about

Kennedy and the polls. The race against Kennedy loomed large enough to affect their discussions about serious policy decisions. A memo from Richard Moe to several top Carter aides on January 8, 1980, notes that Kennedy was criticizing Carter's decision to place a trade embargo on the Soviet Union after its invasion of Afghanistan because of the potential harm to American farmers. Moe suggests several actions to help "effectively answer Kennedy's argument and at the same time build broad public support for our policies."[90]

Even when Carter staffers attended to traditional Democratic constituency groups, they focused on electoral issues. A memo written on January 22, 1980, for example, analyzes support for Carter and Kennedy among African Americans. The author of the memo, while noting that the administration should not be "overly concerned" about Kennedy's lead over Carter among blacks, suggests that the polls could be "helpful in terms of pinpointing who the people are in the black community that we should give some more attention to." As late as April the contest against Kennedy would dominate the administration's thinking about the public; a memo from Powell to Carter before a Walter Cronkite interview advises Carter on how to address the primary campaign, noting that "most of the electorate is beginning to see EMK [Edward M. Kennedy] as a *'big spender'* but has not made the connection between *big spending* and *big deficits* on the one hand and *high interest rates* and *inflation* on the other."[91]

Of course, as the primaries got underway, the whole apparatus of the Carter campaign would be used in analyzing and reacting to public opinion. Over time, the need for information about public opinion had become—by necessity—very precisely linked to worries about reelection.

The Truman, Johnson, and Carter administrations all had various motivations to look to public opinion, and all three changed their motivations over time. The Truman and Carter presidencies began with concern for maintaining dialogue with the public, while the Johnson administration sought to expand its political base by delivering the policies that the public wanted. All three were highly attentive to the public's stance on issues during the popular days of their terms. They were all aware, particularly when they were popular, that the public was an important resource for attaining their objectives. They sought to maintain and expand their support base. As a consequence, the public to which they were attentive was the general public.

The early days of these administrations held the most potential for democratic responsiveness. John Geer's expectation that modern politicians will respond to centrist opinion was possible at that time. The administrations sought out and discussed the public's issue agenda.

Over time, however, these administrations narrowed their scope of attention to public opinion. As their approval ratings began to decline, they developed new strategic objectives for looking to the public. Because they could no longer count on the support of the general public, they found themselves asking questions that could help determine the cause of their support loss. Each administration sensed that there was a cause of growing public disaffection, but any hopes of finding a precise cause were elusive. The presidents and their staffs turned their attention to defining and stabilizing their base of public support.

Eventually, the dominant motive of these administrations for examining public opinion was to consolidate and protect their coalition. As we have seen, this action took two forms. The Truman and Carter administrations, in particular, reacted to the growing discontent of the general public by examining their relationships with the traditional Democratic constituencies. The Truman, Johnson, and Carter administrations each focused on the support they could expect to get in the next election. Through it all their attention was concentrated on their power base.

As they became less popular, the administrations studied here closed off the possibility of being responsive to the general public. Instead, they narrowed the scope of their attention to their core supporters. According to Jacobs and Shapiro, prioritizing the policy objectives of supporters was a major cause of a decline in policy responsiveness to the general public in the 1980s and 1990s. The findings here are consistent with their description of the presidents during those decades as unresponsive, and the cases here suggest that earlier presidents were also closed to the possibility of responding to the public at large.[92] Strategic necessity dictated that the Truman, Johnson, and Carter administrations narrow their scope of attention to public opinion.

None of these administrations were able to sustain the breadth of the attention to public opinion that they had during their popular days, because they needed to change the questions they asked about the public. They did not grow out of touch because of ineptitude or character flaw but rather because of a need to sustain the level of public support necessary for them to work effectively within the political system.

Chapter 5

Conclusion
Implications of the Study

The Truman, Johnson, and Carter administrations watched helplessly as their public support levels declined. To make matters worse, all of these administrations interpreted public opinion and asked questions about the public in a way that failed to bring them closer to understanding the public. By the end of their terms, they had grown out of touch.

The patterns of interpretation seen in chapters 1, 2, and 3 are surprising and perhaps even counter-intuitive. While one might have expected the administrations to become increasingly sensitive to the concerns and attitudes of the American public as support declined, the opposite occurred (sometimes even with an approaching election). Instead, they became increasingly closed to understanding the breadth of public opinion.

During their popular times, all three administrations approached public opinion with a self-congratulatory style, similar to the behavior of Kingdon's winning candidates. Just as with the winners of elections, this pattern of interpreting public opinion led to the belief within the administrations that the public was highly attentive to them. Furthermore, they feared losing public support; this kept them attuned to anything that could lead to its decline. As a result, the relatively popular times of the Truman, Johnson, and Carter terms are marked by attention to a wide scope of public opinion.

Public linkage to these administrations became more difficult as their public support declined. The Truman, Johnson, and Carter administrations all reacted similarly to the decline in public approval. They commonly cited their administration's image and difficulty in communicating their "message" as the culprit. Such an interpretation had the deleterious effect of allowing them to maintain cognitive consonance with their popular times, by dismissing the idea that their decline was serious. Furthermore, unlike their earlier days when their fear of support loss kept them attentive to the public, the interpretation of public opinion while support declined was noticeable for its optimism, another factor that allowed these administrations to downplay the significance of their decline in public approval.

It is unlikely that public opinion could have made itself heard without severe distortion during the unpopular times. The Truman, Johnson, and Carter administrations each dismissed indicators of dissent, either by labeling them as the consequences of actions by manipulative enemies, or by patronizing the public outright. Such behavior mimics Kingdon's losing candidates and is representative of classic cognitive dissonance. Truman and Johnson took this further by developing a deep distrust of pollsters that allowed them to discount the measurements of their slide in public approval. As a result, these three administrations continuously narrowed the size of the population that they considered to be legitimately expressing the public will.

The pattern of interpretation did not solely lead to the estrangement of these administrations from the public. Chapter 4 illustrates that the motivation to look to the public changed as their popularity declined. As a result, the segments of the public that they asked about became increasingly narrow with time. They began, during their popular times, by examining the issue agenda of the American public and by seeking out information that they could use when dealing with other political elites. They sought to maintain and expand their supportive public coalition. When their popularity first began to decline, they looked at public opinion information in an attempt to understanding their declining approval. When explanations proved elusive, they mainly looked to the public to define and stabilize their base of public support. Eventually, with public support falling further, they shrank the scope of their concern to consolidating and protecting their base coalition within the Democratic Party.

Inattention to public opinion did not cause these administrations' difficult relationships with the public. They were attentive, and they all reacted to public opinion. Further, there was never a time when any of them were unaware of the consequences of the decline in public support for their ability to accomplish their policy objectives. The various attempts of these administrations to remedy their political problems by being more attentive to style or by publicizing even the most innocuous evidence of approval illustrate that they wanted to regain public support. Yet while these administrations clearly reacted to public opinion, by changing their interpretation or asking new questions, over time they became increasingly unable to respond to the public in any meaningful way.

Ultimately, of course, the principal question here is about the democratic nature of the presidency. One might argue that the plebiscitary nature of the modern presidency has made it more responsive to the people. The cases examined here suggest otherwise. It is noteworthy that low approval ratings, sometimes accompanied by impending elections, did not result in a heightened attention to the opinions of the people outside of the administration's support base. To the contrary, in each of the cases studied here, the people's voice was most easily heard when it was already supportive of the presidential administration. The administrations responded little to the public at large after their support bases had deteriorated.

There is a tremendous irony in this. The contemporary American polity includes a continuous feeding of public opinion information into the White House. This is due not only to the growth of the mass media but also to the corresponding growth in public opinion polling, an industry that has carved its niche in American politics. Polling had become prominent in Truman's day, but by Johnson's administration polls were being regularly commissioned and routinely analyzed in the White House. With Carter came the institutionalization of an official pollster in the White House. Despite all this information about the public at the fingertips of these presidents and their staffs, the patterns of interpreting public opinion were such that the public guided few presidential actions. While public opinion clearly affected these administrations, their understanding of the public as their terms progressed effectively negated the possibility of democratic control.

This study indicates that there are limits to the degree to which presidents can be responsive to public opinion. Geer has suggested that the scientific public opinion survey has resulted in presidents' being more responsive to the public's policy desires. These three administrations were most open to the public's policy agenda during their popular times. As popularity declined, however, the administrations changed the way that they looked at and interpreted public opinion, and these changes prevented them from responding in any meaningful way.

Polls did little to prevent these presidents from growing out of touch. While Geer asserts that polls leave "less room for rationalization," the evidence presented here contradicts that view. Indeed, these administrations rationalized adverse readings of public opinion, even when the source was a scientific public opinion poll. For example, they dismissed bad news by claiming that the public was being manipulated or did not have all the facts. Despite the scientific nature of polling, White House officials still need to rely on their own perceptions to interpret the meaning of the polls and the thinking of the public. These case studies suggest that Geer's expectation that politicians will be responsive only applies to the presidency when presidents have high levels of public support.

Jacobs and Shapiro, citing evidence that there has been a decline in responsiveness in the last two decades, argue that "politicians don't pander" in part because they place their supporters' interests ahead of centrist public opinion. They also assert that there could someday be a return to pre-1980 levels of responsiveness.[1] The experience of the Truman, Johnson, and Carter administrations suggests that the presidency had limited levels of responsiveness prior to 1980, too. The problem for those seeking a more responsive presidency is that the plebiscitary nature of the modern presidency interferes with the ability of administrations to look to public opinion for policy guidance. The strategic restraints on *why* presidents look to public opinion and the fluctuations in *how* they interpret public opinion information suggest that there are limits to how responsive presidents can be. Presidents will not pander, in part, because they cannot.

In fact, much of what Jacobs and Shapiro criticize in the post-1980 presidency was already present in the Truman, Johnson, and Carter years, though perhaps not to the same extent. For example, Jacobs and Shapiro's claim that administrations look to public opinion for information on how to create "crafted talk" in order to "simulate responsiveness" has a parallel in the earlier administrations studied here. That is, these administrations read their decline in public support as evidence that they needed to improve how they delivered their message. While it is not precisely the same phenomenon as Jacobs and Shapiro observe, it does have the same effect: concern for communicating a message takes precedence over acquiring a fuller understanding of public opinion. In addition, while Jacobs and Shapiro assert that politicians have been more observant of their partisan loyalists than centrist opinion during the 1980s and 1990s, these cases suggest that earlier administrations also focused their attention on their base coalition—at least after their public support dropped. Only when they were popular did they demonstrate an effort to understand and respond to the policy preferences of the public at large.

A peculiar dysfunction results from the importance of public support to the modern presidency. Significantly, the cases examined here illustrate that the need for and attention to public support has interfered with the ability of the modern presidency to be responsive to the public. The priority that the Truman, Johnson, and Carter administrations placed on public support may have drowned out a fuller understanding of public opinion. *For these presidents, growing out of touch did not cause their declining public support; declining public support led to their growing out of touch.*

Public support is a vital concern for those in the White House because it is strategically necessary for the president's ability to deal with other political elites. But public support, quantified today as a "public approval rating," is not a very meaningful source of public opinion. Thus, for example, while declining public approval ratings may suggest to an administration that there is a problem, it does not reveal the causes. Knowledge of lower levels of public approval does not enhance an administration's ability to determine a way out of public disfavor.

The ambiguous meaning of public approval polls contributes to the out-of-touch phenomenon. Administrations know how important public approval ratings are and, thus, closely follow them. The lack of clear meaning forces administrations to develop their own interpretations of these polls. Inevitably, this practice leads to a bias on the part of the interpreter. Kingdon's congratulation-rationalization effect, observed here in the White House, results in an administration's interpreting public approval ratings in the best possible light.

Of course, this problem is not limited to those polls that measure a president's public approval. Any public opinion poll can distract its reader from the nuances of public opinion. Indeed, it has become common for presidents, politicians, and political observers to speak of public opinion primarily as a *measurable* phenomenon. "Polls," Herbst observes, "usually provide only a superficial glimpse of the public mood, not a textured, complex account of popular beliefs."[2] Gone is the notion, discussed in the first chapter, of the "evanescent common will." This too may have the effect of distancing political leaders from the populace. When a poll is used by the supporters of a particular political position, for example, the typical response from detractors is to question the poll's wording, sampling, or survey method. The best way to trump an opponent when caught in such a dispute is to present a "better" poll that purports to reveal a different understanding of the public. However, such an exchange reduces the public to contending sets of numbers. When the leaders of the body politic become reliant on this notion of the public, they risk alienating the public whose favor they seek.

Fortunately, presidents do have many other sources of public opinion information to complement and balance the information they get from polls. The Truman, Carter, and Johnson administrations paid close attention to such things as election results, comments from fellow partisans, mail from the public, media editorials, etc. The administrations did develop from these sources enough of a sense of the public to enable them to speak about public opinion when they deliberated. Yet despite their many sources of information, including non-survey information, they could never escape the uncertainty of attempting to understand public opinion. Furthermore, as noted throughout this book, *they continuously redefined "the public" according to what they needed to attend to at the moment.*

This book has presented an empirical argument based on the observation of three administrations, but the normative question remains to be settled: Should presidents attempt to follow the public's lead when making decisions? More than 200 years ago Edmund Burke devised his classic discussion of the two types of representatives: delegates and trustees. Although Burke's dichotomy was meant to apply to representatives, it is clear that it applies to modern presidents as well. Two of the presidents studied here, Harry Truman and Jimmy Carter are commonly seen as trustees who made their decisions according to their best judgements, while Lyndon Johnson is often seen as the poll-wielding delegate willing to shift his policies according to the latest survey.[3] It is certainly beyond the scope of this book to test these reputations.

Careful observers of American politics, including many cited throughout this book, disagree about what ought to constitute the relationship between the president and the public. Tulis, for example, argues that the contemporary practice—that of continually monitoring public opinion and using rhetoric to lead the public for policy pursuits—creates tensions with the original constitutional order. He advises a "new political education" whereby the polity can evaluate the appropriateness of political uses of rhetoric in modern times.[4] Jacobs and Shapiro, reacting to criticisms of President Clinton for being too responsive to public opinion, call for *more* responsiveness from government officials. They argue, "Democracy does not begin and end with the right to vote." They also assert that the delegate/trustee debate is a false dichotomy and promote "responsive leadership" from American politicians, something they believe is currently lacking.[5] Geer, by contrast, asserts not only that opinion polls have made delegate-style behavior possible but also that politicians will act as delegates on highly salient issues. He cautions, however, that this "places additional responsibility on the shoulders of the public" to be informed.[6]

Whether or not one wishes to reform the presidents, the citizenry, or the constitutional order itself, the Truman, Johnson, and Carter case studies illustrate how difficult it is for the presidency to respond effectively to the public. Reasonable people could disagree about whether ideal presidents should stand by their convictions despite public opinion or should allow the people to guide their actions when taking positions on political issues. The debate sparked by Burke's distinction between delegates and trustees may never be definitively settled. *These case studies suggest, however, that modern presidential administrations operate in a plebiscitary environment that demands continual responsiveness to public opinion while at the same time interferes with their ability to ascertain an understanding of public opinion.* Thus, presidential administrations may react to the public, but not in a way satisfactory to even the most ardent supporters of majoritarian democracy. The degree to which an administration can dismiss or discount mounting public criticism of its policies indicates that even if an administration should deliberately choose to follow the public's lead, it would find it very difficult to do.

These case studies portray how easy it is for a presidential administration to lose touch with the people. Indeed, certain institutional aspects of the modern political order are the prime causes of this problem. The modern presidency operates on a public support base, and public support bases tend to decline. All administrations will have similar strategic concerns, ask similar questions, and face similar problems. Their responses, too, may be similar, such as worrying first about image rather than substance or attempting to manipulate indicators of public support.

Of course, the cases presented here are limited. It is possible that the phenomena observed and the theory presented may not apply to all modern presidents. Clearly, the subject of presidential understanding of public opinion and responsiveness to public opinion deserves further study. Indeed, there are several avenues for further research that could answer remaining questions.

First, the type of study completed here should be applied to Republican presidents as well. Could there be something about the nature of the Republican base constituency that allows administrations to escape the pattern observed here? An ideal case study would be the George H. W. Bush administration. Bush's record drop in the Gallup public approval rating, from a high of 89 percent in early March, 1991, to a low of 29 percent in early August, 1992, could very well have been characterized by self-congratulation followed by rationalization, cognitive dissonance, and a changed set of questions asked about the public.[7] Nixon's presidency could prove equally provocative.

A second similar avenue for research involves studying an administration that is not part of the New Deal tradition. Stephen Skowronek has observed the pattern of "regimes" within the presidency as one president constructs a political regime (e.g., Franklin Roosevelt and the New Deal), others reaffirm the regime and manage the competing interests within (e.g., Kennedy), followed eventually by others who seek to maintain the credibility of the disintegrating regime (e.g., Carter).[8] Given Skowronek's theory, it might prove fruitful to study administrations that are not part of the Roosevelt regime. Some may assert that Reagan is a regime constructor for recent Republican presidents. If so, not only would the Reagan presidency and the two Bush presidencies make useful cases, but so might the Clinton administration, which could plausibly be the first Democratic presidency after the end of the New Deal regime.

A third possible avenue for research involves presidents who were not eligible for reelection. The Twenty-second Amendment to the Constitution did not apply to Truman, and Johnson and Carter were both eligible for terms after the ones studied here. Truman and Johnson each appeared likely to run again. According to Truman biographer David McCullough, Truman actually made his decision to retire in April, 1950, but his decision was known only to his wife until November, 1951, when he privately told his staff. Still, Truman vacillated on the decision until his announcement on March 29, 1952.[9] For Johnson, the evidence presented in the appendix suggests that he was—at very least—strongly considering a run right up to the time of his withdrawal. In both cases, these presidents' administrations had reason to believe that there might be a reelection campaign until fairly late in their terms. Carter ran for a second term but lost. Could there be something about "lame duck" administrations that alters the patterns observed here? Such findings would suggest much about the potential responsiveness of the presidency and the impact of the Twenty-second Amendment.

Fourth, an examination of presidencies that did not have sustained declines in public support or that even had recoveries in public support might provide interesting contrasts to the ones examined here. (Truman, of course, did have a temporary recovery in public support, and earlier chapters note the repeated patterns as his popularity dropped again.) The Clinton presidency, for example, recovered from a low Gallup approval rating of 37 percent in early June, 1993 (less than five months into the president's term), to an average of 61.6 percent in the second term.[10] Reagan and Eisenhower also would provide interesting cases; Reagan's popularity ebbed and flowed over the course of his term, and Eisenhower's, while declining slightly, did not drop as precipitously as some of the presidencies examined here. Of course, high approval ratings do not necessarily connote a close understanding of public opinion. President Clinton, who had high approval ratings at the end of his term, seems to have badly misjudged the public's reaction to his last-minute use of the pardon power and his plan to bring numerous official gifts with him for his personal use as he left the White House. Is this evidence that he too lost touch with public opinion, despite his high approval ratings? One wonders what sorts of problems the popular presidents experience in understanding public opinion.

Fifth, an examination of more recent presidents may be in order. As previously noted, Jacobs and Shapiro suggest that there has been a change in political responsiveness since 1980, and they use sources from the Clinton administration to examine the uses and attitudes about public opinion. This work could be supplemented as the Clinton archives become available. The other presidential administrations of this era could provide an interesting comparison or contrast to the three studied here.

Finally, these cases all involve "modern" presidents of the post–World War II era. Yet presidents prior to Franklin D. Roosevelt had considerable information about public opinion, though not in the form of opinion polls. Indeed, Herbst notes that during the advent of polls in the mid–twentieth century "our conception of public opinion was changing."[11] Did earlier presidents react differently? Many of these presidents have left extensive archives to be examined. What was the Herbert Hoover administration's reaction to his decline in public support? Was it easier or more difficult for it to dismiss or rationalize public disapproval? Did it resort to a focus on communication as a way of explaining the problem? Nineteenth-century presidents may prove fruitful for study as well. Jeffrey Tulis asserts that a fundamental change in the relationship between the president and the public occurred with the Wilson presidency. Do pre-Wilsonian administrations behave differently than the three examined here? In what ways?

The lesson from this study of the Truman, Johnson, and Carter administrations is that the importance of public opinion to the modern presidency does not necessarily translate into a good presidential understanding of the public. The conception of the presidency as an institution of popular leadership, controlled by public opinion, deserves further study and careful reconsideration.

Appendix
But Was Johnson Running in 1968?

The assertion here that LBJ's attention to public opinion was motivated in part by his concern for reelection assumes that he considered himself a candidate in the 1968 election. Although Johnson contends that he never intended to run for reelection, documentary evidence in the Johnson archives suggests that Johnson's withdrawal decision was not made until perhaps the day of or the day before his announcement.

Johnson claims to have decided as early as 1964 not to seek reelection in 1968. According to Johnson, after agonizing in May of 1964 about whether to seek election to the office he inherited from Kennedy, his wife counseled him,

> If you lose in November—it's all settled anyway.
>
> If you win, let's do the best we can for 3 years or 3 years and 4 months—and then, the Lord letting us live that long, announce in February or March 1968 that you are not a candidate for re-election.[1]

When 1968 arrived, Johnson asserts, the real question was not if he would run but when he would announce that he was not running.

Indeed, Johnson contemplated announcing at the end of his January 17, 1968, State of the Union Address that he would not run. In fact, Texas Governor (and Johnson confidant) John Connally called Press Secretary George Christian that day and left him with a list to pass to the president of five reasons why he should conclude that night's State of the Union address with a withdrawal statement.[2] Johnson writes in his memoirs, *The Vantage Point*, that he was seriously considering a surprise announcement on that occasion but was prevented from making it because, "When I arrived at the Capitol that night, I thought I had the statement with me but discovered that I had failed to bring it." He adds that he was also uncomfortable with the timing.[3]

George Christian tells a slightly different story. Although he confirms that Johnson had talked with him about quitting as early as August, 1967, Christian says that it was never a certain thing. On March 30, the day before the announcement, Johnson called his friend Horace Busby and asked, "What do you think we ought to do?"[4] On the morning of March 31, Busby asked the president what the odds were that he would withdraw. "Seven to three against," came the reply.[5] In short, the withdrawal was never a sure thing.

Johnson's papers reflect that he certainly acted like a candidate for the first three months of 1968. The administration acted likewise; Turner notes that the White House staff "proceeded on the assumption that the campaign would soon be in full swing."[6] Johnson sought poll results, communicated with his campaign committee, and worried about improved public relations. For example, on February 16, 1968—six weeks before his surprise withdrawal announcement on March 31—Johnson responded to a memo from Marvin Watson indicating overwhelming support for Johnson over other potential Democratic candidates among Iowa Democratic county chairs. Johnson wrote on the memo, "Send to [columnists] Drew Pearson, [Walter] Winchell, and [Robert] Spivack."[7] Again, it seems unlikely that he was certain about how he would act. On March 22, merely nine days before withdrawing, National Security Adviser Walt Rostow advised Johnson that his longtime friend Justice Abe Fortas and others were discussing the administration's problem "holding and attracting the youth in the coming election." They were concerned that the younger generation's disaffection "draws them towards McCarthy and Bobby Kennedy." The memo passed along the suggestion that the White House should systematically contact campus youth groups. Johnson responded with a note to Harry McPherson, "Harry, you and Joe Califano explore. L."[8] Johnson's willingness to use his staff's time on campaign matters indicates that—at the very least—he was trying to maintain his options. Furthermore, on March 27, 1968, LBJ was still concerned about the potential outcome of the Wisconsin primary and wanted to answer Wisconsin detractors of his Vietnam policy through a forthcoming article by Dwight Eisenhower in *Reader's Digest*.[9] That evening he spoke at length on the telephone with pollster Ed Pauley, who was in Los Angeles, about public poll results showing him losing to Robert Kennedy in California. At the conclusion of the discussion, Johnson told him to work with former White House staff member Irving Sprague.[10] Would Johnson discuss poll results and campaign personnel if he had conclusively decided to withdraw from the race in four days?

Kathleen Turner suggests that Johnson was acting out of "genuine indecision" and a desire not to eliminate his alternatives. Turner observes that the staff was proceeding with campaign planning, often with Johnson's "explicit approval."[11]

Even Johnson's intimate and trusted friends seemed to be in the dark about Johnson's plans to withdraw, and Johnson did nothing to ease the work they were doing for him. James Rowe, for example, wrote to Johnson on March 28, complaining about the fact that supporters were questioning him about why Johnson had not yet officially announced his candidacy. Rowe reported that he was assuring them that Johnson was running. Johnson seemingly did not inform his longtime friend otherwise.[12] Similarly, Johnson met or spoke with his friend Justice Abe Fortas twenty-six times in March, the last time on March 28.[13] The announcement on March 31 surprised Fortas nonetheless; a phone message that night reads, "Well you do have some surprises, don't you?"[14] Because Johnson was still seeking information about his standing in the primaries and not telling his closest associates about his plans to withdraw, it seems likely that it was near the end of March before he really decided to quit.

Of course, even if Johnson knew all along that he would not seek reelection, the election still directed the administration's attention to public opinion. Certainly Johnson acted like a candidate, he and his associates analyzed public opinion information as if he were a candidate, and they focused their attention on presidential pairings as a measure of public support.

Notes

Introduction

1. Doris A. Graber, "Conclusions: Linkage Successes and Failures," in *The President and the Public*, ed. by Graber, p. 289.
2. Lawrence R. Jacobs and Robert Y. Shapiro, *Politicians Don't Pander: Political Manipulation and the Loss of Democratic Responsiveness*, p. 313.
3. Perhaps one of the most forceful arguments of this idea is made by Theodore J. Lowi in *The Personal President: Power Invested, Promises Unfulfilled.*
4. Indeed, the presidents themselves make this argument. Truman and Johnson maintained that they made difficult decisions in favor of foreign interventions; Ford asserts that the pardoning of Richard Nixon was necessary for the nation; and Carter defends his temperate response to the Iranian taking of American hostages as the more level-headed reaction.
5. Richard W. Waterman, Robert Wright, and Gilbert St. Clair, *The Image-Is-Everything Presidency: Dilemmas in American Leadership*, pp. 3–4, 61–62.
6. Ibid., pp. 127–28.
7. Jacobs and Shapiro, *Politicians Don't Pander.*
8. Richard Neustadt, *Presidential Power*, Chapter 5 and p. 74.
9. Michael Baruch Grossman and Martha Joynt Kumar, *Portraying the President: The White House and the News Media*, pp. 83–84. Grossman and Kumar note that the 30 percent figure was ascertained before Carter's establishment of the Office of Assistant to the President for Communication, and therefore should be considered low.
10. *Washington Information Directory, 2001–2002*, p. 333. For a discussion of the role and influence of the White House staff, see Bradley H. Patterson, *The Ring of Power: The White House Staff and Its Expanded Role in Government.*
11. Susan Herbst, *Numbered Voices: How Opinion Polling Has Shaped American Politics*, p. 43–44. The 1965 study cited by Herbst is Harwood Childs, *Public Opinion: Nature, Formation, and Role.*
12. There have been numerous studies examining the history and definition of public opinion. For example, see Wilhelm Bauer, "Public Opinion," in the *Encyclopedia of the Social Sciences*, ed. by Edwin R. A. Seligman, Vol. 12, pp. 669–74. See also Harwood Childs, *Public Opinion*; Hans Speier, "Historical Development of Public Opinion," *American Journal of Sociology* (Jan., 1950): 376–88; Paul Palmer, "The Concept of Public Opinion in Political Theory," in *Essays in History and Political Theory*, pp. 230–57; Bernard Berelson, "The Study of Public Opinion," in *The State of the Social Sciences*, p. 299–318; and Robert Weissberg, *Public Opinion and Popular Government*, pp. 1–5.
13. Bauer, "Public Opinion," p. 670.
14. James Bryce, *The American Commonwealth*, pp. xxxi–xxxii ("Publisher's Note") and p. 923.
15. Ibid., pp. 926, 929.
16. Ibid., pp. 934, 919–20.
17. Jeffrey K. Tulis, *The Rhetorical Presidency*, p. 39, Chapters 2 and 3, pp. 128, 132–37, 146. Samuel Kernell has documented the modern phenomenon of presidents' "going public" to get the public to pressure Congress for desired

policies. See Samuel Kernell, *Going Public: New Strategies of Presidential Leadership*, third edition.

18. David Nichols, "A Marriage Made in Philadelphia: The Constitution and the Rhetorical Presidency," in Richard J. Ellis, *Speaking to the People: The Rhetorical Presidency in Historical Perspective*; Terri Bimes and Stephen Skowronek, "Woodrow Wilson's Critique of Popular Leadership: Reassessing the Modern-Traditional Divide in Presidential History," in Ellis, *Speaking to the People*.

19. Bruce Buchanan, *The Citizen's Presidency: Standards of Choice and Judgment*, pp. 7–15; Dennis M. Simon and Charles W. Ostrom, "The Politics of Prestige: Popular Support and the Modern Presidency," *Presidential Studies Quarterly* 8, no. 4 (fall, 1988): 741–59.

20. Sydney Blumenthal, *The Permanent Campaign*; Lowi, *The Personal President*, p. 20; Paul Brace and Barbara Hinckley, *Follow the Leader: Opinion Polls and Modern Presidents*; Richard Waterman and Hank Jenkins-Smith, "The Expectations Gap Thesis: Public Attitudes Toward an Incumbent President," *Journal of Politics* 61, no. 4 (Nov., 1999): 944–66.

21. John G. Geer, *From Tea Leaves to Opinion Polls: A Theory of Democratic Leadership*; Jacobs and Shapiro, *Politicians Don't Pander*, pp. 8, 44, xvi (emphasis in original), and 27; Jeffrey Cohen, *Presidential Responsiveness and Public Policy Making*.

22. Public opinion can be said to have begrudgingly followed Johnson's leadership on Vietnam until early 1968, and for much of Johnson's term the protestors could have been dismissed as atypical. See Leslie H. Gelb with Richard K. Betts, *The Irony of Vietnam: The System Worked*, p. 293; V. O. Key, "Public Opinion and the Decay of Democracy," *Virginia Quarterly Review* 37, no. 4 (autumn, 1961): 487.

23. George Gallup, "Preserving Majority Rule," in *Polling on the Issues*, ed. by Albert H. Cantril, p. 174.

24. George Gallup and Saul Forbes Rae, *The Pulse of Democracy*, p. 19. See also George Gallup, *The Sophisticated Poll Watcher's Guide*, pp. 18–20; Geer, *From Tea Leaves*, p. 70.

25. For a discussion of the growth of this role, see Michael Barone, "The Power of the President's Pollsters," *Public Opinion* 2, no. 3 (Sept./Oct., 1988): 2–4, 57. Since the institutionalization of the White House pollster during the Carter years, the pollster's salaries have been paid by the national committee of the president's party.

26. Michael X. Delli Carpini and Scott Keeter, *What Americans Know About Politics and Why It Matters*.

27. David Shipler, "Poll Shows Confusion on Aid to Contras," *The New York Times*, Apr. 15, 1986, p. 6. Some have suggested that this poll unfairly denigrated the public, because the word "rebels" was used instead of "contras," and the American people are slow to believe that the United States would support rebels. Nonetheless, the fact that by 1986 the American people could not identify the "rebels" as the "contras" demonstrates a low level of attention to a burning issue of the mid-1980s.

28. George Edwards, *The Public Presidency: The Pursuit of Popular Support*, p. 11.

29. Charles W. Roll and Albert H. Cantril, *Polls: Their Use and Misuse in Politics*, p. 129.

30. Thomas A. Bailey, *The Man in the Street*, p. 132.

31. Stephen Budiansk, et al. "The Numbers Racket: How Polls and Statistics Lie," *U.S. News and World Report,* July 11, 1988, pp. 44–47; Edwards, *The Public Presidency,* p. 9.

32. Gallup approval ratings from *The Roper Center for Public Opinion Research.*

33. Doris A. Graber, *Public Opinion, The President and Foreign Policy: Four Case Studies from the Formative Years;* Melvin Small, "The Impact of the Antiwar movement on Lyndon Johnson, 1965–1968: A Preliminary Report," *Peace and Change* (spring, 1984): 1–22. See also, Small, *Johnson, Nixon, and the Doves;* Kathleen Turner, *Lyndon Johnson's Dual War: Vietnam and the Press;* Bruce Altschuler, "Lyndon Johnson and the Public Polls," *Public Opinion Quarterly* 50, no. 3 (fall, 1986): 285–99; Altschuler, *LBJ and the Polls;* Jacobs and Shapiro, *Politicians Don't Pander.*

34. Lewis Anthony Dexter, "The Representative and His District," *Human Organization* (spring, 1957): 2–13.

35. Richard F. Fenno, *Home Style: House Members in Their Districts,* pp. xiii–xiv. Emphasis in original. The author, in the appendix, expresses a preference for the term "participant observation."

36. Jacobs and Shapiro also note the importance of getting an "insider" perspective. Relying on internal memoranda from the Clinton administration and interviews with White House officials, they attempt to "penetrate the black box of policymaking and investigate how politicians understand, evaluate, and use public opinion." See Jacobs and Shapiro, *Politicians Don't Pander,* p. 68.

37. Altschuler, *LBJ and the Polls,* p. xi; Jacobs and Shapiro, *Politicians Don't Pander,* p. 298.

38. The reader may wonder why the Republican administrations of Richard Nixon, Gerald Ford, and George H. W. Bush were not selected for this study, since they too suffered serious and sustained declines in approval. So much of Nixon's decline in public approval was connected to the Watergate scandal that it would make discussion of other factors less relevant. The short time span of Ford's term makes his presidency less ideal for comparison purposes. And Bush's archives were not sufficiently developed at the time of this writing to provide adequate material for this research.

39. Irving Crespi, "The Case of Presidential Popularity," in *Polling on the Issues,* ed. by Albert Cantril, pp. 29–34. Crespi also notes that Gallup's first four polls contained a slightly different wording: "Do you approve or disapprove of Franklin Roosevelt as president?" This was changed because many who "approved" of him since he was the elected president were not supporters. The question also had a tendency to measure the personal like or dislike of Roosevelt himself. See Crespi, "The Case of Presidential Popularity," p. 41, 45n.

40. Gallup approval ratings from *The Roper Center for Public Opinion Research.*

41. Robert Y. Shapiro and Lawrence R. Jacobs, "Polling and the White House: Public Opinion and Presidential Behavior," in Jeffrey Cohen and David Nice, *The Presidency: Classic and Contemporary Readings.* Emphasis in original.

42. Obviously, "high, moderate, and low" are relative terms. Because I am focusing on how declining public support for these administrations served as a cause for their changing interpretation and political motivation, I use these terms relative to the administrations being studied. Johnson's approval ratings were never as low as Truman's and Carter's lowest, and Carter's were never as high as Truman's and Johnson's highest.

43. John W. Kingdon, "Politician's Beliefs About Voters," *American Political Science Review* (1967): 140.
44. Ibid., p. 141.
45. See Lowi, *The Personal Presidency*; Cohen, *Presidential Responsiveness*, p. 14.
46. Two works have examined the role of cognitive dissonance specifically in President Lyndon Johnson's attitudes towards polls and public opinion. See Altschuler, *LBJ and the Polls*, pp. 101–102, and Michael J. Towle, "Lyndon Baines Johnson and the American People: A Study of Public Opinion Linkage from the Presidential Perspective," Ph.D. diss., University of Texas at Austin, 1990.
47. Leon Festinger, *A Theory of Cognitive Dissonance*, pp. 2–3, 31.

    The field of cognitive psychology is vast, and the reader may wonder why I have chosen cognitive dissonance theory as an operative explanatory theory. One important reason is the parsimony of the theory; the use of dissonance theory requires simply the discovery of contradictory belief sets and subsequent attempts to resolve the contradictions. Yet other theories of social cognition have also achieved prominence, such as attribution theory—which attempts to ascertain how an individual ascribes motivations to others [For a general discussion, see H. H. Kelley and J. Michela, "Attribution Theory and Research," *Annual Review of Psychology*, 1980, pp. 457–501], and schema theory—the prominent theory that individual minds simplify the understanding of information by creating organizational interconnections of knowledge. [For a general discussion, see S. T. Fiske and S. E. Taylor, *Social Cognition*, especially Chapter 6]. While the psychologist might find such theories to be more powerful explanations of human behavior, they are particularly difficult to use to ascribe behaviors to an individual. Schemata, the basic blocks of knowledge according to schema theory, are built upon a lifetime of experiences. It is a monumental task to ascribe a schemata to another individual. Furthermore, it should be noted that consistency theory retains a following among psychologists. Indeed, schema theorists also apply the consistency concept to their work; the ideas are not mutually exclusive. [For a discussion of the processing of schema-consistent and schema-inconsistent theory, see Richard Lau and David O. Sears, "Social Cognition and Political Cognition: The Past, The Present and the Future," in *Political Cognition*, ed. by Richard Lau and David O. Sears, pp. 347–66]. Fiske and Taylor also note that consistency theory's prediction of the selective interpretation of information "makes a complementary point to some of the work on social schemata." See Fiske and Taylor, *Social Cognition*, pp. 361–62.

    Finally, it is important to remember that the use of consistency theory here is to explain administration behavior and to generate hypotheses for future research. As such it is only one of any number of explanatory theories that might be suggested. Indeed, I am arguing that these psychological factors, to the extent that they are crucial, are a direct result of the institutional demands of the modern presidency. (For a discussion of why the institutional surroundings of elite actors should not be considered secondary to cognitive factors, see Paul A. Anderson, "The Relevance of Social Cognition for the Study of Elites in Political Institutions, or Why It Isn't Enough to Understand What Goes on in Their Heads," in *Political Cognition*, ed. by Lau and Sears.)

48. Festinger, *A Theory of Cognitive Dissonance*, p. 47.
49. Fiske and Taylor, *Social Cognition*, pp. 359–62. Considerable evidence exists to support the theory's expectation of selective attention and selective

interpretation, but experiments designed to test the expectation of selective exposure have met with mixed results.

50. Of course, it is certainly plausible that strategic considerations are not the only impetus behind any individual president's attention to public opinion. For example, many have asserted that Lyndon Johnson's life was marked by a need for acceptance and love. See for example, Doris Kearns, *Lyndon Johnson and the American Dream*, p. 48; also, Wilson C. McWilliams, "Lyndon B. Johnson: The Last of the Great Presidents," in *Modern Presidents and the Presidency*, ed. by Marc Landy, p. 165.) Others have observed that he seemed particularly attentive to polls when they showed high levels of approval. See, for example, James David Barber, *The Presidential Experience*, third edition, p. 72. See also Louis Harris, *The Anguish of Change*, pp. 23–24. Was Johnson's attention to polls motivated by a deep burning desire to be loved? Presidents are human, and it is likely that they are interested in public opinion to fulfill their human needs. Nonetheless, the analysis here will focus on the political nature of the concern in an entire administration, as reconstructed from the materials in the presidential archives examined.

Chapter 1

1. Gallup approval ratings from *The Roper Center for Public Opinion Research*.
2. LBJ to Heller, memo, Dec. 23, 1963, WHCF, Ex, Sp 2–4, "State of the Union Message," Speeches, Box 133, LBJ Library.

   Citations from presidential archives will follow a standard format. The cite will first list the author of the correspondence, if known, and then the recipient, if known, followed by the type of document (memo, letter, notes, report, etc.). A date, if known, is indicated next. This is followed by a file name, then the name of the collection in which the document may be found, and finally, the box number in that collection. When citing materials from the vast White House Central Files (WHCF), a code is also given to indicate how the document was filed by White House Archivists. These standard codes are used in all of the archives studied here; the archivists there will be able to locate the appropriate collection by this code. All documents are cited here to allow ease of relocation by archivists. Finally, I label the library where the collection is found: HST Library for the Truman archives, LBJ Library for the Johnson archives, and JEC Library for the Carter archives.

   Whenever a group of documents is stapled together, I always cite the *top* document, so that future researchers may more easily find the document in question. For example, the text may refer to a memo from Jody Powell to President Carter. But that document could be stapled to a covering document from Hamilton Jordan to Stu Eizenstat. In such a case, I will cite the Jordan document. This will prevent future researchers and archivists from having to search through all pages of bound documents to find the material in question. I sometimes include a notation that says "plus attachment(s)" to indicate that the document can be found among papers attached to the cited document.

   Verbatim quotations have occasionally been altered to correct or standardize spelling and grammar. Such rare changes are always minor. For example, I standardized the use of the spelling "Vietnam," although the original documents sometimes use "Viet Nam." Punctuation frequently needed to be added (or corrected), particularly to handwritten documents. Of course, the meaning of the documents cited was never changed. If corrections could not be made without potentially changing the meaning or changing the author's words, the standard [*sic*] was used.

3. For an insider's view of these bills, see Eric F. Goldman, *The Tragedy of Lyndon Johnson*, pp. 76–85.

4. Some later accounting of the transfer of power would question Johnson's sensitivities to the Kennedy family, particularly Robert Kennedy. While many dispute such claims, it is generally acknowledged that the confusing moments after the assassination helped establish Robert Kennedy's ill feelings toward Johnson. See William Manchester, *The Death of a President*, pp. 268–76.

5. Harry McPherson, *A Political Education*, p. 268.

6. Harris, *The Anguish of Change*, p. 23.

7. Kingdon, "Politician's Beliefs About Voters," p. 144.

8. Ross to Truman, memo, Jan. 3, 1946, "The President—Articles on and Memoranda to," Papers of Charles G. Ross, Box 7, HST Library; Proposed Agenda, Jan. 10, 1946, "Cabinet Meetings, 1946–50," PSF, Box 154, HST Library. The document mistakenly refers to the meeting on "Friday, January 10, 1946." The meeting was on Friday, January 11.

9. Minutes of Cabinet Meeting, Jan. 18, 1946, "Notes on Cabinet Meetings, Jan. 11, 18, 25, 1946," Papers of Matthew Connelly, Box 2, HST Library.

10. Keyserling to Clifford, letter, Dec. 20, 1948, "1949 Jan 5 State of Union Drafts (folder 2)," Papers of George M. Elsey, Box 36, HST Library.

11. Minutes of Cabinet Meeting, Sept. 7, 1945, "Notes on Cabinet Meetings, 1945, Sep. 7, 21, 28," Papers of Matthew Connelly, Box 2, HST Library.

12. Minutes of Cabinet Meeting, Jan. 11, 1946, "Notes on Cabinet Meetings, Jan. 11, 18, 25, 1946," Papers of Matthew Connelly, Box 2, HST Library.

13. Busby to LBJ, memo, Jan. 14, 1964, "Memos to Mr. Johnson—April," Office Files of Horace Busby, Box 53, LBJ Library; Nelson to LBJ, memo, Mar. 26, 1964, filed in the George Gallup Name File, LBJ Library; Busby to LBJ, memo, Apr. 16, 1964, "Political Polls," Office Files of Horace Busby, Box 41, LBJ Library. Emphasis in original.

14. Goldman, *The Tragedy of Lyndon Johnson*, p. 294. Johnson attracted wide attention and gained many followers because of this speech. But he lost Louisiana in the election.

15. Busby to LBJ, memo, (undated, but the contents indicate that it was written October 12, 1964), "Memos to the President, 1964," Office Files of Bill Moyers, Box 10, LBJ Library. Emphasis in original.

16. Small, *Johnson, Nixon, and the Doves*, p. 28.

17. Busby to LBJ, memo, Feb. 27, 1965, "Memos to the President—February 1965," Office Files of Horace Busby, Box 52, LBJ Library.

18. Hayes Redmon to unknown recipient, June 17, 1965, and Hayes Redman to unnamed recipient, undated (The latter memo is undated, but appears to follow the first. It has a handwritten notation, however, that it was *filed* August 9, 1965), "PR 16 Public Opinion Polls (April '66–June '65)," Confidential File, Box 80, LBJ Library.

19. Redmon to Califano, memo, Dec. 28, 1965, "1967 State of the Union Categories: Youth, Labor, Manpower," Statements Box 224, LBJ Library; Redmon to Moyers, memo, Jan. 22, 1966, "Manatos: Leg General—1966 Jan. Feb. March," Office Files of Manatos, Box 3, LBJ Library; Redmon to Moyers,

memo, Jan. 27, 1966, "Polls," Office Files of Henry Wilson, Box 14, LBJ Library.

20. *Gallup Political Index,* Report No. 2, 1965. The figures do not add up to 100 percent because of the undecided respondents.

21. Hodges to LBJ, two memos, Aug. 10, 1964, and Ellington to LBJ, Aug. 10, 1964, in "Elections-Campaigns (1964–1966)," Confidential File, Box 77, LBJ Library; Busby to LBJ, memo, July 13, 1964, "Memos to the President—July," Busby 52, LBJ Library.

22. Redmon to Moyers, memo, Jan. 22, 1966, "Manatos: Leg General—1966 Jan Feb March," Manatos 3, LBJ Library.

23. Busby to LBJ, memo, Feb. 27, 1965, "Memos to the President, February 1965," Office Files of Horace Busby, Box 52, LBJ Library; Notes of meeting in the President's Office, May 16, 1965, Meeting Notes, Box 1, LBJ Library; Memorandum for the record, Aug. 4, 1965, "Publicity (1963–1965)," Confidential File, Box 83, LBJ Library.

24. Notes of meeting in the Cabinet Room, Dec. 17, 1965, Meeting Notes, Box 1, LBJ Library; Valenti to LBJ, memo, Dec. 18, 1965, "SP 2–4, Exec, State of the Union Messages," Speeches 133, LBJ Library.

25. Johnson's dread of how Vietnam would affect his public standing was intense. Turner notes that Johnson feared being labeled "the first American President to lose a war" because loss would be "completely inconsistent with his values and perceptions." But he also was deeply distressed by his policy options. See Turner, *Lyndon Johnson's Dual War,* pp. 108–10.

26. Notes of National Security Council Meeting No. 548, Feb. 10, 1965, Meeting Notes, Box 1, LBJ Library.

27. Redmon to Moyers, Feb. 27, 1966, "Public Opinion Polls (1 of 5)," Confidential File, Box 81, LBJ Library.

28. Caddell to Carter, memo, Dec. 21, 1976, "Caddell, Patrick, [12/76–1/77]," Staff Secretary, Box 1, JEC Library; Jagoda to Carter, memo, Jan. 23, 1976 [*sic*— should be dated 1977], "Fireside Chats, 1977," Powell, Box 59, JEC Library; Rafshoon to Carter, memo, Jan. 25, 1977, "Fireside Chats, 1977," Powell, Box 59, JEC Library. Ellipses in original. The memo is referring to Carter's decision to walk the inaugural parade route; the inaugural address; the inaugural ball; Carter's pardoning of all Vietnam-era draft dodgers; Carter's issuing of an executive order to reduce the thermostats in federal buildings to sixty-five degrees (in an effort to save energy); the release of detailed notes, contrary to custom, of the president's first cabinet meeting; and a trip to western Europe and Japan by the vice president to explain American foreign policy for the new administration.

29. Caddell to Carter, memo, Feb. 3, 1977, "Caddell, Pat H.," Name File, JEC Library; Hutcheson to Powell, memo, Feb. 24, 1977, "2/24/77," Staff Secretary, Handwriting File, Box 10, JEC Library; Schneiders to President, memo, July 1, 1977, Staff Secretary, Box 36, JEC Library.

30. Caddell to Carter, memo, Dec. 21, 1976, "Caddell, Patrick, [12/76–1/77]," Staff Secretary Box 1, JEC Library.

31. Jordan to Carter, memo, Mar., 1977, "Early Months Performance, H.J. memos to Pres, 1977," Jordan, Box 34, JEC Library. The typed memo is undated but a handwritten notation at the top reads "77 (March?)."

32. Rafshoon to Carter, memo, June 14, 1977, "Image 1977," Jordan, Box 34, JEC Library. Emphasis in original.

33. Van Dyk to Eizenstat, memo plus attachments, July 26, 1977, "Pollster Reports—Public Opinion (2)," Domestic Policy Staff, Box 254, JEC Library.

Chapter 2

1. Festinger observes that dissonance can result from incongruity with past experiences. See Festinger, *A Theory of Cognitive Dissonance*, p. 4.
2. *Statistical Abstract of the United States*.
3. Ibid.
4. See Turner's *Lyndon Johnson's Dual War* for an extensive discussion of Johnson's press relations.
5. George Gallup, *The Gallup Poll: Public Opinion 1935–1971*, Volume 3, 1959–1971.
6. *Statistical Abstract of the United States*.
7. Jimmy Carter, *Keeping Faith*, pp. 114–21.
8. J. William Holland, "The Great Gamble: Jimmy Carter and the 1979 Energy Crisis," *Prologue* (spring, 1990): 73.
9. Ibid., pp. 73–74. Carter himself has written, "I handled the cabinet changes very poorly." Carter, *Keeping Faith*, p. 121.
10. Minutes of Cabinet Meeting, Oct. 11, 1946, "Notes on Cabinet Meetings, May 17–Dec. 20, 1946," Papers of Matthew Connelly, Box 2, HST Library. Hannegan may have been referring to informal comments made by the president on September 24 to Democratic congressional candidates, in which he denounced Republicans as "obstructionists."
11. Truman to Cannon, letter, Jan. 9, 1947, "General," PSF, Box 54, HST Library.
12. Minutes of Cabinet Meeting, May 19, 1950, "Notes on Cabinet Meetings, 1950, Jan. 6–Dec. 29," Papers of Matthew Connelly, Box 2, HST Library; Hechler, memo, Oct. 24, 1950, "Politics—1950, Election," Papers of George Elsey, Box 92, HST Library.
13. Hechler, memo, Nov. 6, 1950, "Politics—1950, Election," Papers of George Elsey, Box 92, HST Library; Hechler, memo, Nov. 15, 1950, "Politics—1950—Election post-mortems," Papers of George Elsey, Box 92, HST Library; Nash to Hechler, memo, Nov. 22, 1950, "Political 1950—Campaign Analysis of 1950 Election Results," Papers of Philleo Nash, Box 64, HST Library.
14. Altschuler makes a similar observation in "Lyndon Johnson and the Public Polls," pp. 288–89, and in *LBJ and the Polls*, pp. 71–72, and 105. Altschuler gives seven examples of the administration's attempt to "emphasize the positive," all of which occur in the transitional period of public approval discussed in this Chapter.
15. Redmon to Moyers, memo, May 26, 1966, "BDM memos, April–May 1966," Office Files of Bill Moyers, Box 12, LBJ Library.
16. Redmon to Roche, memo, July 26, 1966, filed in the George Gallup Name File, WHCF, LBJ Library.
17. Panzer to LBJ, memo, Feb. 17, 1967, "Presidential Memo Backup Material, Office Files of Fred Panzer, Box 399, LBJ Library.
18. Panzer to LBJ, memo, Mar. 13, 1967 filed in George Gallup name File, WHCF, LBJ Library.
19. Redmon to Moyers, memo, May 26, 1966, "BDM Memos, April–May 1966," Office Files of Bill Moyers, Box 12, LBJ Library; Jones to LBJ, memo, Jan. 28, 1967, filed in George Gallup Name File, WHCF, LBJ Library; Panzer to LBJ,

memo, Feb. 17, 1967, "February," Office Files of Fred Panzer, Box 398, LBJ Library; LBJ to Mary S., memo attachment, Apr. 5, 1967, filed in the George Gallup Name File, WHCF, LBJ Library; Panzer to LBJ, memo, May 12, 1967, "May," Office Files of Fred Panzer, Box 398, LBJ Library.

20. George E. Reedy, *The Twilight of the Presidency: From Johnson to Reagan*, pp. 87 and 81; Altschuler, *LBJ and the Polls*, p. 50. See also p. 103.

21. Eizenstat to Carter, memo, Feb. 21, 1978, "2/21/78 [1]," Staff Secretary Box 73, JEC Library; Hutcheson to Jordan, memo plus attachment, Mar. 21, 1978, "Economic Development Administration," Jordan Box 44, JEC Library; Mondale to Eizenstat, memo, Aug. 14, 1978, "Pollster Reports—Public Opinion," Domestic Policy Staff, Eizenstat, Box 253, JEC Library.

22. Moore and Eizenstat to Carter, memo, Sept. 27, 1978, "PR 15, 6/1/78–12/31/78," WHCF PR, Box PR-75, JEC Library; Jordan to Carter, Sept. 29, 1978, "Informal Advisors Group," Jordan Box 47, JEC Library; Powell to Carter, memo, Oct. 13, 1978, "10/3/78–10/30/78," Powell Box 37, JEC Library.

23. Rafshoon to Jordan, et al., memo, Feb. 22, 1979, "1/4/79–8/3/79," Powell Box 46, JEC Library; Cover note plus attachments, "Pres Address to Nation 7/15/79 [3]," Staff Secretary Box 139, JEC Library. The cover sheet is labeled "HJ has seen."

24. ABC News—Harris Survey, undated, "ABC News—Harris Surveys, 1978–80," Powell Box 50, JEC Library. Content indicates that the poll was taken as late as November 29, 1979.

25. Elsey to Clifford, memo plus attachment, June 6, 1947, "Wallace, Henry," Papers of Clark Clifford, Box 20, HST Library.

26. Minutes of cabinet meeting, June 20, 1947, "Notes of Cabinet Meetings, 1947, Jan. 3–Dec. 19," Papers of Matthew Connelly, Box 2, HST Library.

27. Elsey to Clifford, memo, Mar. 5, 1948, "1948, March 17, St. Patrick's Day Speech (Folder 2)," Papers of George Elsey, Box 21, HST Library; *The Public Papers of the Presidents of the United States, Harry S. Truman, 1948*.

28. Davis to Clifford, memo, Apr. 13, 1948, "Miscellaneous Correspondence 1948 Campaign (1 of 2)," Papers of Clark Clifford, Box 23, HST Library.

29. Report, undated (content suggests June, 1948), "Miscellaneous Correspondence 1948 Campaign (1 of 2)," Papers of Clark Clifford, Box 23, HST Library.

30. Hechler to Elsey, memo, Oct. 27, 1950, "Scare Words," Papers of Kenneth Hechler, Box 4, HST Library; *The Public Papers of the Presidents of the United States, Harry S. Truman, 1950*.

31. Minutes of cabinet meeting, Dec. 22, 1950, "Notes of Cabinet Meetings, 1950, Jan. 6–Dec. 29," Papers of Matthew Connelly, Box 2, HST Library.

32. Hechler to Truman, memo, Jan. 2, 1951, "Politics—Democratic National Committee," Papers of George Elsey, Box 92, HST Library.

33. Minutes of cabinet meeting, Feb. 2, 1951, "Notes of Cabinet Meetings, 1951, Jan. 2–Dec. 31," Papers of Matthew Connelly, Box 2, HST Library.

34. Elsey to Hechler, memo, Mar. 19, 1951, "Politics—Democratic National Committee," Papers of George Elsey, Box 92, HST Library; Hechler to Bell, memo, Mar. 23, 1951, "Budget and Fiscal Policy," Papers of Kenneth Hechler, Box 4, HST Library; Hechler to Bell, memo, Apr. 2, 1951, "Budget and Fiscal Policy," Papers of Kenneth Hechler, Box 4, HST Library.

35. Short to Truman, memo, Apr. 2, 1951, "1951–April 1–15, PSF, Box 96, HST Library. ECA was the Economic Cooperation Administration, which was

responsible for administering the Marshall plan. Point Four was a program of American technical assistance to underdeveloped countries that began in 1950.

36. Elsey to Cantril, letter, Apr. 20, *1951*, "Cantril, Dr. Hadley," Papers of George Elsey, Box 102, HST Library; Unknown author to Claxton, memo, May 24, 1951, "Memorandum on 'Our Foreign Policy,'" Papers of Kenneth Hechler, Box 4, HST Library.

37. Unknown author and recipient, memo, Oct. 17, 1951, "Campaign 1952," PSF, Box 55, HST Library. An author is indicated in a handwritten notation on a copy of this memo in "Politics—Democratic National Committee," Papers of George Elsey, Box 92, HST Library. Unfortunately, the handwriting is illegible.

38. See Turner's *Lyndon Johnson's Dual War* for an extensive discussion of Johnson's press relations; Kintner to LBJ, Moyers, Watson, et al., memo, May 17, 1966, Confidential File, "Speeches (1966)" WHCF, Box 86, LBJ Library; Memo to LBJ, May 20, 1966, "Speeches (1966)," Confidential File, Box 86, LBJ Library. Although the portion of the memo in this file does not indicate the author, other documents in the box suggest that Robert Kintner probably wrote it.

39. Redmon to Moyers, two memos, June 9, 1966, "BDM Memos, June–July 11, 1966," Office Files of Bill Moyers, Box 12, LBJ Library; Moyers to LBJ, memo, June 9, 1966, "Public Opinion Polls (1966) 4 of 5," Confidential File, Box 82, LBJ Library.

40. Markman to Watson, memo, June 9, 1966, "Public Opinion Polls (1966) 4 of 5," Confidential File, Box 82, LBJ Library.

41. Kintner to LBJ, memo, June 9, 1966, "Public Opinion Polls (1 of 5)," Confidential File, Box 81, LBJ Library.

42. Moyers to LBJ, memo, June 10, 1966, "Public Opinion Polls (1966) 4 of 5," Confidential File, Box 82, LBJ Library; Redmon to Moyers, memo, June 27, 1966, "BDM Memos, July 12–August 1966," Office Files of Bill Moyers, Box 12, LBJ Library; Moyers to LBJ, memo, Aug. 4, 1966, "BDM Memos, July 12–August 1966," Office Files of Bill Moyers, Box 12, LBJ Library.

43. Sparks to Kintner, memo, Aug. 26, 1966, "Speeches (1966)," Confidential File, Box 86, LBJ Library.

44. Maguire to Kintner, memo, Nov. 7, 1966, "Speeches (1966)," Confidential File, Box 86, LBJ Library. See also Turner's discussion of this memo; Turner, *Lyndon Johnson's Dual War*, p. 168.

45. Altschuler makes a similar point regarding the administration's analysis of polls about Vietnam. See Altschuler, *LBJ and the Polls*, p. 49.

46. See, for example, Rowland Evans and Robert Novak, *Lyndon B. Johnson: The Exercise of Power*, pp. 117–18; and Kearns, *Lyndon Johnson and the American Dream*, pp. 317–18.

47. See Daniel Patrick Moynihan, *Maximum Feasible Misunderstanding*, especially Chapters 7 and 8.

48. George Gallup, *The Gallup Poll: Public Opinion 1935–1971*.

49. See Small, *Johnson, Nixon and the Doves*, Tables 1 and 2. For a discussion of the high costs of the rather minimal war progress by 1967, See George C. Herring, *America's Longest War: The United States and Vietnam, 1950–1975*, second edition, pp. 149–56; Altschuler, *LBJ and the Polls*, p. 37.

50. Hutcheson to Carter, memo plus attachments, June 10, 1977, "PR 15, 1/20/77–8/31/77," WHCF PR, Box PR-75, JEC Library; Powell to Carter, memo, June 21, 1977, "President/Rafshoon/Powell—T.V. Image, 1977," Powell Box 69, JEC Library.

51. Eizenstat to Carter, Jordan, and Powell, memo, Jan. 9, 1978, "1/9/78–2/28/78," Powell, Box 36, JEC Library; Jordan to Carter, memo, Jan. 17, 1978, "President Carter—Misc. Memos, 1978," Jordan, Box 51, JEC Library.

52. Moe to Mondale, Jordan, Powell, and Butler, memo, Apr. 3, 1978, "Memoranda: Vice President's Staff, 4/3/78–10/11/78," Powell, Box 47, JEC Library.

53. *The Public Papers of the Presidents of the United States, Jimmy Carter, 1978.*

54. Vertical File, "Rafshoon, Gerald." JEC Library. The document is a copy of Dom Bonafede, "Telling Us Who's on First," *National Journal,* May 27, 1978.

55. Cutter to Jordan, memo, May 30, 1978, "4/1/78–5/30/78," Powell Box 36, JEC Library; Rafshoon to Carter, memo, July 19, 1978, "Memoranda: Rafshoon, Jerry. May 18/78–8/25/78," Powell Box 46, JEC Library.

56. Hutcheson to Rafshoon, memo plus attachments, June 19, 1978, "Energy—Misc.," Rafshoon Box 44, JEC Library.

57. Eizenstat to Rafshoon, memo, July 8, 1978, "Harris Polls," Rafshoon Box 3, JEC Library.

58. Notes, Aug. 4, 1978, "Staff Meeting—August 4, 1978," Rafshoon Box 31, JEC Library; Eizenstat to Carter, memo, Aug. 15, 1978, "Pollster reports—Public Opinion," Domestic Policy Staff, Eizenstat Box 253, JEC Library; Rafshoon to Carter through Powell, memo, Aug. 25, 1978, "Camp David Summit," Rafshoon Box 24, JEC Library. Ellipses and emphasis in original. Rafshoon to Carter, memo, Sept. 1, 1978, "9/1/78," Staff Secretary Box 101, JEC Library.

59. Jordan to Carter, memo plus attachment, Sept. 1, 1978, "9/1/78," Staff Secretary Box 101, JEC Library. Emphasis in original. Jordan to Carter, memo, Sept. 29, 1978, "Informal Advisors Group," Jordan Box 47, JEC Library. Emphasis in original.

60. Rafshoon to Marshall, memo, Nov. 7, 1978, "Labor, Dept. of," Rafshoon Box 3, JEC Library; Giannini to Schneider, memo, Oct. 31, [1978], "Camp David Summit," Rafshoon Box 24, JEC Library; Powell and Rafshoon to Carter, memo, Dec. 1, 1978, "9/22/78–12/6/78," Powell Box 40, JEC Library. Emphasis in original. Powell to Rafshoon, memo, undated, "Memoranda: Rafshoon, Jerry, 5/18/78–8/25/78." Powell, Box 46, JEC Library.

61. Hamilton to Carter, memo, Mar. 16, 1979, "Economics 1978–79," Jordan Box 34, JEC Library.

62. WHCF, Vertical File, "Rafshoon, Gerald," JEC Library. The article is Dom Bonafede, "Has the Rafshoon Touch Left its Mark on the White House?" *National Journal,* Apr. 14, 1979.

63. Powell to Carter, memo, June 7, 1979, "9/2/79–9/28/79," Powell Box 37, JEC Library; Watson to Carter, memo, June 21, 1979, "6/23/79," Staff Secretary Box 137, JEC Library; Jesse Jackson to Carter, memo, July 7, 1979, "Camp David, 7/5/79–7/21/79 [1]," Staff Secretary Box 137, JEC Library.

64. Mondale and Jordan to Carter, memo, June 28, 1979, "Memoranda, Vice Pres. Staff, 2/7/79–10/11/79," Powell Box 48, JEC Library; Rafshoon and Powell to Carter, memo, June 29, 1979, "5/1/79–9/24/79," Powell Box 40, JEC Library; Rafshoon to Carter, memo, June 13, 1979, "1/4/79–8/3/79," Powell Box 46, JEC Library.

65. Notes, "Dinner with Bill Moyers, et al., May 30, 1979," Powell Box 55, JEC Library.

66. Jordan to Carter, memo, July 3, 1979, "Speech, Presidents 7/15/79," Jordan

Box 37, JEC Library. Another copy of that memo was also sent to Rosalynn Carter by Hamilton Jordan. Emphasis in original.

67. Matthews to Powell, memo, July 27, 1979, "7/2/79–7/31/79," Powell Box 37, JEC Library; Rafshoon to Carter, memo, Aug. 2, 1979, "1/4/79–8/3/79," Powell Box 46, JEC Library.

68. *The Public Papers of the Presidents of the United States, Jimmy Carter, 1979.*

69. Rafshoon to Powell, Cutler, Voorde, and Wise, action request, Aug. 17, 1979, "5/1/79–9/24/79," Powell Box 40, JEC Library.

70. Caddell to Carter, memo, Nov. 6, 1979, "Caddell (Pat) (3)," Jordan Box 33, JEC Library. Emphasis in original.

71. McDonald to Powell, memo, Nov. 26, 1979, "11/1/79–12/28/79," Powell Box 38, JEC Library.

72. Rafshoon to Dobelle, memo, 1979, "Campaign Themes Memorandum, 1979," Rafshoon, Box 24, JEC Library; Rick [?] to Greg [Schneiders], memo, undated, "Campaign Themes Memorandum, 1979," Rafshoon, Box 24, JEC Library. At the time, there were three people who went by the name Rick working for the White House. One was Hendrik Hertzberg, chief speechwriter. Another was Richard Hutcheson, staff secretary. Still another was Richard M. Neustadt on the Domestic Policy staff.

73. Rafshoon to Carter, memo (draft), 1979, "Campaign Themes Memorandum, 1979," Rafshoon, Box 24, JEC Library.

74. Wexler and From to Carter, memo, Jan. 9, 1980, "1/1/80–1/15/80," Powell Box 38, JEC Library; Wexler, Eizenstat, and McDonald to Carter, memo, Apr. 9, 1980, "ABC News—Harris Surveys, 1978–80," Powell Box 50, JEC Library; Eizenstat to Carter, memo, June 4, 1980, "4/10/80–6/27/80," Powell Box 40, JEC Library. Emphasis in original. Wexler to Powell and Watson, memo, Dec. 17, 1980, "memo, Jody Powell 1/30/80–12/28/80," Powell Box 39, JEC Library.

75. Presidential rhetorical style, of course, can be a genuine problem or a tremendous asset. Reagan's reputation as the "great communicator" underscores the importance of a president's ability to connect with the American people when attempting to garner public support. Some presidents are gifted public orators, and others are deficient in that regard.

   Presidential rhetoric can frequently be *important* as well. Karlyn Kohrs Campbell and Kathleen Hall Jamieson have analyzed the importance of various "genres" of presidential address in their work *Deeds Done in Words*. Different forms of presidential address, such as inaugural addresses or State of the Union addresses, fulfill particular functions. Thus, for example, Campbell and Jamieson argue that inaugural addresses serve an "investiture" function of bestowing legitimacy on the new president. Various genres of presidential address also allow an individual to be "seen as, and acting as, the president" (p. 213). Campbell and Jamieson comment on the importance of various forms of presidential address: "These words are deeds; in their speaking, the presidency is constituted and re-constituted" (p. 214). See Karlyn Kohrs Campbell and Kathleen Hall Jamieson, *Deeds Done in Words: Presidential Rhetoric and the Genres of Governance.*

   Clearly, there are times when it is appropriate for presidential administrations to focus on their rhetoric. Of course, concerns about rhetoric in other circumstances can overshadow important concerns and can fog the interpretation of public opinion.

76. This phenomenon may be common in the rhetorical presidency of today. Jacobs and Shapiro note in their discussion of "crafted talk" in the Clinton administration that the focus on teaching the public acted as a substitute for reconsidering the administration's policy direction. See Jacobs and Shapiro, *Politicians Don't Pander,* p. 115.

Chapter 3

1. Fiske and Taylor, *Social Cognition*, pp. 360–61.
2. Altschuler, "Lyndon Johnson and the Public Polls," pp. 294–96, and *LBJ and the Polls*, pp. 76–78.
3. Herbert Y. Schandler, *The Unmaking of a President: Lyndon Johnson and Vietnam*, p. 197.
4. George Gallup, *The Gallup Poll: Public Opinion, 1935–1971.*
5. See Turner, *Lyndon Johnson's Dual War*, p. 248.
6. Francis X. Clines, "First Lady Attributes Inquiry to 'Right Wing Conspiracy,'" *The New York Times*, Jan. 28, 1998, p. l.
7. Truman to Hannegan, memo plus attachments, Mar. 19, 1946, "Hannegan, Robert E.," PSF, Box 122, HST Library.
8. Truman to Hannegan, letter, Sept. 10, 1946, "Hannegan, Robert E.," PSF, Box 122, HST Library.
9. Elsey to Clifford, memo, June 6, 1947, "Wallace, Henry," Papers of Clark Clifford, Box 20, HST Library; Sheppard to Truman, letter, Apr. 13, 1948, "California: James Roosevelt," PSF, Box 54, HST Library.
10. Batt to Elsey, memo, Aug. 31, 1948, "1948 Presidential Campaign, September 6–Labor Day," Papers of George Elsey, Box 24, HST Library; Batt to Clifford, memo, Sept. 3, 1948, "1948 Presidential Campaign, September 6, Labor Day," Papers of George Elsey, Box 24, HST Library.
11. L [Max Lowenthal] to Clifford, letter, Oct. 5, 1948, "Miscellaneous Correspondence 1948 Campaign (1 of 2)," Papers of Clark Clifford, Box 23, HST Library. Truman archives officials have identified the author as Max Lowenthal. Unknown author and recipient, report, undated, "Miscellaneous Political File 1948 (2 of 2)," Papers of Clark Clifford, Box 22, HST Library.
12. Unknown author and recipient, memo, June 29, 1948, "Campaign 1948–HST acceptance speech," Papers of Samuel Rosenman, Box 9, HST Library.
13. See Robert Ferrell, *Off the Record: The Private Papers of Harry S. Truman.*
14. Truman, draft letter, "The President—Articles on and Memoranda to," Papers of Charles G. Ross, Box 7, HST Library.
15. Hechler, memo, June 19, 1950, "Chron File—June–Sept. 1950," Papers of Kenneth Hechler, Box 1, HST Library. The Hoover Commission, chaired by former President Herbert Hoover, was appointed by President Truman to make recommendations for the reorganization of the executive branch. Though Hechler criticizes their broadcast, the Citizen's Committee was supportive of the commission's report, which Truman also supported. Minutes of Cabinet Meeting, Dec. 12, 1950, "Notes on Cabinet Meetings, 1950, Jan. 6–Dec. 29," Papers of Matthew Connelly, Box 2, HST Library.
16. Minutes of Cabinet Meeting, Dec. 19, 1950, "Notes on Cabinet Meetings, 1950, Jan. 6–Dec. 29," Papers of Matthew Connelly, Box 2, HST Library.
17. Author and recipient unknown, memo, Apr. 19, 1951, "1951–May," PSF,

Box 96, HST Library. The memo seems to be addressed to the president. Minutes of Cabinet Meeting, Apr. 20, 1951, "Notes on Cabinet Meetings, 1951, Jan. 2–Dec. 31," Papers of Matthew Connelly, Box 2, HST Library.

18. Truman to Clifford, letter plus attachments, Apr. 27, 1951, "Clark Clifford," PSF-General File, Box 117, HST Library.

19. Minutes of Cabinet Meeting, Aug. 18, 1950, "Notes on Cabinet Meetings, 1950, Jan. 6–Dec. 29," Papers of Matthew Connelly, Box 2, HST Library; Ickes to Truman, letter, Sept. 15, 1950, "Ickes, Harold E.," PSF, Box 123, HST Library.

20. Hechler to unknown recipient, memo, Nov. 15, 1950, "Politics—1950—Election post-mortems," Papers of George Elsey, Box 92, HST Library; Truman to Secretary of Agriculture, memo, Mar. 30, 1951, "Agriculture, Secretary of, Misc. (folder 1)," PSF, Box 155, HST Library; Minutes of cabinet meeting, Apr. 2, 1951, "Notes of Cabinet Meetings, 1951, Jan 2–Dec 31," Papers of Matthew Connelly, Box 2, HST Library.

21. Routing slip plus attachments, undated (attached article is hand-dated March 24, 1951), "Politics—Democratic National Committee," Papers of George Elsey, Box 92, HST Library. The article referred to is Miles McMillin, "Probes Threaten Democratic Party," *Capital Times*.

22. Kenneth Hechler, memo, Apr. 12, 1951, "Working with Truman: MacArthur, Douglas," Papers of Kenneth Hechler, Box 6, HST Library; Kenneth Hechler, memo, Apr. 16, 1951, "Working with Truman: MacArthur, Douglas," Papers of Kenneth Hechler, Box 6, HST Library.

23. Minutes of Cabinet Meeting, May 4, 1951, "Notes on Cabinet Meetings, 1951, Jan. 2–Dec. 31," Papers of Matthew Connelly, Box 2, HST Library; Memo, Oct. 17, 1951, "Politics—Democratic National Committee," Papers of George Elsey, Box 92, HST Library. There is illegible handwriting on the memo, suggesting an author's name. The paper is also marked "Dem Nat Committee" in handwriting at the top of the memo. Minutes of Cabinet Meeting, "Notes on Cabinet Meetings, 1951, Jan. 2–Dec. 31," Papers of Matthew Connelly, Box 2, HST Library. Minutes are dated simply "Last Meeting of Year."

24. Truman to Chapman, memo, Dec. 20, 1951, "Ickes, Harold E.," PSF, Box 123, HST Library; Truman to McKinney, memo, May 23, 1952, "McKinney, Frank E., Meetings," PSF, Box 58, HST Library.

25. Minutes of Cabinet Meeting, Sept. 5, 1952, "Notes on Cabinet Meetings, Jan. 4, 1952–Jan. 16, 1953," Papers of Matthew Connelly, Box 2, HST Library; Minutes of Cabinet Meeting, Nov. 7, 1952, "Notes on Cabinet Meetings, Jan. 4, 1952–Jan. 16, 1953," Papers of Matthew Connelly, Box 2, HST Library. The anticommunist activities of Joseph McCarthy and Richard Nixon are widely known, but the third name may be less familiar. "Jenner" referred to the anticommunist Senator William Jenner of Indiana.

26. Panzer to LBJ, memo, Mar. 31, 1967, filed in the George Gallup Name File, WHCF, LBJ Library.

27. Ronald Steel, *Walter Lippmann and the American Century*, pp. 521–22, 554–55. In fact, Steel writes that in 1964 Lippmann almost considered LBJ to be "a savior"; Panzer to LBJ, memos, Oct. 31, 1967, filed in the George Gallup Name File, WHCF, and Oct. 30, 1967 and Oct. 31, 1967, "November 1967 (Watson)," Office File of Fred Panzer, Box 433, LBJ Library.

28. Panzer to LBJ, memo, Feb. 15, 1968, filed in George Gallup Name File, WHCF, LBJ Library.

29. Kintner to LBJ, letter, Jan. 15, 1968, "State of the Union 1968, Memorandum 12/2/66–1/12/68," Statements, Box 260, WHCF, LBJ Library.

30. Memorandum for the Record, "Vietnam [folder 1 of 2]," Office Files of Marvin Watson, Box 32, LBJ Library.

   The memo is undated, but it was probably written in late 1967 or early 1968. The memo speaks of problems "as we approach the 1968 campaign." Although the attached report has been largely dismantled, the latest date on a clipping that is obviously part of the report is dated June 22, 1967. This is, therefore, the earliest possible date for the report.

   The memo refers to Herbert Aptheker, a history professor and communist; Stokely Carmichael, one of the founders of the Black Panther Party; and Paul Booth, a leader of the militant antiwar organization Students for a Democratic Society.

31. Unknown author to LBJ, memo, Mar. 8, 1968, "Political Affairs (St 15–St 32)," Confidential File, Box 77, LBJ Library.

32. Kintner to LBJ, memo, May 18, 1967, and Kintner to Attorney General Clark, May 19, 1967, "Publicity (1967—)," Confidential File, Box 83, LBJ Library.

33. Unknown author to LBJ, memo, May 25, 1967, "Speeches (SP/FG-11-15)," Confidential File, Box 86, LBJ Library.

34. Panzer to LBJ, memo, Oct. 9, 1967, "October," Panzer 398, and undated draft to "Mr. Speaker" in the same file, LBJ Library.

35. Caddell to Carter, memo, Jan. 10, 1977, "Caddell, Patrick [12/76–1/77]," Staff Secretary Box 1, JEC Library; Jordan to Carter, memo, Mar., 1977, "Early Months Performance, HJ Memos to Pres. 1977," Jordan Box 34, JEC Library; Butler to Jordan memo, Mar. 17, 1977, "SALT, 1977," Jordan Box 37, JEC Library.

36. Note, "1/14/80 [1]," Staff Secretary Box 164, JEC Library.

37. Powell to Carter, memo, Nov. 19, 1979, "11/1/79–12/28/79," Powell Box 38, JEC Library; Powell to Carter, memo, Dec. 7, 1979, "11/1/79–12/28/79," Powell Box 38, JEC Library; Phil Wise to Carter, memo, Dec. 7, 1979, "10/1/79–12/31/79," Powell Box 40, JEC Library.

38. Lipshutz to Jordan, Powell, and Rafshoon, memo, Aug. 8, 1979, "Memoranda: Jody Powell 8/3/79–8/31/79," Powell Box 37, JEC Library; Hutcheson to Brzezinski, memo plus attachment, Apr. 29, 1980, "4/3/80–4/30/80," Powell Box 38, JEC Library.

39. Carter to Maier, memo, Nov. 3, 1977, "9/6/77–12/27/77," Powell Box 39, JEC Library; Powell to Carter, memo, May 8, 1980, "5/1/80–5/30/80," Powell Box 38, JEC Library.

40. Powell to Scheduling Office, memo, Aug. 19, 1980, "Memoranda: Jody Powell, 8/1/80–8/29/80," Powell Box 39, JEC Library; McDonald to Jordan, et al., memo, Aug. 25, 1980, "Memoranda: Jody Powell, 8/1/80–8/29/80," Powell Box 39, JEC Library; Carter to Powell, Eizenstat, and Kirbo, memo, Oct. 3, 1980, "Memoranda: Jody Powell, 10/3/80–12/29/80," Powell Box 39, JEC Library.

41. Truman to Hannegan, memo plus attachments, Mar. 19, 1946, "Hannegan, Robert E.," PSF, Box 122, HST Library; Davis to Clifford, memo, Apr. 13, 1948, "Miscellaneous Correspondence 1948 Campaign (1 or 2), Papers of Clark Clifford, Box 23, HST Library.

42. Keenan to Clifford, letter, Oct. 21, 1948, "Miscellaneous Correspondence 1948

Campaign (2 of 2)," Papers of Clark Clifford, Box 23, HST Library; Webb to Clifford, memo plus attachments, Dec. 30, 1948, "State of the Union 1949, Labor Phase," Papers of Clark Clifford, Box 39, HST Library.

43. Hechler to unknown recipient, memo, Nov. 15, 1950, "Politics—1950—election post-mortems," Papers of George Elsey, Box 92, HST Library; Hechler to Elsey, memo, Mar. 20, 1951, "Bipartisan Foreign Policy Study by Hechler," Papers of Kenneth Hechler, Box 4, HST Library. The reference to the mink coat involved an influence-peddling scandal in which a law firm gave a White House stenographer an expensive mink coat after her husband, a former examiner for the Reconstruction Finance Corporation, arranged a loan for the firm. See David McCullough, *Truman*, p. 863.

44. Panzer to Watson, memo, Sept. 16, 1967, "September 1967 (Watson)," Office Files of Fred Panzer, Box 432, LBJ Library; Goldstein to LBJ, memo, Nov. 14, 1967, "Vietnam [folder 2 of 2]," Office Files of Marvin Watson, Box 32, LBJ Library.

45. Panzer to LBJ, memo, Oct. 13, 1967, "October," Office Files of Fred Panzer, Box 398, LBJ Library; Panzer to LBJ, memo, Nov. 9, 1967, filed in the George Gallup Name File, WHCF, LBJ Library.

46. *The Public Papers of the Presidents of the United States of American, Jimmy Carter, 1979.*

47. Caddell to Carter, memo, July 12, 1979, "7/15/79—Address to the Nation—Energy/Crisis of Confidence," Staff Secretary Box 139, JEC Library.

48. *The Public Papers of the Presidents of the United States of American, Jimmy Carter, 1979.*

49. Aronson to Powell, memo, June 6, 1979, "6/1/79–6/28/79," Powell Box 37, JEC Library; Voorze to Jordan, Powell, and Rafshoon, memo, July 2, 1979, "7/2/79–7/31/79," Powell Box 37, JEC Library; Kahn to Carter, memo, July 11, 1979, "Camp David, 7/5/79–7/12/79 [2]," Staff Secretary Box 138, JEC Library.

50. Hutcheson to Powell, et al., action request, July 17, 1979, "5/1/79–9/24/79," Powell Box 40, JEC Library; Wexler and From to Carter, memo, Jan. 9, 1980, "1/1/80–1/15/80," Powell Box 38, JEC Library; McDonald to Jordan, memo, Apr. 28, 1980, "4/3/80–4/30/80," Powell Box 38, JEC Library.

51. The Carter archives, however, reveal very few instances of finding fault with the polls. John Geer, in *From Tea Leaves to Opinion Polls*, argues that older politicians who did not grow up with polls are less trusting of them. Although Carter grew up before polls became widely accepted, many on his staff did not. This may explain the relative absence of distrust in polling in the Carter White House.

52. Keenan to Clifford, letter, Oct. 21, 1948, "Miscellaneous Correspondence 1948 Campaign (2 of 2)," Papers of Clark Clifford, Box 23, HST Library. In 1936, *Literary Digest* predicted a decisive victory for Republican Alf Landon against Franklin Roosevelt. It was Roosevelt who was the decisive victor. Poor sampling technique is commonly seen as the culprit. See Stephen J. Wayne, *The Road to the White House, 2000*, pp. 266–67.

53. The President's Appointments, Dec. 2, 1948, "1948–December," PSF Appointments, Box 90, HST Library.

54. Anderson to Truman, letter, Nov. 30, 1948, "Anderson, Clinton P.," PSF, Box 54, HST Library; Knopf to Truman, letter, Feb. 23, 1949, "505 (1949–51)," Official File, Box 1373, HST Library. Knopf's letter indicates that Truman did not mention the book by name. The book was *The Pollsters*, by Lindsay Rogers.

55. Jones to Vaughan, letter, May 6, 1950, "Gallup Poll 505A," Official File, Box 1373, HST Library.

56. McKinney to Elsey, letter, Feb. 5, 1952, "Politics—Democratic National Committee," Papers of George Elsey, Box 92, HST Library.

57. Short to Mitchell, memo, Aug. 28, 1952, "Gallup Poll 505A," Official File, Box 1373, HST Library.

58. Louis Harris, *The Anguish of Change*, p. 23.

59. Altschuler makes a similar observation. See Altschuler, "Lyndon Johnson and the Public Polls," p. 293, and *LBJ and the Polls*, p. 75.

60. Panzer to LBJ, memo, Feb. 17, 1967, "February," Office Files of Fred Panzer, Box 398, LBJ Library.

61. Panzer to LBJ, memo, Sept. 8, 1967, "President: telecopies sent to ranch," Office Files of Fred Panzer, Box 399, LBJ Library; Panzer to LBJ, memo, Oct. 10, 1967, "October," Office Files of Fred Panzer, Box 398, LBJ Library.

62. Panzer to LBJ, memo, Oct. 3, 1967, filed in George Gallup Name File, WHCF, LBJ Library; Panzer to LBJ, memo, Oct. 24, 1967, "October," Office Files of Fred Panzer, Box 398, LBJ Library; Panzer to LBJ, memo, Nov. 3, 1967, "November," Panzer 398, LBJ Library; Panzer to LBJ, memo, Dec. 1, 1967, "Memos to the President December 1967," Panzer 397, LBJ Library. Altschuler also notes Panzer's annoyance at "buried" information. See, for example, Altschuler, "Lyndon Johnson and the Public Polls," p. 289, and *LBJ and the Polls*, p. 71.

63. Panzer to Watson, memo, Dec. 21, 1967, filed in George Gallup Name File, WHCF, LBJ Library.

64. Maguire to Kintner, memo, Nov. 7, 1966, "Speeches (1966)," Confidential File, Box 86, LBJ Library; assignment progress record, LBJ to Jones, Feb. 13, 1967, "Polls—Backup to Memos to President," Office Files of Fred Panzer, Box 395, LBJ Library.

65. Panzer to LBJ, memo, Oct. 7, 1967, "October," Panzer 398, LBJ Library.

66. LBJ to Levinson, memo, Nov. 18, 1967 (filing date), filed in George Gallup Name File, WHCF, LBJ Library.

67. Altschuler, "Lyndon Johnson and the Public Polls," pp. 295–98, and *LBJ and the Polls*, pp. 77–80.

68. Christian to Watson, memo, Dec. 1, 1967, George Gallup Name File, LBJ Library.

69. See Altschuler, "Lyndon Johnson and the Public Polls," pp. 293–96, and *LBJ and the Polls*, pp. 75–78, for additional discussion of the Johnson administration's efforts to manipulate polling studies or influence the pollsters.

70. Memo with photocopied top cover, "The President's reactions relayed to Christian from the LBJ Ranch," May 17, 1967, filed in the George Gallup Name File, LBJ Library.

71. Panzer to LBJ, memo, Oct. 17, 1967, "10–1-67–10–31–77," WHCF, PR 16, Box 349, LBJ Library. Altschuler elaborates on the "New York Poll" mentioned. The poll was taken by Archibald Crossley, who was hired by a friend of Johnson, Arthur Krim. When Krim asked Crossley to take the poll in New York without New York Governor Nelson Rockefeller as one of the candidates, Crossley agreed with the provision that his permission be obtained prior to the polls being released. Crossley also conducted a few other polls for Krim. The polls seemed to show Johnson's strength, but Crossley only gave permission to release the polls in their entirety. In response, the White House decided to leak the polls to selected

reporters. Crossley responded to the leaked polls by pointing out some methodological problems. The White House tried unsuccessfully to dispute Crossley. See Altschuler, *LBJ and the Polls*, p. 74–75.

72. LBJ to Christian, memo, Oct. 27, 1967, filed in the Drew Pearson Name file, LBJ Library. This memo is interesting for another reason. Many have claimed that Lyndon Johnson never understood the press or how to deal with it. Note Johnson's chiding expectation that the press easily can be convinced to write a positive story. Indeed, George Reedy, one of Johnson's press secretaries, claimed that one of Johnson's major weaknesses was his "inability to understand the press"; he expected the press to act like *political* actors. See George Reedy, *Lyndon B. Johnson, A Memoir*, p. 59. Panzer to Christian, memo, Nov. 16, 1967, "11–1-67–11–21–67," WHCF, PR 16, Box 349, LBJ Library; LBJ, memo, Feb. 4, 1968, filed the George Gallup Name File, LBJ Library.

73. LBJ to Christian, memo, Mar. 29, 1967, "3–1-67–4–20–67," WHCF, PR 16, Box 348, LBJ Library; Watson to LBJ, memo, Oct. 24, 1967, filed in Drew Pearson Name File, LBJ Library.

74. Watson to Panzer, memo, Oct. 18, 1967, "Watson, Marvin, (Incoming)," Panzer Box 433, plus attachments. See also Panzer to LBJ, memo plus attachments, Oct. 17, 1967, "October," Panzer Box 398, LBJ Library; Panzer to LBJ, memo, Nov. 9, 1967, filed in the George Gallup Name File, LBJ Library.

75. Panzer to LBJ, memo, July 28, 1967, "SP 3–195, President's Address to Nation on Civil Disorders," Confidential File, Box 89, LBJ Library; LBJ to Jim Jones, Dec. 13, 1967, filed in the George Gallup Name File, LBJ Library. The note is an attachment to a Gallup "Advance Promotion."

76. It is possible that the Truman administration may also have wanted to skew poll questions to get favorable outcomes. On July 8, 1952, Kenneth Hechler sent a memo to DNC Research Director Bert Gross. It is not clear what Hechler is referring to, but the statement he makes speaks for itself. "Would you please change question 40 (page 8) to read as follows: Do you agree with Herbert Hoover who branded a Democratic public works-unemployment relief bill on December 9, 1930, as 'playing politics at the expense of human misery'?" (Hechler to Gross, memo, July 8, 1952, "General Research—Truman White House," Papers of Kenneth Hechler, Box 4, HST Library). Such a loaded question does not seem designed to get a true picture of public opinion!

77. Altschuler, *LBJ and the Polls*, p. 99. See also p. 101.

78. Kingdon, "Politician's Beliefs About Voters," pp. 140–41.

79. There is reason to believe that this reaction occurs in other administrations as well. Jacobs and Shapiro observe that the Clinton White House believed that opposition to their health care reform policies was due to "faulty cognitive capacity" on the part of the public and "misleading information" being espoused by the opposition. See Jacobs and Shapiro, *Politicians Don't Pander*, p. 322.

80. The terms *selective attentions* and *selective interpretation* are taken from Fiske and Taylor, *Social Cognition*, pp. 354–62.

Chapter 4

1. See, for example, numerous memos to the president that report about polls in "Trends (Public Opinion)," PSF, Box 138, HST Library.

2. Minutes of Cabinet Meeting, Nov. 16, 1945, "Notes on Cabinet Meetings, 1945, 11/2–11/30," Papers of Matthew Connelly, Box 2, HST Library.

3. Minutes of Cabinet Meeting, Sept. 28, 1945, "Notes on Cabinet Meetings, 1945, Sep. 7, 21, 28," Papers of Matthew Connelly, Box 2, HST Library; Minutes of Cabinet Meeting, Nov. 23, 1945, "Notes on Cabinet Meetings, 11/2–11/30, 1945," Papers of Matthew Connelly, Box 2, HST Library.

4. Note, Nov. 30, 1945, "Notes on Cabinet Meetings, 11/2–11/30, 1945," Papers of Matthew Connelly, Box 2, HST Library; Minutes of Cabinet Meeting, Mar. 1, 1946, "Notes on Cabinet Meetings, "March 1, 8, 22, 29, 1946," Papers of Matthew Connelly, Box 2, HST Library.

5. Elsey to Clifford, memo, Mar. 7, 1947, "1947, March 12, 'Truman Doctrine' Speech," Papers of George Elsey, Box 17, HST Library.

6. Minutes of Cabinet Meeting, Apr. 9, 1948, "Notes on Cabinet Meetings, 1948—Jan. 9–Dec. 31," Papers of Matthew Connelly, Box 2, HST Library; Humelsine to Clifford, memo, July 10, 1948, "Palestine—United States Policy with regard to Palestine," Papers of Clark Clifford, Box 15, HST Library; Howe, memo for the record, Oct. 5, 1948, "Palestine—Correspondence, Misc.," Papers of Clark Clifford, Box 13, HST Library.

7. Goldman to LBJ, et al., memo, Dec. 21, 1963, WHCF SP2–4, "State of the Union," Box 133, LBJ Library; Cater to LBJ, two memos, Oct. 8, 1964, and Cater to Busby, Oct. 12, 1964, "Political Polls," Busby Box 41, LBJ Library.

8. Shapiro and Jacobs argue that Johnson continued to be responsive to public opinion after it was obvious that he would be reelected "in order to solidify his public support for purposes of leading the public on his racial and social policy agenda *after* the election." (See Shapiro and Jacobs, p. 165. Emphasis in original.) They argue, however, that there was a decline in responsiveness after the 1964 election. The research here suggests that the Johnson administration was still somewhat attentive to the public's issue agenda into 1966. After that, as the remainder of this Chapter argues, attention to the public's issue agenda declined.

9. Irving Crespi to Hayes Redmon, letter, June 10, 1965, filed in the George Gallup name file, LBJ Library. See also, Redmon to Moyers, memo, July 21, 1965, "Immigration," Office Files of Mike Manatos, Box 8, LBJ Library.

10. Cater to LBJ, Aug. 3, 1965, Ex Sp 2–4, "State of the Union Messages," Box 133, LBJ Library; Redmon to Califano, Dec. 28, 1965, "1967 State of the Union Categories: Youth Labor Manpower," Statements 224, LBJ Library.

11. Redmon to Moyers, Nov. 9, 1965, filed in the Louis Harris Name File, LBJ Library. Altschuler notes that there is no indication that the poll was ever done. See Altschuler, "Lyndon Johnson and the Public Polls," p. 296, and *LBJ and the Polls*, p. 98.

12. Redmon to Moyers, Jan. 27, 1966, "Polls," Personal Papers of Henry Wilson, Box 14, LBJ Library.

13. Caddell to Carter, memo, Dec. 21, 1976, "Caddell, Patrick, [12/76–1/77]," Staff Secretary, Box 1, JEC Library.

14. Caddell to Carter, memo, Jan. 10, 1977, "Caddell, Patrick, [12/76–1/77]," Staff Secretary, Box 1, JEC Library.

15. Schneiders to Carter, memo, Feb. 8, 1977, "Memorandum, Schneiders, Greg, 2/8/77–6/ 23/77," Powell, Box 47, JEC Library; Schneiders to Carter, memo, Feb. 10, 1977, "Memorandum, Schneiders, Greg, 2/8/77–6/23/77," Powell, Box 47, JEC Library.

16. Hutcheson to Schneiders, memo plus attachments, Feb. 28, 1977, "Handwriting File 2/28/77 [1]," Staff Secretary, Box 10, JEC Library; Hutcheson to Hugh

Carter, memo plus attachments, Mar. 2, 1977, "Handwriting File, 3/2/77," Staff Secretary, Box 10, JEC Library.

17. Schneiders to Carter, memo, Mar. 8, 1977, "Memorandum: Watson, Jack, 1/27/77–4/20/77," Powell, Box 48, JEC Library.

18. Hutcheson to Hugh Carter, memo plus attachments, July 5, 1977, "7/5/77 [2]," Staff Secretary, Box 35, JEC Library; Hutcheson to Costanza, memo plus attachments, July 6, 1977, "7/6/77," Staff Secretary, Box 36, JEC Library; Caddell to Carter, letter, Oct. 21, 1977, "Caddell, (Patrick) (1)," Jordan, Box 33, JEC Library.

19. Mondale to Carter, memo, Sept. 6, 1977, "Vice President," Jordan, Box 37, JEC Library.

20. Minutes of Cabinet Meeting, Sept. 7, 1945, "Notes on Cabinet Meetings, 1945, Sep. 7, 21, 28," Papers of Matthew Connelly, Box 2, HST Library; Minutes of Cabinet Meeting, Nov. 30, 1945, "Notes on Cabinet Meetings, 11/2–11/30, 1945," Papers of Matthew Connelly, Box 2, HST Library.

21. Minutes of Cabinet Meeting, Jan. 11, 1946, "Notes on Cabinet Meetings, Jan. 11, 18, 25, 1946," Papers of Matthew Connelly, Box 2, HST Library; Minutes of Cabinet Meeting, May 10, 1946, "Notes on Cabinet Meetings, May 3, 10, 17, 24, 1946," Papers of Matthew Connelly, Box 2, HST Library.

22. Minutes of Cabinet Meeting, Mar. 7, 1947, "1947, Jan. 3–Dec. 19," Papers of Matthew Connelly, Box 2, HST Library.

23. Wilson to O'Brien, Nov. 9, 1964, "Larry O'Brien, Wilson," Box 4, LBJ Library.
   Actually, the memo was incorrect. Although Johnson did receive more total votes than Moore, Johnson led Goldwater by 175,295 votes, whereas Moore defeated his opponent by 184,178 votes.

24. Goldman, *The Tragedy of Lyndon Johnson*, pp. 301–304.

25. Watson to LBJ, memo, Apr. 1, 1966, "3-1-66–4-7-66," WHCF, PR 16, Box 347, LBJ Library.

26. Moyers to LBJ, memo, Apr. 12, 1966, "Public Opinion Polls (1 of 5)," Confidential File, Box 81, LBJ Library; Manatos to LBJ, memo, Jan. 25, 1966, "Manatos: Leg. General—1966. Jan. Feb. March," Office Files of Michael Manatos, Box 3, LBJ Library.

27. G[reg Schneiders] to Gael [?], memo plus attachment, Apr. 5, 1977, "Citizen Response—mass participation feedback," Rafshoon (Schneiders) Box 38, JEC Library. I am unable to determine who the recipient is, but it may have been *Gail* Harrison, assistant to the vice president for domestic policy, or Gael Summer in the First Lady's Office. Hutcheson to Moore, memo, Apr. 23, 1977, "4/23/77," Staff Secretary Box 20, JEC Library.

28. Butler to Jordan, memo, Mar. 17, 1977, "Salt, 1977," Jordan Box 37, JEC Library; Butler to Jordan, memo, May 11, 1977, "Salt, 1977," Jordan Box 37, JEC Library; Jordan to Carter, June 1977, "Foreign Policy/Domestic Politics Memo HJ Memo 6/77," Jordan Box 34, JEC Library.

29. Hodding Carter to Jordan, memo, Sept. 19, 1977, "Fireside Chats, 1977," Powell Box 59, JEC Library; list plus attachment, Nov. 5, 1977, "9/1/77–5/31/78," WHCF, PR, Box 75, JEC Library.

30. Eizenstat to Schlesinger, et al., memo plus attachments, Oct. 14, 1977, "Energy Legislation," Jordan Box 34, JEC Library; Jordan to Carter and Mondale, memo, undated, "Energy Legislation," Jordan Box 34, JEC Library.

31. Moe to Mondale, Jordan, Moore, Brzezinski, and Butler, memo, Apr. 10, 1978,

"SALT, 1978," Jordan Box 37, JEC Library. The memorandum is also interesting for another reason. Moe suggested that the administration should submit SALT as an executive agreement rather than risk the embarrassment of failing to get the treaty approved. Ultimately, Carter had to withdraw the treaty because of a lack of support.

32. Brzezinski to Caddell, letter, Apr. 24, 1978, "Caddell, Pat. H," Name File, JEC Library.

33. Rafshoon to Mondale, et al., memo, June 1, 1978, "Memoranda: Rafshoon, Jerry, 5/18/78–8/25/78," Powell Box 46, JEC Library.

34. Rick Hutcheson to Jack Watson, et al., action request, June 8, 1978, "Memoranda: Rafshoon, Jerry 5/18/78–8/25/78," Powell Box 46, JEC Library. The memo does not identify the means by which the public was to pressure Congress. Indeed, Rafshoon continues, "We are not asking the people to contact their Congressman (although hopefully they will) or to conserve or to do anything else."

35. Connelly to Truman, memo, Oct. 2, 1945, "Cabinet—General, 1945–51," PSF, Box 154, HST Library; Truman to Hannegan, memo plus attachments, Mar. 19, 1946, "Hannegan, Robert E.," PSF, Box 122, HST Library.

36. Niles to Connelly, memo, Oct. 8, 1946, "Polls," PSF—Political File, Box 60, HST Library; Minutes of Cabinet Meeting, Oct. 11, 1946, "Notes on Cabinet Meetings, May 17–Dec. 20, 1946," Papers of Matthew Connelly, Box 2, HST Library.

37. Analysis, undated, "Voting Statistics," PSF, Box 61, HST Library.

38. Kenneth Hechler, memo, July 21, 1950, "Letters and memoranda to and with House and Senate Members," Papers of Kenneth Hechler, Box 5, HST Library.

39. Minutes of Cabinet Meeting, Nov. 14, 1950, "Notes on Cabinet Meetings, 1950, Jan. 6–Dec. 29," Papers of Matthew Connelly, Box 2, HST Library; Hechler, memo, Nov. 15, 1950, "Politics—1950—Election post-mortems," Papers of George Elsey, Box 92, HST Library; Lloyd to Murphy, memo, Nov. 16, 1950, "Politics—1950—Election post-mortems," Papers of George Elsey, Box 92, HST Library.

40. Elsey to Murphy, memo plus attachments, Nov. 17, 1950, "Politics—1950—Election post-mortems," Papers of George Elsey, Box 92, HST Library; Minutes of Cabinet Meeting, Dec. 12, 1950, "Notes on Cabinet Meetings, 1950, Jan. 6–Dec. 29," Papers of Matthew Connelly, Box 2, HST Library.

41. Hechler to Elsey, memo, Apr. 9, 1951, "Korea—MacArthur Dismissal—Jefferson Jackson Day Speech," Papers of George Elsey, Box 75, HST Library; Hechler to Elsey, Carroll, Bell and Neustadt, memo, July 16, 1951, "Memoranda on our Foreign Policy," Papers of Kenneth Hechler, Box 4, HST Library.

42. Redmon to Moyers, May 27, 1966, "BDM Memos, June-July 1966," Moyers Box 12, LBJ Library; Redmon to Moyers, June 9, 1966, "BDM Memos June–July 11, 1966," Moyers, Box 12, LBJ Library; Bill Moyers to the President, memo, June 9, 1966, "BDM Memos, June–July 11, 1966," Office Files of Bill Moyers, Box 12, LBJ Library.

43. Markman to Watson, June 9, 1966, "Public Opinion Polls (1966) 4 of 5," Confidential File, Box 82, LBJ Library; Jones to Watson, June 24, 1966, "Public Opinion Polls (1966) 4 of 5," Confidential File, Box 82, LBJ Library; Redmon to Moyers, July 19, 1966, George Gallup Name File, LBJ Library.

44. Redmon to Moyers, memo, Aug. 31, 1966, "BDM Memos, July 12–August

1966," Office Files of Bill Moyers, Box 12, LBJ Library; Redmon to Moyers, memo, Sept. 27, 1966, "BDM Memos September 1966–February 1967," Office Files of Bill Moyers, Box 12, LBJ Library.

45. Altschuler and Towle each observe the dominance of the question of approval in the Johnson administration. See Altschuler, *LBJ and the Polls*, pp. 37, 107, and 109, and Towle, "Lyndon Baines Johnson and the American People," pp. 221, 234–35.

46. Poll Report, May 27, 1977, "Public Communications, Relations, Appearances, and Pollster Reports," Domestic Policy Staff Box 264, JEC Library; Poll Report, Oct. 15, 1977, "Public Communications, Relations, Appearances, and Pollster Reports," Domestic Policy Staff Box 264, JEC Library.

47. Hutcheson to Jordan, memo plus attachment, Mar. 21, 1978, "Economic Development Administration, 1977," Jordan Box 44, JEC Library.

48. Strauss to Jordan and Powell, memo, May 1, 1978, "4/1/78–5/30/78," Powell Box 36, JEC Library.

49. Cutter to Jordan, memo, May 30, 1978, "4/1/78–5/30/78," Powell Box 36, JEC Library; Stern to Eizenstat, memo, July 11, 1978, "Pollster reports—public opinion [2]," Domestic Policy Staff Box 254, JEC Library.

50. Jacobs and Shapiro, *Politicians Don't Pander,* p. xiii.

51. Ross to Truman, memo, Jan. 3, 1946, "The President—Articles on and Memoranda to," Papers of Charles G. Ross, Box 7, HST Library; McCullough, *Truman,* p. 566.

52. Sullivan to Clifford, memo, June 14, 1947, "Labor—HR 3020—Taft-Harley Bill—Correspondence (1 of 2)," Papers of Clark Clifford, Box 7, HST Library.

53. McCullough, *Truman,* p. 566.

54. For discussion of the political merits of the veto, see Alonzo L. Hamby, *Man of the People: A Life of Harry S. Truman,* p. 424; Bert Cochran, *Harry Truman and the Crisis Presidency,* p. 239; and Harold I. Gullan, *The Upset that Wasn't: Harry S Truman and the Crucial Election of 1948,* p. 214.

55. Clifford to the president, memo, Nov. 19, 1947, "Confidential Memorandum to the President" (Clifford-Rowe Memorandum of Nov. 19, 1947), Papers of Clark Clifford, Box 22, HST Library. Emphasis in original. For a discussion of the story and impact of the memorandum, see Gullan, *The Upset that Wasn't,* pp. 60–64 and 112–14.

56. Clifford to the President, memo, Nov. 19, 1947, "Confidential Memorandum to the President" (Clifford-Rowe Memorandum of November 19, 1947), Papers of Clark Clifford, Box 22, HST Library.

57. Nash to Truman, memo, Nov. 6, 1948, "Misc.—Political File 1948 (2 of 2)," Papers of Clark Clifford, Box 22, HST Library; Chart, undated, "Voting Statistics," PSF, Box 61, HST Library.

58. Anderson to Truman, letter, Nov. 30, 1948, "Anderson, Clinton P.," PSF, Box 54, HST Library; Webb to Clifford, memo plus attachments, Dec. 30, 1948, "State of the Union 1949—Labor Phase," Papers of Clark Clifford, Box 39, HST Library.

59. Hechler to unknown recipient, memo, Nov. 15, 1950, "Politics—1950—Election post-mortems," Papers of George Elsey, Box 92, HST Library; Lloyd to George, memo, Nov. 16, 1950, "Politics—1950—Election post-mortems," Papers of George Elsey, Box 92, HST Library.

60. Moyers to LBJ, memo, June 10, 1966, "Public Opinion Polls (1966) 4 of 5," Confidential File, Box 82, LBJ Library.

The survey indicates that the members of the House believed that the primary issues of concern to their constituents were Vietnam (88 percent mentioned it), inflation (61 percent), the war on poverty (34 percent), civil rights (29 percent), and education (19 percent). In the Senate, the response was Vietnam (76 percent), inflation (56 percent), agriculture (40 percent), civil rights (28 percent), and education (20 percent). Note that the survey only indicates the issues of concern, not the beliefs about the constituents' opinions on the issues.

61. Moyers to LBJ, July 17, 1966, "BDM Memos, July 12–August 1966," Office Files of Bill Moyers, Box 12, LBJ Library.

62. President's Diary cards. Also, audio visual archivist's records, LBJ Library.

63. WHCF, Press Office Files, LBJ Library.

64. Watson to LBJ, memo plus attachments, Jan. 12, 1967, "Elections, Campaigns (1967—)," Confidential File, Box 77, LBJ Library; Moyers to LBJ, Dec. 7, 1967, Bill Moyers Name File, LBJ Library.

65. See Manchester, *The Death of a President*; Kintner to LBJ, memo plus attachments, Jan. 27, 1967, "Elections Campaigns (1967—)," Confidential File, Box 77, LBJ Library. Attachments include two advance releases by Louis Harris. The quote is from the Harris release for January 30, 1967.

66. Kintner to LBJ, memo, Mar. 3, 1967, "2–1-67–3–15–67," PR 16, Box 348, LBJ Library; Panzer to LBJ, memo, Mar. 23, 1967, "3–1-67–4–20–67," PR 16, Box 348, LBJ Library.

67. Panzer to LBJ, memo, May 5, 1967, "May," Office Files of Fred Panzer, Box 398, LBJ Library.

68. Panzer to LBJ, memo, May 8, 1967, filed in the George Gallup Name file, LBJ Library.

69. Markman to Watson, memo, Feb. 20, 1967, "2–1-67–3–15–67," PR 16, Box 348, LBJ Library; Jones to Watson, memo plus attachments, Apr. 19, 1967, filed in the George Gallup Name File, LBJ Library; Panzer to Watson, memo, Apr. 20, 1967, filed in the George Gallup Name File, LBJ Library.

70. Panzer to LBJ, memo, Dec. 1, 1967, "Memos to the President, December 1967," Office Files of Fred Panzer, Box 397, LBJ Library; Panzer to LBJ, memo, Jan. 27, 1968, filed in the Oliver Quayle Name File, LBJ Library.

71. Panzer to LBJ, memo, Jan. 10, 1968, "12–28–67–1–23–68," PR 16, Box 350, LBJ Library.
    This memo is also noteworthy for its foresightful analysis. Eugene McCarthy, of course, would ultimately do surprisingly well in the New Hampshire primary; although Johnson would win, McCarthy's surprise showing would help Johnson decide to withdraw from the election. Curiously, Quayle foresaw the outcome. Panzer wrote that Quayle was "nervous" about how the undecided voters would vote. "He believes they would mostly go for McCarthy or someone else—not LBJ. Thus, he counsels LBJ supporters to be very cautious in making claims about how well they will do, lest it give McCarthy or Kennedy an opportunity to claim any kind of victory even though Johnson gets more write-ins than others combined. Poor mouthing the vote is always good advice." Quayle's advice, if heeded, may have downplayed McCarthy's strong showing and kept Johnson in the race. See Altschuler, *LBJ and the Polls*, p. 92, and Towle, "Lyndon Baines Johnson and the American People," p. 184.

72. Panzer to Watson, memo with LBJ handwritten message, Jan. 22, 1968, and Panzer to LBJ, memo, Jan. 23, 1968, "12–28–67–1–23–68," PR 16, Box 350, LBJ Library.

73. Stanley Karnow, *Vietnam: A History*, p. 546.

74. For Johnson's reaction, see Lyndon Baines Johnson, *The Vantage Point: Perspectives on the Presidency*, p. 537–38.

75. *The Public Papers of the Presidents of the United States, Lyndon Johnson, 1968*.

76. Caddell to Carter, memo, Dec. 21, 1976, "Caddell, Patrick [12/76–1/77]," Staff Secretary Box 1, JEC Library.

77. Van Dyk to Eizenstat, memo, July 26, 1977, "Pollster reports—public opinion (2)," Domestic Policy Staff Box 254, JEC Library; E. to Jordan, memo, July 13, 1977, "Middle East, 1977 [1]," Jordan Box 35, JEC Library; Hutcheson to Jordan, memo plus attachment, July 7, 1977, "7/7/77 [2]," Staff Secretary Box 36, JEC Library.

78. Mondale to Carter, memo, Sept. 6, 1977, "Vice President," Jordan Box 37, JEC Library; Jordan, Moe, and Kraft, memo, Nov. 21, 1977, "Vice-President—Agenda 11/77," Jordan Box 37, JEC Library; Report, Dec. 14, 1977, "Democratic National Committee 1977–79," Jordan Box 34, JEC Library.

79. Powell to Carter, memo, Jan. 12, 1978, "1/10/78–5/18/78," Powell Box 39, JEC Library.

80. *The Public Papers of the Presidents of the United States, Jimmy Carter, 1978*.

81. Mondale and Eizenstat to Carter, memo, Feb. 13, 1978, "2/14/78 [1]," Staff Secretary Box 73, JEC Library.

82. *The Public Papers of the Presidents of the United States of American, Jimmy Carter, 1978*.

83. Hutcheson to Eizenstat, memo plus attachment, Feb. 16, 1978, "2/16/78," Staff Secretary Box 73, JEC Library.

84. Jordan to Carter, memo, Mar. 24, 1978, "Urban Policy, 3/24/78," Jordan Box 37, JEC Library. Emphasis in original. Rick [?] to Jordan, memo, Mar. 24, 1978, "Economic Development Administration [1977]," Jordan Box 44, JEC Library. The author could have been either Hendrik Hertzberg, chief speechwriter, or Richard Hutcheson, staff secretary.

85. Moore to Powell, memo, May 1, 1979, "4/2/79–5/31/79," Powell Box 37, JEC Library; Phil [Wise] to Jordan and Powell, memo plus attachments, Oct. 25, 1979, "10/1/79–10/31/79," Powell Box 37, JEC Library; Samuels to Jordan, Powell, and Bario, memo, Jan. 22, 1980, "1/16/80–1/31/80," Powell Box 38, JEC Library.

86. Jordan to Carter, memo, Mar., 1977, "Foreign Policy/Domestic Politics Memo HJ Memo 6/77," Jordan Box 34, JEC Library; Report, Dec. 14, 1977, "Democratic National Committee 1977–79," Jordan Box 34, JEC Library; Stern to Eizenstat, memo, July 11, 1978, "Pollster reports—public opinion (2)," Domestic Policy Staff Box 254, JEC Library; Jordan to Carter, memo, undated, "Comprehensive Test Ban Treaty/SALT, 1978," Jordan Box 34, JEC Library.

87. Rafshoon to Jordan, Eizenstat, Powell, Moore, and Kraft, memo, Feb. 22, 1979, "1/4/79–8/3/79," Powell Box 46, JEC Library; Kamarck to White, memo, Mar. 20, 1979, "2/6/78–3/30/79," Powell Box 37, JEC Library; Caddell to Democratic National Committee, memo, May 25, 1979, "Caddell, Pat (3)," Jordan Box 33, JEC Library.

88. CSP to Dick [Moe], memo, undated, "10/1/79–10/31/79," Powell Box 37, JEC Library. Jordan's notation is on the memo, sending it to Jody Powell "F.Y.I." The Carter Library has identified the likely identity of CSP as Carla Perantoni, secretary to the chief of staff to the vice president.

89. Powell to Carter, memo, Dec. 7, 1979, "11/1/79–12/28/79," Powell Box 38, JEC Library; Free to Carter, memo, Dec. 7, 1979, "10/1/79–12/31/79," Powell Box 40, JEC Library.
90. Unknown author [probably Powell] to Carter, memo, Dec. 31, 1979, "10/1/79–12/31/79," Powell Box 40, JEC Library; Moe to Jordan, Powell, Brzezinski, and McDonald, memo, Jan. 8, 1980, "Soviets in Afghanistan (3)," Powell Box 79, JEC Library.
91. Samuels to Jordan, Powell, and Bario, memo, Jan. 22, 1980, "1/16/80–1/31/80," Powell Box 38, JEC Library; Powell to Carter, memo, Apr. 21, 1980, "4/3/80–4/30/80," Powell Box 38, JEC Library. Emphasis in original.
92. See Jacobs and Shapiro, *Politicians Don't Pander*. See also Shapiro and Jacobs, "Polling in the White House," p. 159.

Chapter 5

1. Jacobs and Shapiro, *Politicians Don't Pander*, pp. 4–5, 296.
2. See Herbst, *Numbered Voices*, p. 162. This volume offers an insightful discussion of the view that public opinion is a measurable phenomenon.
3. Truman's reputation is the stuff of political lore, yet some have made the same observation of President Carter. See, for example, Charles O. Jones, *The Trusteeship Presidency: Jimmy Carter and the United States Congress*.
4. Tulis, *The Rhetorical Presidency*, p. 204.
5. Jacobs and Shapiro, *Politicians Don't Pander*, pp. 302–303, 298.
6. Geer, *From Tea Leaves*, pp. 187–91, 196.
7. Gallup approval ratings from *The Roper Center for Public Opinion Research*.
8. Stephen Skowronek, "Presidential Leadership in Political Time" in *The Presidency and the Political System*, sixth edition, ed. by Michael Nelson, pp. 125–70.
9. McCullough, *Truman*, pp. 770–71, 873–74, 888–93.
10. Gallup approval ratings from *The Roper Center for Public Opinion Research*.
11. Herbst, *Numbered Voices*, p. 109.

Appendix

1. Johnson, *The Vantage Point*, p. 94.
2. Christian to LBJ, Jan. 17, 1968, "Elections-Campaigns (1967—)," Confidential File, Box 77, LBJ Library.
3. Johnson, *The Vantage Point*, p. 430.
    George Christian writes about Johnson's claim that he lost the statement, "I've always believed he was joshing." See George Christian, "The Night Lyndon Quit," *Texas Monthly*, (Apr., 1988): 109, 168–69.
4. Christian, "The Night Lyndon Quit," p. 168.
5. Ibid.
6. Turner, *Lyndon Johnson's Dual War*, p. 235.
7. Watson to LBJ, Feb. 16, 1968, "1–24–68–3–5-68," PR 16, Box 350, LBJ Library.
8. Rostow to LBJ, Mar. 22, 1968, "March 1968," filed in the Abe Fortas Name File, LBJ Library.
9. Roche to LBJ, Mar. 27, 1968, "Vietnam, 1 of 2," Office Files of Marvin Watson, Box 32, LBJ Library.

10. Notes of Johnson's telephone conversation with Ed Pauley of Los Angeles about polls, Mar. 26, 1968, "MMW Conversations," Office Files of Marvin Watson, Box 32, LBJ Library.
11. Turner, *Lyndon Johnson's Dual War,* pp. 244–45.
12. Rowe to LBJ, memo, Mar. 28, 1968, "James Rowe," Name File, LBJ Library.
13. Johnson's Diary cards, LBJ Library.
14. Fortas to Johnson, message taken by Jim Jones, "March 1968," filed in the Abe Fortas Name File, LBJ Library.

Bibliography

Altschuler, Bruce. *LBJ and the Polls.* Gainesville: University of Florida Press, 1990.
———. "Lyndon Johnson and the Public Polls." *Public Opinion Quarterly,* fall, 1986.
Anderson, Paul A. "The Relevance of Social Cognition for the Study of Elites in Political Institutions, or Why It Isn't Enough to Understand What Goes on in Their Heads." In *Political Cognition,* ed. by Richard Lau and David O. Sears. Hillsdale, N.J.: Lawrence Erlbaum Associates, 1986.
Bailey, Thomas A. *The Man in the Street.* New York: Macmillan Company, 1948.
Barber, James David. *The Presidential Experience,* third edition. Englewood Cliffs, N.J.: Prentice-Hall, 1985.
Barone, Michael. "The Power of the President's Pollsters." *Public Opinion* 2, no. 3 (September/October, 1988): p. 2–4, 57.
Bauer, Wilhelm. "Public Opinion." In *Encyclopedia of the Social Sciences,* ed. by Edwin R. A. Seligman. New York: Macmillan Company, 1934.
Berelson, Bernard. "The Study of Public Opinion." In *The State of the Social Sciences.* Chicago: University of Chicago Press, 1956.
Bimes, Terri, and Stephen Skowronek. "Woodrow Wilson's Critique of Popular Leadership: Reassessing the Modern-Traditional Divide in Presidential History," in Richard J. Ellis, *Speaking to the People: The Rhetorical Presidency in Historical Perspective.* Amherst: University of Massachusetts Press, 1998.
Blumenthal, Sydney. *The Permanent Campaign.* New York: Simon and Schuster, 1982.
Bonafede, Dom. "Has the Rafshoon Touch Left its Mark on the White House?" *National Journal,* April 14, 1979.
———. "Telling Us Who's on First." *National Journal,* May 27, 1978, p. 852.
Brace, Paul, and Barbara Hinckley. *Follow the Leader: Opinion Polls and Modern Presidents.* New York: Basic Books, 1992.
Bryce, James. *The American Commonwealth.* Indianapolis: The Liberty Fund, 1995.
Buchanan, Bruce. *The Citizen's Presidency: Standards of Choice and Judgment.* Washington, D.C.: CQ Press, 1987.
Budiansky, Stephen, Art Levine, Ted Gest, Alvin P. Sanoff, and Robert Shapiro. "The Numbers Racket: How Polls and Statistics Lie." *U.S. News and World Report,* July 11, 1988, pp. 44–47.
Campbell, Karlyn Kohrs, and Kathleen Hall Jamieson. *Deeds Done in Words: Presidential Rhetoric and the Genres of Governance.* Chicago: University of Chicago Press, 1990.
Carter, Jimmy. *Keeping Faith.* New York: Bantam Books, 1982.
Childs, Harwood. *Public Opinion: Nature, Formation, and Role.* Princeton, N.J.: D. Van Nostrand, 1965.
Christian, George. "The Night Lyndon Quit." *Texas Monthly,* April, 1988, pp. 109, 168–69.
Clines, Francis X. "First Lady Attributes Inquiry to 'Right Wing Conspiracy.'" *The New York Times,* January 28, 1998, p. l.
Cochran, Bert. *Harry Truman and the Crisis Presidency.* New York: Funk and Wagnalls, 1973.
Cohen, Jeffrey. *Presidential Responsiveness and Public Policy Making.* Ann Arbor: University of Michigan Press, 1997.

Crespi, Irving. "The Case of Presidential Popularity." In *Polling on the Issues,* ed. by Albert Cantril. Washington, D.C.: Seven Locks Press, 1980.

Delli Carpini, Michael X., and Scott Keeter. *What Americans Know about Politics and Why It Matters.* New Haven: Yale University Press, 1996.

Dexter, Lewis Anthony. "The Representative and His District." *Human Organization* 16, no. 1 (spring, 1957): pp. 2–13.

Edwards, George. *The Public Presidency: The Pursuit of Popular Support.* New York: St. Martin's Press, 1983.

Evans, Rowland, and Robert Novak. *Lyndon B. Johnson: The Exercise of Power.* New York: The American Library, 1986.

Fenno, Richard F. *Home Style: House Members in Their Districts.* Boston: Little, Brown and Company, 1978.

Ferrell, Robert. *Off the Record: The Private Papers of Harry S. Truman.* New York: Harper and Row, 1980.

Festinger, Leon. *A Theory of Cognitive Dissonance.* Stanford, Calif.: Stanford University Press, 1957.

Fiske, S. T., and S. E. Taylor. *Social Cognition.* New York: Random House, 1984.

Gallup Political Index, Report No. 2, 1965.

Gallup, George. "Preserving Majority Rule." In *Polling on the Issues,* ed. by Albert H. Cantril. Washington, D.C.: Seven Locks Press, 1980.

———. *The Gallup Poll: Public Opinion 1935–1971.* New York: Random House, 1972.

———. *The Sophisticated Poll Watcher's Guide.* Princeton, N.J.: Public Opinion Press, 1972.

Gallup, George, and Saul Forbes Rae. *The Pulse of Democracy.* New York: Simon and Schuster, 1940.

Geer, John G. *From Tea Leaves to Opinion Polls: A Theory of Democratic Leadership.* New York: Columbia University Press, 1996.

Gelb, Leslie H., with Richard K. Betts. *The Irony of Vietnam: The System Worked.* Washington, D.C.: Brookings, 1979.

Goldman, Eric F. *The Tragedy of Lyndon Johnson.* New York: Dell Publishing Company, 1969.

Graber, Doris A. "Conclusions: Linkage Successes and Failures." In *The President and the Public,* ed. by Graber. Philadelphia: Institute for the Study of Human Issues, 1982.

———. *Public Opinion, The President and Foreign Policy: Four Case Studies from the Formative Years.* New York: Holt, Rinehart and Winston, Inc., 1968.

Grossman, Michael Baruch, and Martha Joynt Kumar. *Portraying the President: The White House and the News Media.* Baltimore: Johns Hopkins University Press, 1981.

Gullan, Harold I. *The Upset that Wasn't: Harry S Truman and the Crucial Election of 1948.* Chicago: Ivan R. Dee, 1998.

Hamby, Alonzo L. *Man of the People: A Life of Harry S. Truman.* New York: Oxford University Press, 1995.

Harris, Louis. *The Anguish of Change.* New York: W. W. Norton and Company, 1973.

Herbst, Susan. *Numbered Voices: How Opinion Polling Has Shaped American Politics.* Chicago: University of Chicago Press, 1993.

Herring, George C. *America's Longest War: The United States and Vietnam, 1950–1975,* second edition. New York: Alfred A. Knopf, 1986.

Holland, J. William. "The Great Gamble: Jimmy Carter and the 1979 Energy Crisis." *Prologue: Quarterly of the National Archives* 22, no. 1 (spring, 1990): pp. 63–79.

Jacobs, Lawrence R., and Robert Y. Shapiro. *Politicians Don't Pander: Political Manipulation and the Loss of Democratic Responsiveness.* Chicago: University of Chicago Press, 2000.

Johnson, Lyndon Baines. *The Vantage Point: Perspectives on the Presidency.* New York: Holt, Rinehart and Winston, 1971.

Jones, Charles O. *The Trusteeship Presidency: Jimmy Carter and the United States Congress.* Baton Rouge: Louisiana State University Press, 1988.

Karnow, Stanley. *Vietnam: A History.* New York: The Viking Press, 1983.

Kearns, Doris. *Lyndon Johnson and the American Dream.* New York: Holt, Rinehart and Winston, 1970.

Kelley, H. H., and J. Michela. "Attribution Theory and Research." *Annual Review of Psychology,* 1980.

Kernell, Samuel. *Going Public: New Strategies of Presidential Leadership,* third edition. Washington, D.C.: CQ Press, 1997.

Key, V. O. "Public Opinion and the Decay of Democracy." *Virginia Quarterly Review* 37, no. 4 (autumn, 1961): pp. 481–94.

Kingdon, John W. "Politicians' Beliefs About Voters." *American Political Science Review,* 1967.

Lau, Richard, and David O. Sears. "Social Cognition and Political Cognition: The Past, The Present, and the Future." In *Political Cognition,* ed. by Lau and Sears. Hillsdale, N.J.: Lawrence Erlbaum Associates, 1986.

Lowi, Theodore J. *The Personal President: Power Invested, Promises Unfulfilled.* Ithaca, N.Y.: Cornell University Press, 1985.

Manchester, William R. *The Death of a President, November 20–November 25, 1963.* New York: Penguin Books, 1967.

McCullough, David. *Truman.* New York: Touchstone, 1992.

McMillin, Miles. "Probes Threaten Democratic Party." *Capital Times,* March 24, 1951.

McPherson, Harry. *A Political Education.* Boston: Little, Brown and Company, 1972.

McWilliams, Wilson C. "Lyndon B. Johnson: The Last of the Great Presidents." In *Modern Presidents and the Presidency,* ed. by Marc Landy. Lexington, Mass: D. C. Heath and Company, 1985.

Moynihan, Daniel Patrick. *Maximum Feasible Misunderstanding.* New York: The Free Press, 1969.

Neustadt, Richard. *Presidential Power.* New York: John Wiley and Sons, 1980.

Nichols, David. "A Marriage Made in Philadelphia: The Constitution and the Rhetorical Presidency." In *Speaking to the People: The Rhetorical Presidency in Historical Perspective,* ed. by Richard J. Ellis. Amherst: University of Massachusetts Press, 1998.

Palmer, Paul. "The Concept of Public Opinion in Political Theory," in *Essays in History and Political Theory.* Cambridge, Mass.: Harvard University Press, 1936.

Patterson, Bradley H. *The Ring of Power: The White House Staff and Its Expanded Role in Government.* New York: Basic Books, 1988.

Public Papers of the Presidents of the United States.

Reedy, George Reedy. *Lyndon B. Johnson, A Memoir.* New York: Andrews and McMeel, 1982.

————. *The Twilight of the Presidency: From Johnson to Reagan.* New York: New American Library, 1987.

Rogers, Lindsay. *The Pollsters.* New York: Alfred A. Knopf, 1949.

Roll, Charles W., and Albert H. Cantril. *Polls: Their Use and Misuse in Politics.* New York: Basic Books, 1972.

Schandler, Herbert Y. *The Unmaking of a President: Lyndon Johnson and Vietnam.* Princeton, N.J.: Princeton University Press, 1977.

Shapiro, Robert Y., and Lawrence R. Jacobs. "Polling and the White House: Public Opinion and Presidential Behavior." In *The Presidency: Classic and Contemporary Readings*, ed. by Jeffrey Cohen and David Nice. New York: McGraw-Hill, 2003.

Shipler, David. "Poll Shows Confusion on Aid to Contras." *The New York Times*, April 15, 1986, p. 6

Simon, Dennis M., and Charles W. Ostrom. "The Politics of Prestige: Popular Support and the Modern Presidency." *Presidential Studies Quarterly* 8, no. 4 (fall, 1988): pp. 741–59.

Skowronek, Stephen. "Presidential Leadership in Political Time." In *The Presidency and the Political System*, sixth edition, ed. by Michael Nelson. Washington, D.C.: CQ Press, 2000.

Small, Melvin. *Johnson, Nixon, and the Doves.* New Brunswick, N.J.: Rutgers University Press, 1988.

————. "The Impact of the Antiwar Movement on Lyndon Johnson, 1965–1968: A Preliminary Report." *Peace and Change* 10, no. 1 (spring, 1984): pp. 1–22.

Speier, Hans. "Historical Development of Public Opinion." *American Journal of Sociology* 55, no. 4 (January, 1950): pp. 376–88.

Statistical Abstract of the United States.

Steel, Ronald. *Walter Lippmann and the American Century.* New York: Random House, 1981.

Towle, Michael J. "Lyndon Baines Johnson and the American People: A Study of Public Opinion Linkage from the Presidential Perspective." Ph.D. diss., University of Texas at Austin, 1990.

Tulis, Jeffrey K. *The Rhetorical Presidency.* Princeton, N.J.: Princeton University Press, 1987.

Turner, Kathleen. *Lyndon Johnson's Dual War: Vietnam and the Press.* Chicago: University of Chicago Press, 1985.

Washington Information Directory, 2001–2002 (Washington, D.C.: CQ Press, 2001)

Waterman, Richard W., and Hank Jenkins-Smith. "The Expectations Gap Thesis: Public Attitudes Toward an Incumbent President." *Journal of Politics* 61, no. 4 (November, 1999), pp. 944–66.

Waterman, Richard W., Robert Wright, and Gilbert St. Clair. *The Image-Is-Everything Presidency: Dilemmas in American Leadership.* Boulder, Colo.: Westview Press, 1999.

Wayne, Stephen J. *The Road to the White House, 2000.* Boston: Bedford/St. Martin's, 2000.

Weissberg, Robert. *Public Opinion and Popular Government.* Englewood Cliffs, N.J.: Prentice-Hall, 1976.

Index

Aaron, David, 94
Ackley, Gardiner, 46
Afghanistan, Soviet Invasion of, 14, 110
Altschuler, Bruce: analysis of Fred Panzer's role in Johnson administration by, 39, 141 n. 62; comments on advantages of archival research, 13; observations of Johnson administration's attempts to manipulate poll data, 58, 141 n. 69; observations about inability of polls to convince Johnson and his administration of their problems, 48, 83; observations about polls and pollsters in Johnson administration, 12, 80, 132 n. 14, 134 n. 45, 141 n. 59, 141–42 n. 71, 143 n. 11, 146 n. 45, 147 n. 71; use of cognitive dissonance theory to explain Johnson administration, 128 n. 46
American Association of Retired Persons, 108
American Farm Bureau Federation, 66
American Federation of Government Employees, 108
American GI Forum, 108
American Medical Association (AMA), 97
Amherst College, 74
Anderson, Clinton P., 24, 41, 76, 77, 101
Anderson, Jack, 71
Anderson, Paul A., 128 n. 47
Annenberg, Walter, 75
Aptheker, Herbert, 68, 139 n. 30
Aragon, Joseph (Joe), 50
archival documents, citing, 129 n. 2
Articles of Confederation, 74
attribution theory, 128 n. 47

Barber, James David, 129 n. 50
Barkley, Alben, 43, 66
Batt, William, 63
Bean, Louis, 76
Begin, Menachem, 35
Berlin Airlift, 32
Biden, Joseph, 40
Bimes, Teri, 8
black news organizations, 107
Black Panther Party, 139 n. 30
Blumenthal, Michael, 51
Blumenthal, Sydney, 8–9
Bolling, Richard, 42–43
Bonafede, Dom, 49, 51
Booth, Paul, 68, 139 n. 30
Brace, Paul, 9

Brown, Jerry, 29, 70, 109
Bryce, James, 6–7
Brzezinski, Zbigniev, 71, 91, 94, 95
Buchanan, Bruce, 8
Bunker, Ellsworth, 60, 105, 106
Burke, Edmund, 116, 117. *See also* delegate/trustee
Busby, Horace, 25, 26, 27, 28, 121
Bush, George H. W., 4, 117, 127 n. 38
Bush, George W., 5, 117
Business Roundtable, The, 108
Butler, Landon, 49, 91

Caddell, Patrick, 28, 29, 52, 53, 70, 74, 89–90, 91, 95, 107, 109
Califano, Joseph, 89, 98, 122
Camp David Summit, 40, 50
Campbell, Karlyn Kohrs, 136 n. 75
Cannon, Clarence, 37
Cantril, Hadley, 44
Carmichael, Stokely, 68, 139 n. 30
Carter, Hodding, III, 94
Carter, Hugh, 90
Carter, James Earl, III (Chip), 40
Carter, Jimmy: and the 1980 election, 29, 109; and approval ratings on handling the economy, 49, 50; the Camp David Summit and, 35; and canceling of U.S. participation in 1980 summer Olympic Games, 61; pattern of public approval for, 14–15; popular times of, 22; and problems with speaking style, 54; public approval ratings of, 14–15, 19, 34, 35, 36, 57, 60–61, 109; staff's trust of polls, 140 n. 51; as trustee, 116, 149 n. 3 (ch 5); use of symbolism, 22
Carter, Rosalynn (Mrs. Jimmy Carter), 40, 50, 135–36 n. 66
Carter Administration: attempt to understand support loss, 99; attention to base coalition of, 107–110; belief that declining public approval was temporary, 39–40; belief in need for better communication, 48–55; communications about energy policy and, 36, 49, 50, 52, 53; defining and dismissing the "manipulative" opposition, 70–71; desire to learn public's issue agenda, 89–91; and energy policy, 33–34, 52, 53, 74, 94, 95, 131 n. 28; engaging the public in dialogue about policy issues, 86; fear of support loss in, 29–30; gasoline prices